To Bob Davidson

From a grateful
doctor to a helpful
friend –

Sam

# Doctor and Teacher, Hospital Chief

# DOCTOR AND TEACHER, HOSPITAL CHIEF

## Dr. Samuel Proger and the New England Medical Center

HERBERT BLACK

The Globe Pequot Press   Chester, Connecticut

Publication of this book was made possible in part
by grants from Mr. Bingham's trusts for charitable purposes.
Library of Congress Number 81-82605
ISBN: 0-87106-960-1

# Acknowledgments

I thank the following:

My wife, Marion Black, who gave moral support as I researched, wrote and rewrote this book at a time when she expected to be free of deadlines after my 45 years of newspapering.

William Davis Taylor, chairman of Affiliated Publications and former publisher of the *Boston Globe*, who suggested that the life of Dr. Samuel Proger, the development of the New England Medical Center, and the work of the Bingham Program were major events in the history of Boston and American medicine that should be recorded.

Henry T. Wilson, public relations director of the Tufts-New England Medical Center, who spent many hours checking the manuscript for accuracy and who allowed complete access to his voluminous files. Also his helpful staff.

Charles B. Everitt, president of the Globe Pequot Press, who served as editor, critic and general manager of production of this volume. Also, Jessie Howland, who copy edited the book superbly; Sarah W. Bartlett, Sc.D., assistant to the president of New England Medical Center, who helped pull together the final chapter; and Mrs. Beverly Nuss, who typed the manuscript with great care and precision.

Dr. John T. Bowers, president of the Floating Hospital Alumni Association, who provided information about that hospital's history, as did Henry Brainerd, a trustee. The latter drew on his own experiences and those of his father, William Hungerford Brainerd, architect, who planned modernization of the first Floating Hospital ship, supervised construction of the Jackson building and served as a trustee and clerk of the corporation of the Boston Floating Hospital for 40 years, beginning in 1905.

I am indebted to Joseph E. Garland, author of *Experiment in Medicine,* a book about the first 20 years of the Bingham Program, written in 1960, which provided important information about the beginnings of the Bingham Program and the hospital.

Herbert Black

# Contents

Preface    ix

1   Young Doctor from Atlanta    1

2   A Remarkable Yankee Doctor    9

3   The Boston Dispensary    15

4   The Boston Floating Hospital    24

5   Tufts Medical and Dental Schools    36

6   Boston and Heidelberg    43

7   Dr. John George Gehring    50

8   William Bingham, 2nd, Philanthropist    54

9   Birth of the Bingham Program    61

10   The Boston-Maine Connection    68

11   A New Hospital for Boston    74

12   People at the Pratt    81

13   The Bingham Program Makes History in Maine    88

14   Surgery Comes to the Pratt    95

15   A Watershed Period    102

16   Recruiting and Paying the Players    110

17   Dr. Proger's Patients   118

18   The Parts Finally Come Together   127

19   A Tribute in Glass and Stone   135

20   The Bingham Program at Age Fifty   141

21   Doctors and Their Patients   152

22   A Modern Berth for the Floating Hospital   160

23   New England Medical Center Today   169

24   A View of the Future   182


*Appendices*

Building Diagram   190

Founders of the Boston Dispensary:
Original Subscribers, 1796   193

Governors, Trustees and Medical Staff of
the New England Medical Center, 1982   194

Institutional Affiliations of
the New England Medical Center   202


Index   203

# Preface

In August 1928, when Herbert Hoover was running for President, he said, "We are nearer to the final triumph over poverty than ever before in the history of any land. The poorhouse is vanishing from among us. We have not yet reached that goal, but we soon shall be in sight of the day when poverty will be banished from the nation."

A few months later, in 1929, when Mr. Hoover was in the White House and his optimistic campaign forecast was still representative of the national view, a group of concerned men and women started a series of meetings in Boston to map their own effort to combat poverty and illness. They represented three institutions that historically had provided care for the sick poor of the city: the Boston Dispensary, oldest private medical care institution in the city; the Boston Floating Hospital for Infants and Children, which had provided free treatment aboard ships for generations of sick youngsters; and the Tufts Medical and Dental Schools, which for years had conducted clinics for the medically indigent in the South End and on Huntington Avenue.

Their plan was to develop the nation's first regional academic medical center to provide health care for the poor, to expand the training of private-practice doctors, to provide research facilities, and to promote health-care programs for the benefit of all New England citizens.

The loose federation they planned — each component would maintain independence — was given the ambitious name, "New England Medical Center." Some of the planners thought the name a bit pretentious in view of the limited financial resources available; but the majority, encouraged by the forecasts of continued prosperity, opted for a goal and a name that indicated service to the region and not just the city.

Official announcement of the formation of the New England Medical Center was made at the Boston Chamber of Commerce on October 16, 1929. Eight days later, on Thursday, October 24, the stock market began to collapse, with $13 million worth of shares traded during the one day. October 29, "Black Tuesday", was another disastrous day, with $16 million worth of stocks traded. Within three weeks, a staggering total of $30 billion in stock market values and hopes for perpetual prosperity had vanished into thin air.

Economic conditions grew so desperate that many stock-market losers jumped out of windows; jobless men sold apples on street corners; and the Ford Motor Company, trying to sell a few cars, lowered the price of its popular Model A coupe from $550 to $500, and its Phaeton from $460 to $440.

Instead of surrendering to the grim outlook, so different from what everyone had anticipated, the founders of the New England Medical Center decided to proceed — because the need for their combined contributions was increased by the economic disaster. The projected cost of their pioneering medical center was set at $1.5 million. This was to cover construction of a new, land-based Floating Hospital, $200,000; renovation of the Boston Dispensary, $130,000; construction of a Center building for use by all three institutions, $450,000; land purchases, $190,000; and endowments for operating costs, $530,000.

Appeals for funds emphasized the need to continue the free care the Dispensary had provided since 1796, shortly after the birth of the nation. They also stressed the increased urgency of continuing free care for infants and children at the Floating. A third reason for giving, designed to appeal to a sense of enlightened self-interest on the part of donors, was the argument that the Center would enhance the training of private practice doctors. This had considerable appeal, because already a trend toward specialization and scientific research had developed. Already people were complaining that the family physician was disappearing and that they couldn't get a doctor to make a house call.

The representatives of Tufts, the Dispensary, and the Floating Hospital continued an intensive fund drive through 1930; and in January 1931 they were in a position to begin construction of their new Center. During 1931 they also strengthened their confederation by obtaining official sanction for it from the state legislature. The New England Medical Center was opened in November 1931, and was officially dedicated on National Hospital Day, May 12, 1932.

At the beginning of all this activity, in July of 1929, a young doctor from Georgia, Samuel H. Proger, had arrived in Boston. He intended to work for one year under the tutelage of Dr. Joseph H. Pratt, physician-in-chief at the Boston Dispensary and professor of medicine at Tufts Medical School.

Fifty-three years later, in 1982, Dr. Proger was still at the New England Medical Center, although in emeritus positions, after having guided the Center to its present eminence. He was the chief architect, money raiser, medical authority, and ethical force behind the growth of the New England Medical Center.

During a half-century of building a hospital from scratch, Dr. Proger also became an outstanding cardiologist, a widely recognized researcher in heart disease, an eminent teacher, and a nationally known innovator in methods of delivering health care to rural areas. Above all, he was a healer, friend, and counselor to hundreds of patients.

Dr. Proger and his role in the development of the New England Medical Center is the central theme of this book, which does not pretend to provide the definitive description of all the medical and surgical advances made at the center. The concern of the book is with dozens of individuals who helped develop the center — patients, doctors, trustees, educators, staff members, philanthropists, and politicians.

These were very human people, who had faults as well as virtues, who made mistakes as well as good judgments; men and women who made a difference in American medicine, in New England health care, and in the well-being of the public.

These people, what they did, how they did it, and why they gave of themselves, provide lessons for the future as well as interesting history. It is becoming apparent that in the 1980s, with limited government resources, the private sector again is being called upon to help in a major way to provide and maintain health care institutions. What the private sector was able to accomplish fifty years ago may provide clues for meeting future problems.

During interviews in preparation for my writing this book, Dr. Proger expressed concern that some of his associates might not be given proper recognition for their efforts in developing the hospital. If so, those unnamed may take solace in Dr. Proger's tribute to all who helped him when he accepted the Robert H. Williams "Distinguished Chairman of Medicine" award, given him in Washington in 1980 by the Association of Professors of Medicine. He said,

"On an occasion like this, it is important to call attention to the obvious; namely, that an achievement of any consequence is always built upon the achievements of others, and with the help of still others. It is easy for a child on his father's shoulders to see himself as taller than his father. I have had many such metaphorical fathers, and also many metaphorical right arms.

"In support of the indispensable role of others, let me cite a remark by Casey Stengel, that quaint philosopher and verbal gymnast who, for a time, as everybody knows, managed the Yankees baseball team. He was being congratulated after his team had won yet another World Series. Stengel responded with thanks. Then, as you may recall, he added, 'But, you know, I couldn't have done it without the boys.' He proved his point shortly thereafter when, as manager of the Mets, but with another group of boys, he finished last several years in a row."

This book tells the story of the manager and some of the men and women on his team: men and women who made many hits, runs, and errors; scored numerous victories and recorded many defeats; but kept trying until they flew some pennants over the New England Medical Center.

The writer, a professional journalist for 45 years and one who always prided himself on his objectivity, confesses that, during a year of interviews with Dr. Proger, he became increasingly fond of him and appreciative of his humor and humanity. One of Dr. Proger's traits is his ability to view events involving himself with objectivity and dispassion, almost as an observer himself.

One of his pertinent stories illustrates the spirit of our interviews. He tells about the young reporter who was having his first experience as a war correspondent, in China, during the Boxer Rebellion: "In his initial dispatch to the *New York Globe,* he wrote, 'It is impossible to exaggerate the importance of what is going on here — but I shall do my best.'" Dr. Proger said he would try to avoid exaggeration, for he recognized that achievements are apt to loom large if you are very close to them, and especially if you tend to be pleased with them.

Doctor and Teacher, Hospital Chief

# CHAPTER 1

# Young Doctor from Atlanta

Dr. Samuel Herschel Proger, age 23, arrived in Boston on July, 1, 1929, a steaming hot day with the thermometer at 90° even during the morning hours. Fifty years later, he could still recall the events that followed his stepping down from a train at South Station, then one of the world's busiest rail terminals.

Most passengers stumbled in disarray from the distinctly non-air-conditioned coaches onto the stifling platform. The young doctor, come north from Georgia to continue his formal training in medicine, was among them, but not disheveled. His clothing, he recalled, was light in color and texture to absorb a minimum of the muggy heat of his home-town of Atlanta. One can guess that his suit was still pressed, his shirt white and buttoned, his tie neatly tied, and his appearance in general cool and calm. Nobody in the next half-century would see him looking rumpled. Furthermore, he was so pleased to be in Boston, that mecca of medicine, that he hardly noticed the heat. Nor did he feel weary from having been train-bound for 30 hours, a time span during which, in later years, he would fly halfway around the world to treat patients.

Dr. Proger weighed 154 pounds at the time, a weight that never would vary more than a pound or two for the next half-century. He was of medium height, probably even then carrying himself with a measure of dignity. In his right hand he swung a shiny suitcase, which one would guess was neatly packed. Under his left arm was a tennis racket. He wondered, as he moved quickly toward the station concourse, whether he would find time to keep up his tennis in Boston.

Dr. Proger walked out of the station, asked directions from a police officer, and boarded a subway train for Boston City Hospital. As soon as he was seated, he patted his coat to make certain his credentials were safe in his inside pocket. These included documents indicating he had graduated Phi Beta Kappa from Emory University in 1925 after three years of undergraduate work and a year in medical school; also that he had graduated with highest honors from Emory Medical School in 1928, served a summer internship at New York's Bellevue Hospital, and completed a year of internship at Atlanta's Piedmont Hospital. Most important, at the moment, was a letter accepting him as a resident physician (second year of postgraduate training) at the Boston Dispensary.

Dr. Proger felt quite confident about meeting the challenges ahead. He had been a top student all through Boys High School in Atlanta, college, and medical school. His self-assurance had been developed by playing golf and tennis well, and by playing violin as a member of the Atlanta Symphony Orchestra. He had given violin lessons long enough to afford to buy a prized Model T Ford. He had had several prestigious medical residencies offered him, and had chosen Boston because of the exciting advances being reported by its academic and hospital physicians.

Other thoughts occurred to him as the train emerged from the subway onto the elevated tracks. He was one of the very first graduates of Emory Medical School to seek a career in academic medicine; most other graduates had gone into private practice, and pressure had come from several quarters for him to do likewise. He would, he realized, be a Southerner in Yankeeland. In addition, he was Jewish. He knew from personal experience that there were quotas, although this was never admitted, for accepting Jewish students in many medical schools of that day. He had heard that Jewish physicians had difficulty finding senior staff positions at teaching hospitals, although some had done so. He also had been told that the only "Jews" who had become full professors and chiefs of services in American universities and teaching hospitals were a few Unitarians who had attended temple as youths.

When the train stopped at Northampton Street, Samuel Proger got out and walked along Massachusetts Avenue to Boston City Hospital. He entered the lobby, presented his credentials, and was told in a never-to-be-forgotten moment that nobody there had ever heard of him. He explained that he had been accepted for a residency training post at the

Boston Dispensary and displayed his letter of acceptance. He was told, "No, the Boston Dispensary is not a part of Boston City Hospital. It is a completely separate institution over on Bennet Street."

Disappointed to discover that Boston City Hospital, about which he had heard so much — which was affiliated at that time with Harvard, Tufts, and Boston University — was not the place where he had been accepted, the young doctor picked up his hat, his bag, and his tennis racket, and headed back toward the downtown area.

When he finally found Bennet Street, in Boston's South Cove area back of the Metropolitan Theatre, the neighborhood did little for his somewhat wilted self-confidence. The area was a slum, worse than anything in rundown sections of Atlanta. He could see no open spaces, not even a vacant lot. There were rows of old brick houses, proud homes in earlier days but now reduced to housing the city's poorest immigrants. The red brick Dispensary building was no prize, and presented a rather gloomy exterior. As he looked at it, Samuel Proger thought sorrowfully of the appointments he had rejected at Johns Hopkins and New York Hospital to come to this bleak place. Just then, the east wind blew in and dropped the temperature 20 degrees in minutes. The visitor decided at least to go inside and make an appearance.

He was greeted by Dr. Joseph Hersey Pratt, chief of medicine, who had hurried from his office to meet the newcomer and welcome him to Boston. When he heard what had happened, Dr. Pratt turned on the full charm he reserved for special occasions. He wanted this young man, highly recommended by an old friend in Atlanta, to stay. The younger man began to reconsider leaving town. After all, it was to work with Dr. Pratt that he had come to town. What did it matter if Dr. Pratt was at some place called the Boston Dispensary, and not at Boston City Hospital?

Dr. Pratt had been chosen as Dr. Proger's mentor by Dr. James E. Paullin, a professor at Emory and an internist who was one of Franklin D. Roosevelt's doctors at Warm Springs. Dr. Paullin had been a friend of Dr. Pratt at Johns Hopkins Medical School and had followed the career of the latter with great interest. He considered Dr. Pratt one of America's great practitioners and teachers of medicine.

In many ways the careers of Dr. Pratt and Dr. Paullin had run parallel courses. Both were considered fine researchers in addition to being excellent teachers and clinicians. Doctors who possessed that combination of abilities were scarce for much of the first half of this century in the United States. In fact, research and patient care were considered by many doctors of that time to be incompatible.

Dr. Proger had dreams of combining teaching, research, and patient care, visions triggered by the example of Dr. Paullin. He said in a memorial lecture in 1953 that Dr. Paullin was "a complete physician, a superb clinician, a solid scientist, an inspiring teacher and a major medical statesman; a unifying figure in the midst of divisive influences." He added, "In saying this, I have in mind a tendency sometimes noted nowadays of viewing clinical medicine and scientific medicine separately, the one being 'practical' and the other 'theoretical'. When Dr. Paullin began his practice in Atlanta, he had what at that time was an impressive background in, and concern for, the laboratory as an aid to medical practice. He was, therefore, accused of being a theoretical and not a practical doctor. He stood his ground, however, and was able to demonstrate that one could combine laboratory with bedside observations to the great advantage of the patient."

Dr. Proger continued, "This conflict between the scientific and so-called practical approach to the sick must be as old as science itself. But, as we look about us and see flame photometers, ultracentrifuges, Tiselius apparatuses and the like, it is important to remember that a century ago the stethoscope was considered just a scientific gadget."

Dr. Proger always believed, beginning with the days when he sat at Dr. Paullin's feet, that a person could be a good laboratory investigator and a successful practitioner at the same time. He said, in his 1953 lecture, "This is so despite the fact that the good practitioner must be all assurance, the sound researcher all doubt. Doubt and assurance need not be mutually exclusive. They can indeed be wisely combined both in the laboratory and at the bedside. Here, as in so many other aspects of human endeavor, apparent irreconcilables are nothing more than reciprocal antagonisms which need only to be brought into some sort of equilibrium."

The matter of equilibrium was in Dr. Proger's mind that morning as he weighed his disappointment over not being at Boston City Hospital against his favorable impression of Dr. Pratt. The opportunity to study under a great teacher, to learn about the innovative procedures and imaginative practices that Dr. Pratt had brought to medicine, tipped the scales; he decided to stay.

In later years, Dr. Proger was to consider Drs. Paullin and Pratt as his medical fathers. He considered Dr. William Osler, in turn, to be his medical grandfather; because the great Osler had taught both Pratt and Paullin at Hopkins. Also, Dr. Proger, as a medical student, had read Dr. Harvey Cushing's biography of Osler and it had inspired him to seek a career in academic medicine. Cushing's book had provided his first exposure to the larger academic world outside of Atlanta. In 1930 the medical academic world was largely confined to Boston, New York, Philadelphia, and Baltimore.

Dr. Proger was to find in Boston a whole new world of academic medicine. When he was in medical school in the South, the teachers were all practicing physicians who taught part-time; men who accepted, rather than challenged, the precepts of medicine. Boston was the kind of academic world he had read about in the biography of Osler, where nobody accepted anything without substantiating evidence.

His first summer at the Dispensary, however, was more clinical than academic for Dr. Proger. He worked closely with Dr. Pratt and took a month's turn on the Home Medical Service, the Dispensary's program of caring for the poor in the midst of their families. He began to gain an appreciation of the world of the urban poor.

Dr. Joseph Rosenthal, a 1926 graduate of Tufts Medical School, head of the Home Medical service in 1939 and a director of the program during Dr. Proger's first year, described in an interview what the Home Service was like in those days.

"We provided home care in the North End, in Hyde Park, Charlestown, East Boston, South Boston, Brighton, Allston, Dorchester, Mattapan, Jamaica Plain, Roslindale, and part of Roxbury. The Boston University home care program served the South End and another part of Roxbury. Probably our greatest efforts were in South Boston where, for some reason, there seemed to be large numbers of acutely sick children and adults. The illnesses among children ranged from acute respiratory diseases to scarlet fever, and included strep throats, chicken pox, measles, German measles, and pneumonia. We had a large geriatric practice, with many elderly people living in South Boston.

"We tried hard to control strep throat infections, realizing that the streptococcus that carried it was an underlying cause of rheumatic fever. We had a difficult time treating infectious diseases because the antibacterial agents, such as penicillin, were still in the future. But Dr. Pratt, and later Dr. Proger, insisted that we make the effort. We eventually used some of the sulfonamides, but at the beginning we hardly knew what we were doing. Little by little we learned.

"During influenza outbreaks, we would make a hundred calls a day to treat sick children. Dr. Proger, when he first came, went out on house calls with the students and interns. Sometimes the young doctors and medical students — the district service was utilized as an important teaching arm of Tufts Medical School — would run into strange and sometimes dangerous situations. Once, two students heard shots ring out as they entered a South Boston tenement. When they rushed up to see what they could do, they found two men and a woman, all dead."

The very first days of Dr. Proger's stay in Boston served to cheer him up. He learned something of the distinguished history of the Boston Dispensary and Boston Floating Hospital. He met some of the professors at Tufts Medical and Dental Schools. And, on the Fourth of July, he attended the historic first Esplanade Concert ever given by Arthur Fiedler and the Boston Pops Orchestra. He was enthralled by the then young maestro and, after going on to the Common to view the fireworks, determined to meet him. He soon did, and they became close friends. In later years, Dr. Proger played chamber music with Arthur Fiedler and a small group of his musicians. Later, Fiedler became his patient.

As the weeks went along, he found that Boston City Hospital was not far away, and that some of the great medical men working there were approachable and friendly. He was particularly impressed by the researchers at the Thorndike Laboratory at BCH. "They were an extraordinary group of medical giants in the 1930s and 1940s."

During the period of initiation in his work at the Dispensary, Sam Proger at times longed for Atlanta. He missed his home, where music and culture had been traditional. His father, an Atlanta businessman, his mother, a gifted and gentle woman, and his talented sister, Pearl, had made up a closely knit family.

He was also lonesome for his fiancee, Evelyn Levinson, whom he had met at a party given by her sister, back when he was in college. Evelyn

Dr. and Mrs. Samuel Proger about the time that the Proger Health Services building was dedicated in 1973.

Proger would later recall that Sam spent that evening helping her with her homework (she was in high school at the time).

Dr. Proger said in later years that the reason he and Evelyn did not get married earlier was that "people didn't marry in those days while they were still in medical school." They were eventually wed in Atlanta, on September 8, 1929, several months after he first came to Boston.

During a 50th wedding anniversary party, given by their family and friends on September 7, 1979, Dr. Proger made these remarks:

"I remember reading many stories as a child that ended with the cheery statement, 'And they lived happily ever after.' I often wondered just what that meant. Now I know. And I hope that Evelyn knows, too; for it is *they* who lived happily ever after and it is *she* who has made it all a reality. That is no mean accomplishment. For, to create happiness is surely one of the greatest of all human achievements.

"In the world at large, the half-century we are marking today has been characterized by unrelieved turmoil. But through it all Evelyn has provided a fixed point of comfort, tranquility, happiness and love.

"That fixed point has been here in Boston, a city with a Puritan background, a background that we have been told is not conducive to unbounded joy. Indeed, I have heard Puritanism defined among other things as 'the haunting fear that someone somewhere is having fun.' We have not been tainted by that grim view. For if to have fun is to sin, then we have been sinning blissfully for 50 years.

"Events like this, a 50th wedding anniversary, and occasions like this, a happy gathering of family and friends are what heaven must be all about.

"There is a story, said to be one of Adlai Stevenson's favorites, of a child in a drawing class. When the teacher came by, she asked what the child was drawing. The child said, 'I am drawing God.' 'But,' the teacher said, 'no one knows what God looks like.' 'Yes,' the child replied, 'but they will when I get through.' I may not be able to draw a picture of God, but I believe I could draw a pretty good picture of heaven, what with 50 years of experience."

# CHAPTER 2

# A Remarkable Yankee Doctor

Dr. Joseph Hersey Pratt, an innovative, eminent, and controversial figure in the history of Boston medicine, was 57 on that July day in 1929 when he sat down with Dr. Samuel Proger, then 23, and convinced the younger man to remain for a year as his pupil.

He related some of the illustrious history of the Boston Dispensary, which recently had become affiliated with Tufts Medical School, and his belief that a new era of academic medicine was about to begin there. Dr. Pratt emphasized that there would be opportunities to combine clinical research with patient care. He offered considerable freedom for scientific investigation. He noted that there would be opportunities to treat all types of illness in the Dispensary's Home Medical Service clinics.

Dr. Proger said later that he was attracted to the older man, who, in turn, seemed to like him enough to urge him to stay. If Dr. Pratt was an example of a Yankee doctor, Dr. Proger thought, the Boston experience could prove both enjoyable and instructive.

If a stranger from the South had had an idea that all Yankee doctors were tall, cold, stiff, and austere, the illusion would have been dispelled by Dr. Pratt. He was warm, friendly, and kind; quick to smile and joke, but dignified in appearance despite the fact that he was a bit portly and of only medium height. He could also be quick-tempered and blunt with colleagues who refused to try new ways of doing things, a trait that led to several serious conflicts during his career.

Joe-Joe Pratt, as he was widely known, was born in Middleboro, Massachusetts, on December 5, 1872, the son of Martin van Buren and

Rebecca Adams (Dyer) Pratt. He grew up in the Pilgrim tradition of service to people, in what then was farming country near Plymouth. The first of his family to go to college, he chose Yale because its Sheffield Scientific School offered the only biology course in the country tailored specifically as a prelude to medical school.

He entered Harvard Medical School after graduation from Yale, but transferred after a year to Johns Hopkins so that he could study under the famed pathology professor, Dr. William H. Welch, and be taught by Dr. William Osler, considered the leading clinician and teacher of his time. Dr. Osler advocated combining patient care with clinical research, and Dr. Pratt said often that nobody had a greater influence on his life than Dr. Osler.

On returning to Boston after his graduation from Hopkins, Dr. Pratt was welcomed by his former Harvard Medical School professor, Dr. William T. Councilman, who invited him to join his pathology department at Boston City Hospital. Dr. Pratt quickly accepted and worked there with Dr. Frank B. Mallory, for whom the Mallory Institute of Pathology at Boston City Hospital was later named.

Within a few months of Dr. Pratt's arrival, Dr. Councilman sent him to Germany to study under Dr. Ludolf Krehl, who was then 42 and at the height of his fame. While in Germany, Dr. Pratt developed the first accurate method for counting blood platelets. He also treated patients in the wards.

Over the course of his early years at Boston City, Dr. Pratt made important contributions to knowledge about the bacteriology and diagnosis of typhoid fever, the function of the pancreas, the treatment of gout, and the effects of digitalis in the treatment of heart disease.

Dr. Jean A. Curran, a longtime associate of Dr. Pratt, noted that the latter's lifelong interest in patients was evident in his early days at Boston City. Curran wrote the following in a manuscript unpublished because of his death:

"As an early evidence of Dr. Pratt's innovative originality, he received approval for the institution of the first elective clerkships for Harvard medical students who wished to pursue special interests. Among them, significantly, were Francis W. Peabody and Paul Dudley White, both destined for careers of international leadership characterized by deep personal and continuing care for their patients. Both, during their formative years, must have derived inspiration from Dr. Pratt's warm interest in his patients.

"It was Dr. Peabody, first director of Boston City Hospital's Thorndike Laboratory, who, writing in 1927 in the *Journal of the American Medical Association*, made a simple statement that rang around the world, but is not often quoted today: "The secret of the care of the patient is caring for the patient."

Reminiscing years later about caring for patients, Dr. Proger said that Dr. Pratt was a genius in that regard. He added, however, that he had known two doctors who were even better at making each patient think that he or she was the doctor's favorite. These were Dr. Paul Dudley White, the famed cardiologist, and Dr. Elliott P. Joslin, who founded the Joslin Clinic for the treatment of diabetes.

In 1903, Dr. Pratt shifted his major interest to internal medicine and joined Dr. Richard Cabot, a noted Harvard physician, in the tuberculosis clinic he directed at the Massachusetts General Hospital. By 1905, Dr. Pratt had initiated a do-it-yourself program for the treatment of tuberculosis (which was then known as consumption). He sometimes referred to the treatment as a labor-saving device because it consisted of group therapy. He met patients in groups because of the pressures — there were 14,000 cases of tuberculosis that year in Massachusetts, with 5,000 deaths.

The *MGH News*, official publication of the Massachusetts General Hospital, noted the following in November 1975, the 70th anniversary of the group therapy program: "Dr. Pratt pioneered the idea of gathering together tuberculosis victims to teach them how to put themselves back on the road to good health." The article stated that retreats where patients could recover from tuberculosis were few and catered mainly to the affluent. Dr. Pratt reasoned that recovery could be obtained at home if the same strict rules enforced at institutions could be carried on voluntarily. One of his rules was that patients must sleep on the roofs of their homes.

Emmanuel Church, on Newbury Street, subsidized the program, providing funds for the purchase of tents, chairs, and extra wraps for the patients and the compensation of visiting social workers.

Dr. Richard Cabot, who encouraged Dr. Pratt's therapy programs at the MGH, said later: "His method of treatment in the homes of the poor was an astonishing success from the beginning. In 1907, when his Boston colleagues were having pretty poor success with the outpatient treatment of tuberculosis, Dr. Pratt's patients showed as large a measure of recovery in Boston as did the more affluent who went to Saranac Lake and other first-class sanatoriums. These patients lived on the roofs of their own homes in Boston, and there a large fraction of them got well."

Once, when asked the secret of his success, Dr. Pratt answered, "I give a large amount of time to a small number of patients." Dr. Cabot noted that Dr. Pratt also gave "vast patience, ingenuity, optimism and the milk of human kindness." He added, "No one else was as warm-hearted as Dr. Pratt, no one else enjoyed meeting his patients so much, and was as pleased with each little success and as confident of eventual recovery."

During the course of establishing his program, Dr. Pratt enlisted the aid of women to visit homes and determine if his rules were being adhered to as prescribed. He called these women "Friendly Visitors." He considered them key elements in his concept of the cottage sanatorium. The work of the Friendly Visitors was so successful that Dr. Cabot and Miss Ida Cannon at the MGH followed up on it and established a program at that hospital that many consider the beginning of modern medical social service.

Dr. Pratt's pioneering home care of tuberculosis in the early decades of this century eventually forced other doctors to revise their treatment of the disease. "Other men were advocating some rest, but exercise with it," Dr. Pratt said once. "I thought that long bed rest was the most important thing of all." Even with the drugs in use today to combat tuberculosis, bed rest is still considered an important part of treatment.

It is evident, then, that when he and Dr. Proger met in 1929 Dr. Pratt already had completed what would be for most people a distinguished career. In addition to his work with tubercular patients, he had become an authority on diseases of the pancreas and the chest. He had written 120 medical papers. He had held a commission in World War I. He had headed some of America's most prestigious medical and scientific societies. He had taught for many years at Harvard and Tufts Medical Schools. He had served on the staffs of great hospitals.

Neither Dr. Pratt nor Dr. Proger could know on the day they met that for the next quarter-century their lives would be intertwined as they launched the Tufts–New England Medical Center and the Bingham

Associates Program for the Advancement of Rural Medicine. Nor could they know that in the coming years Dr. Pratt, utilizing the group therapy techniques of the tuberculosis clinics, would break new ground in the treatment of psychiatric patients through group therapy.

The fact that Dr. Pratt was at the Dispensary to greet Dr. Proger at the outset, and that he remained there to participate in the development of the Medical Center, was partly due to his distinguished career and partly due to another side of his life. He had forfeited opportunities to achieve high posts at both the Peter Bent Brigham and Massachusetts General Hospitals by his bluntness, his outspokenness, and his uncompromising stands on medical issues.

Dr. Proger said many years later, when asked how Dr. Pratt came to the Dispensary, "He was rambunctious in many ways and in others the sweetest person in the world. He said what was on his mind and this irritated people at times. He became unpopular at the MGH and the Brigham. In the middle 1920s, he went into private practice at 270 Commonwealth Avenue, and did his hospital work at New England Baptist Hospital. A colleague told him in 1927 that the Dispensary was looking for a chief of medicine. He applied and was given the post." In two years Dr. Pratt had accomplished much in upgrading the Dispensary.

During the 1930s and later, Dr. Pratt became more and more involved in psychotherapy. He specialized in psychoneurotic cases and gradually got farther away from internal medicine. The only medical patients he always remained interested in were tuberculosis, gout, and angina cases.

Dr. Proger said of this period: "Dr. Pratt stands as having made a unique contribution to psychiatry, group therapy. He learned in his tuberculosis groups how important patients can be to one another in providing mutual support. For example, in the tuberculosis clinics, when one patient learned from another that he could stay outside even when it was cold, the second patient was encouraged to do the same.

"Dr. Pratt called his psychiatric clinics thought control clinics, and he used applied psychology for many people who were worrying themselves sick. They would provide reassurance for each other. They would discuss in general sessions how much better they felt and how they were controlling their emotions. The group effect was greater than any individual therapy they received.

"I remember taking a class when Dr. Pratt was absent one day. And it was fun. I felt better, myself, when I came out. Dr. Pratt always came out of the sessions with an increased sense of well-being. I think he obtained psychotherapy himself from the sessions."

Dr. Pratt's "thought control" clinics often have been described as the world's first experiment in group psychotherapy. Nothing is more dangerous in medicine than claiming "firsts," as people almost never arrive alone at new ideas and techniques. Dr. Pratt owed something to the French psychiatrist, Joseph Jules Dejerine, whom he had met in 1913, and to Dr. John George Gehring of Bethel, Maine, who was to become Dr. Pratt's patient in 1931 and who for many years had been practicing a form of group therapy for business leaders and professional people who had suffered "nervous breakdowns."

The Pratt technique involved relaxation exercises, periods of constructive thinking, reports by patients on their progress, and mutual encouragement of one another. There also were inspirational talks by the doctor. By the time Dr. Pratt was 80, more than 3,400 patients had been treated and his ideas were being adopted throughout the world.

On Dr. Pratt's eightieth birthday in 1952, during a reception at the Harvard Club, he gave the following advice to young doctors who would come after him:

"Never forget that patients are persons. There is too much tendency today to overlook that. As a person, you cannot treat your patient without considering his emotional life, all his surroundings — everything that bears on his life either as a well or a sick person."

Dr. Pratt, who had lived in Brookline much of his life, spent his last years in Andover, where he lived with one of his five children, Sylvia Kemp, whose husband was headmaster of Phillips Academy.

When he died in 1956, at age 84, the *Boston Globe* concluded an editorial by saying: "Still vigorously pioneering in the alleviation of man's ills at an age when lesser men were being pushed into retirement, Dr. Pratt earned a place in the group of Boston's medical immortals who have done so much to raise the whole standard of medicine in this country."

In 1981, Dr. Jerome Grossman, Director of the New England Medical Center, launched plans to restore the Pratt Clinic in a new form to serve patients during the 1980s and beyond.

# CHAPTER 3

# The Boston Dispensary

If Dr. Proger had been aware of the illustrious history of the Boston Dispensary — the oldest civilian health care institution in New England, and the third oldest in the nation — he might have been less depressed by having been sent there instead of to Boston City Hospital for post-doctoral training. The Dispensary, founded in 1796, had been providing quality care free of charge to the sick poor of the city for 68 years before the Boston City Hospital opened its doors in 1864.

The founding charter of the Dispensary, signed at the Boston Chamber of Commerce in September 1796, was printed in the same month and year that George Washington, after two terms as President, wrote his famed Farewell Address. One document signified the end of a political era in American history, and the other a new commitment on the part of Boston's private citizens to provide medical care for people too poor to otherwise obtain it.

In what may now be seen as a precedent, even though the dispensary idea was imported from London, the public-spirited and prominent sponsors of the original Boston institution organized what amounted to a privately funded Medicaid program to provide home care for the medically indigent of their day.

The well-to-do citizens of Boston in that post-Revolutionary period were treated in their homes by private physicians. The poor were treated by "town" doctors, paid by town funds. The founders of the Dispensary were stirred to action by discovering that the needy sick were being sent to an almshouse on an island in the harbor when they became too destitute to shift for themselves. Most of those who went there never came back.

There were no hospitals for rich or poor in Boston when the Dispensary was opened. There had been several military hospitals during the war, and there were quarantine stations on harbor islands, designed to limit new waves of disease every time a ship came in. The city's first hospital, Massachusetts General, would not open until 1821 (delayed by the War of 1812), 25 years after the Dispensary began providing care.

Medicine had been very rudimentary in the colonies. Physicians depended on bleeding and purging as standard treatments. Benjamin Franklin was fond of saying that sick people were better off without doctors. The major illnesses of the day included smallpox, yellow fever, dysentery, malaria, respiratory ailments, pleurisy, and venereal disease.

Two events had served to improve somewhat the medical care offered by some Boston doctors even before the opening of the Dispensary. One was the experience gained by treating sick and wounded soldiers during the Revolution. The second was the opening of Harvard Medical School in 1783.[1]

The Dispensary was in no sense a hospital, or even a clinic, when it started. Headquarters was the pharmacy shop of Thomas Bartlett at 61 Cornhill, now Washington Street, across from the Old South Meetinghouse. Doctors fanned out from there to visit sick people whose care was paid for by contributions.

Three tenets, drawn up by a committee of the Dispensary's founding group, all business and professional leaders of the town, guided policy:

" . . . the sick, without being pained by a separation from their families, may be attended and relieved in their own homes;

" . . . the sick can, in this way, be assisted at less expense to the public than in any hospital;

" . . . those who have seen better days may be comforted without being humiliated; and all the poor receive the benefits of a charity, the more refined as it is the more secret."

The need for public assistance was great in the 1790s because Boston, then a city of 18,000, was in the midst of a deep postwar depression.

[1] Harvard Medical School was the third in the United States. The Medical Department of the College of Philadelphia (now the University of Pennsylvania) was first in 1765. The Medical School of King's College (now Columbia University) was second in 1767.

Jobs were scarce, food costs high, and sickness widespread. The dozen founders, encouraged by the example of the Good Samaritan, traveled about town to seek sponsors for their program.

Their appeal was simple: "Contribute $5.00 and receive a pair of tickets to be given to two patients of your choice." Each ticket entitled the bearer to a year of care by a Dispensary doctor. A $10.00 donation paid for four persons for a year; and a $50.00 lump sum guaranteed health care for one person for life.

Among 104 original Dispensary sponsors were citizens with such well-known Boston names as Allen, Amory, Brooks, Coffin, Codman, Cutler, Eliot, Greene, Higginson, Lowell, Parker, Parkman, Payne, Pratt, Stillman, Taylor, Tudor, Tuckerman, Wendell, and McDonough. (See Appendix for complete list.)

Food was often prescribed as a medicine by early Dispensary doctors, who recognized that malnutrition was a cause of many recurring illnesses among the poor of the city. The Dispensary governing board agreed and allowed the doctors to consider food as medicine and dispense it free of charge. (When, 170 years later in 1967, doctors from Tufts Medical School and the Dispensary tried to prescribe free food for malnourished black children in Mississippi, under a federal Office of Economic Opportunity program, U.S. bureaucrats were less cooperative; they refused to allow prescription of food as "medicine.")

Wine was another prescribed drug in early Dispensary days, but by 1805 prescriptions for sherry and port had become so numerous that doctors were restricted to a single quart per prescription. In 1818, wine was removed entirely from the drug list.

Dr. John Fleet, a graduate of the first class at Harvard Medical School, was the Dispensary's first physician, receiving a salary of $20.00 a month. He cared for 80 patients the first year. The records show: "Polly Lewis had slow fever and worms. Mary Adams had fits. Poor Sally Trefarthen was afflicted with bilious fever. Nicholas Freaney suffered with singular scrofulous complications. John Spear's wife presented a remarkable case of hysteria. Cato Green's dyspepsia gradually improved. Henry Cunston got rid of erysipelas. John Thompson died of tabes [atrophy of the body]. Rachel Milton gave up the battle with consumption."

As the numbers of patients increased, the Dispensary moved along what is now lower Washington Street at various times in its early days. At one time, it was in the old Thompson's Spa building; at another, in the old *Boston Globe* building, both gone.

In 1833 Dispensary doctors had begun the first comprehensive medical record keeping, using uniform nomenclature for diseases and identifying patients by country of origin, economic standing, and "social habits." This early effort at public-health profiling listed three designations under the heading, "Manner of Life." These were: (1) comfortable, (2) decent, (3) wretched. Scales of drinking were listed as (A) temperate, (B) moderate, (C) drunkard, (D) child of intemperate parent.

During the 1830s, as Boston grew, so did the complexity of providing health care to the needy by personal recommendations of sponsors. By 1853 the use of tickets was discontinued completely. The responsibility for making the difficult decisions concerning eligibility for aid was placed on Dispensary officials, pioneer social service workers, and physicians.

One of the latter, Dr. Oliver Wendell Holmes, had suggested in 1837 that a central house be obtained in Boston where patients able to leave their beds could present themselves and be seen by a group of doctors. He said such a clinic would save time and money, provide opportunity to serve larger numbers of patients, and reserve home visits for the seriously ill.

But, as so often happens in medicine between proposal and implementation, it was years before Holmes's suggestion could be effected. In 1856, when the estate of Benjamin Dearborn was settled and a legacy of $90,000 cleared, Dispensary officials finally had the means to proceed with a clinic. They purchased a small house on the corner of Ash and Bennet Streets in the South Cove area. The house had a "green lawn in the front and the ocean at its back," according to the records, as in those days the South Cove extended at high tide to Harrison Avenue.

Benjamin Dearborn was the first of a series of wealthy, sometimes eccentric, men who were to help finance the Dispensary and the New England Medical Center which grew out of it. He was an educator, inventor, and philanthropist. Among his accomplishments was the writing and publishing of the first American grammar in 1785. He was the first to urge useful employment of convicts in state prisons. He suggested to Congress in 1819 that steam carriages be built to run on steel rails, a suggestion that antedated the introduction of the steam locomotive in England.

A medical and a surgical clinic were opened in the building whose purchase Mr. Dearborn's will had made possible. Miss Abbie Dunks, for nearly 50 years an official of the Dispensary and its administrator during the years preceding 1965, found in the records that in the first year in the new building two and one-half times as many patients were seen, and at half the cost of those who were treated in their homes during the same period. "This marked the beginning of what we know today as group medicine, with its growing attention to the vertical patient and the corresponding increase in the protection of the public health," Miss Dunks wrote in a New England Medical Center publication in 1948.

She noted that the number of patients and their maladies increased year by year, and that this brought new interest in the development of medical specialties. The work of the Dispensary grew so rapidly, with increasing immigration, that only 27 years after the first building was opened it became necessary to rebuild and enlarge the clinics. The second building, which still stands, was completed in 1883. It was considered luxurious at the time, but it looked worn and dingy when Dr. Proger first saw it in 1929 — and it looks old and decrepit today.

Over the door of the Dispensary building still may be seen a brick bas-relief of the Good Samaritan, the symbol of the Dispensary from the day of its founding. When the Dispensary first opened in the apothecary shop, the site was marked by a four-foot by five-foot wooden signboard, which was constructed by Thomas Clement, a local carpenter, at a cost of $7.00. On it, John Johnston, a recognized artist, painted his version of the Good Samaritan ministering to the sick man. The artist was paid $30.00. That sign, now estimated to be worth $30,000, is on display today in administrative offices in the Oliver Wendell Holmes building at the New England Medical Center.

The following are some of the most significant of the Dispensary's early accomplishments:

— Programs of vaccination against smallpox in Boston in 1803, believed to be the first in the nation.

— Assignment of nurses to needy home-care patients in 1814, a pioneer venture.

— Establishment in 1821 at the Dispensary of the first public bath in New England, "because a clean skin is often more potent in the treatment of ailments than the administration of drugs."

— Formation in 1873 of the first venereal disease clinic in the United States, a clinic still in existence at the New England Medical Center.

— Opening of the first dental clinic for the sick poor in 1873.

The activity at the Dispensary attracted the great names of Boston medicine, many of them Harvard doctors who worked at the Dispensary as volunteers. They included John Homans, John Collins Warren, Jacob Bigelow, John G. Coffin, Samuel Cabot, James G. Shattuck, Francis Minot, and David W. Cheever, in addition to Holmes.

Developments in medicine continued at the Dispensary in the early part of the 20th century. By 1900 the first lung clinic was established and serving patients. In 1900, also, the first clinical laboratory was opened, one in which Dr. William A. Hinton in 1927 would develop his famous diagnostic test for syphilis, still used today. In 1949, Dr. Hinton became Clinical Professor of Bacteriology and Immunology at Harvard Medical School, the school's first black professor. Treatment of syphilis had been undertaken as early as 1873 despite the general opinion of the day that such patients were "victims of their own sensual indulgence."

Diet and nutrition were important components of Dispensary therapy from the beginning. Physicians who visited the "wretched" in slums of the city noted not only a lack of food, but also a lack of knowledge of even the rudiments of nutrition. New immigrants from other countries, unable to speak English, found it especially difficult to reconcile their native eating habits with foodstuffs found in America.

In 1847 a group of Boston ladies established what they called the South End Diet Kitchen to furnish nutritious food to the indigent, many of whom were Dispensary patients. For many years these ladies doled out nourishing food after being advised of the nutritional value of various vegetables and meats by Dispensary specialists.

Dispensary officials, seeing a need for even closer supervision of diet, and for more scientific approaches to the study of nutrition, opened the Frances Stern Nutrition Center in 1918. The new center, directed by Miss Stern, a widely known nutritionist, received financial aid from the ladies of the Diet Kitchen.

Still an integral part of the New England Medical Center, the Nutrition

Patients on way to Boston Dispensary in the early 1900s. At that time the average number of patients daily was 350, with one-third of them children. Scene is at corner of Ash and Bennet Streets. Car is parked in front of Dispensary door. Pratt Diagnostic Hospital was built in 1930s in area to the right of horse and cart.

The first Visiting Nurse Association in New England was organized in Boston in 1886.
The first nurse, with an office at the Boston Dispensary, accompanied a district doctor
on his rounds.

Center was described in a 1957 article by Dorothy Crandall, then food editor of the *Boston Globe*. She wrote, "Boston is the first city in the world to add warmth and understanding to the nutrition education it gives sick people. At the time, the clinic was serving 31 different nationalities. Wax food models and cards printed in various languages were used to overcome verbal communication barriers."

In 1908, as costs began to mount, the Dispensary set an admission fee of ten cents per visit. Responsibility for determining eligibility was placed on social workers. The first evening clinics in the nation were opened in 1913 to accommodate working people who could not come in the daytime and who earned enough to pay their way. The fee for these people was $1.00, which approximately covered the costs of the care they received.

In 1918, with costs continuing to rise, the Dispensary established a "Health Clinic," placing emphasis on the early diagnosis of diseases, an idea again in vogue in the 1980s.

The end of World War I put new demands on scientific equipment and trained personnel at the Dispensary. A fact-finding committee reported in 1926 that, in order to provide the quality of care for which the institution had always had been known, it would be necessary to establish a limited number of hospital beds, secure a definite affiliation with a medical school, and accept some patients who could pay their way.

These requirements led to negotiations for affiliation with Tufts Medical School and, in 1927, the employment of Dr. Pratt as Medical Director. Affiliation became a fact in the 1929–1930 period.

This was the stage the Dispensary had reached when Dr. Proger joined its staff in 1929 to participate in future events, including its absorption into the New England Medical Center Hospital.

# CHAPTER 4

# The Boston Floating Hospital

When Dr. Samuel Proger arrived in Boston, everybody knew how the Boston Floating Hospital for Infants and Children had obtained what many people today consider to be its unusual name. Up to 1927, for a period of 33 years, the hospital had been located aboard two successive widely-publicized vessels that provided havens for sick children while cruising Boston Harbor.

The floating mercy missions were fresh in memory at that time, as was the disastrous fire that had burned the second Floating Hospital ship at its North End Pier dock on the night of June 1, 1927, while being fitted out for a 34th season of voyages. It was following the fire, and during initiation of plans to build a new hospital on shore, that directors of the Boston Floating Hospital joined with trustees of the Boston Dispensary and Tufts to form the fledgling New England Medical Center.

The idea for the original Boston Floating Hospital arose one hot summer evening in July of 1893, when the Reverend Rufus Babcock Tobey, assistant pastor and social service worker at Berkeley Temple, a Congregational church in Boston's South End, was walking on the Dover Street bridge while waiting to board a train at the South Boston railroad station for his home in Wollaston.

Mr. Tobey saw women, some of whom he knew personally from his social service work, walking back and forth on the bridge with infants in their arms or in carriages, trying to find some relief from the oppressive heat that had settled in their tenements. He was accompanied by his friend and assistant, Mr. Lewis Freeman, a large, strong black man who

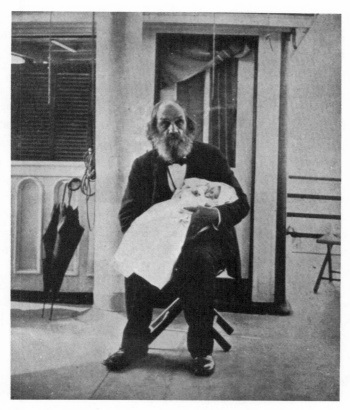

Rev. Rufus B. Tobey, founder of Boston Floating Hospital, with one of his charges aboard the original Floating Hospital boat in 1894.

had insisted on walking along to provide protection in the rough waterfront area. Mr. Freeman later wrote an account of what they saw:

"We noticed numbers of women trundling children in carriages and carts across the bridge up to the midnight hours, in search of some relief from the unsanitary and miasmatic conditions surrounding their home neighborhoods. Occasionally we would meet a man with an infant on a pillow in his arms, pacing backward and forward on the Dover Street bridge, the child suffering from infantile debility of some character, for which the doctor had prescribed salt air as a source of relief; but the ebb and flow of the tide brought not salt air but fetid odors which were almost fatal to the weak and sickly infants who were subjected to its influence. It seemed that if in some way these people could be got away from their surroundings for a few hours, conditions might be improved."

The next day, Mr. Tobey and Mr. Freeman discussed what they had seen. Both were compassionate men and as social workers had first-hand knowledge of the hardships endured by immigrants in Boston. They resolved to do something. Mr. Tobey recalled that his friend, the Reverend Edward Everett Hale, had suggested to him that a hospital be built by the sea for treatment of children. Mr. Tobey adapted this idea to plan a hospital afloat.

Mr. Tobey and Mr. Freeman were very different in appearance and background, but seem to have complemented one another. Mr. Freeman was a giant of a man, easy-going and good-natured; Mr. Tobey was smaller, a bit irascible and quick-tempered. Mr. Freeman was born in Washington and had grown up there after the Civil War. His mother was a freed slave and his father had become an attache at a South American Embassy. As a young man, Mr. Freeman had carried messages between the two factions of the Hayes-Tilden controversy, who had their headquarters at opposite ends of the same hotel. He remained a part of the Boston Floating organization until 1930, when he died at the age of 83. The Reverend Mr. Tobey was a descendant of John Alden who had attended Phillips Academy, Andover; Amherst College; and Andover Theological Seminary. He devoted his life to service, for years coming into daily contact with the immigrants who came in waves during the 1890s from Ireland, Germany, Italy, Russia, and other countries to flood tenements never built to hold them all. Boston at the time of Mr. Tobey's walk had grown from a town of 18,000 persons (as it was at the time of the founding of the Dispensary) to more than a half million.

Learning that a ship hospital for children was operating in New York, Mr. Tobey publicly suggested that one be founded in Boston. His suggestion was reported by the *Boston Herald* as a firm decision, and the news story brought a flood of donations. There now was no turning back. A formal fund drive was launched, aided by the Christian Endeavor Society of Berkeley Temple.

In the spring of 1894, the Monday Evening Club endorsed the project and provided major funding. Mr. Tobey chartered the 237-ton excursion barge *Clifford,* which had no engines and was tugged by a towboat, to

The Boston Floating Hospital, from 1906 to 1927, was located aboard this ship, which carried sick children on cruises in the harbor. A smaller vessel, pulled by a tug, was used from 1896 to 1904.

make a pilot trip and determine if the idea was feasible. The date was July 25. The voyage proved so successful that five trips were made that summer, carrying 1100 infants and children.

The *Clifford* was used as a cruise boat at night, so that partying equipment had to be removed and hammocks slung for children on the upper and lower decks on days when it was to serve as a hospital. Tickets for the free hospital trips, which departed from Snow's Arch Wharf, and later from Commercial Wharf, each Tuesday and Friday morning when the weather was pleasant, were distributed by doctors and hospitals. When the harbor was calm, the engineless barge rocked gently and proved soothing to the children and their mothers. One well child was allowed aboard with a mother and sick child if nobody was at home to care for the sibling. Harvard Medical School doctors participated in the program, with Dr. Samuel Breck of Commonwealth Avenue in charge of the medical team. Mr. J. R. Anderson was superintendent. Doctors from the Boston Dispensary cooperated, beginning in 1895. Patients came from Boston, East Boston, Brighton, Dorchester, Revere, South Boston, Charlestown, Cambridge, Hull, West Roxbury, Allston, Roxbury, Jamaica Plain, Medford, Malden, and Chelsea.

A strict rule was that no food or drink could be brought aboard. For one thing, the doctors and nurses were trying to teach good nutritional practices; for another, they didn't want any tipsy parents falling overboard.

In 1896 sponsorship of the Floating Hospital was taken over by the Ten Times One Society, later known as Lend-a-Hand Clubs. The Reverend Dr. Hale, who wrote *The Man without a Country,* also wrote several inspirational books, including *Ten Times One Is Ten* and *In His Name,* and he was president of the Ten Times One Society in 1896. In that year 3,564 infants and children were taken on cruises aboard the *Clifford* in Boston Harbor. Hundreds were treated successfully for various illnesses. Three died, two just after being brought aboard the ship.

Dr. Hale's leadership and writing led to formation of dozens of philanthropic organizations, many of which supported the Boston Floating Hospital. The theory behind the Ten Times One Society was that, if ten workers for good were multiplied by ten every three years, the whole world would accept faith, hope, and love as rules of life at the end of 27 years. Unfortunately, the chain seems to have been broken somewhere along the line. The motto of the Lend-a-Hand Clubs was, "Look up and not down, look forward and not back, look out and not in, Lend a Hand."

The Ten Times One Society purchased the *Clifford* in 1897 and installed permanent hospital equipment aboard. By this time, several thousand children had been taken on one-day trips. Doctors and nurses were concerned, however, that in a single outing they could do little more than provide a day of relief. They did diagnose diseases, recommend additional treatment ashore in some instances, instruct mothers in care techniques at home, and emphasize the necessity of sterilization of milk.

The most critical problem for children in the 1890s was infectious summer diarrhea. Mortality rates were four to five times greater in summer than in winter. There were also many cases of anemia, pneumonia, otitis, teething, hernia, and malnutrition.

On September 23, 1901, the Floating Hospital Corporation was formed and a start was made on raising funds to build a large boat, to be called The Boston Floating Hospital for Infants and Children. When completed, the hull of the new ship was steel, divided into seven compartments to make it practically unsinkable. It was 170 feet long and had a 46-foot beam to increase stability. There was room for 100 beds. A vast improvement was that children now could be kept aboard when they required hospitalization, and there was space for pediatric research. The cost of the boat was $100,000 without engines, which were installed a year later. It was launched on Saturday, July 7, 1906, at the Atlantic Works Wharf, Border Street, East Boston, and was berthed at North End Pier. The initial trip was made on August 15. It was the only vessel in the world designed and built as a hospital ship. Mr. G. Loring Briggs was manager, and later Mr. Edward Pope.

Over the years, The Boston Floating Hospital contributed much to American pediatrics, especially in the treatment of diarrhea. Many experts attribute the decline of infant diarrhea to research and treatment developed on the ships and to the requirement of pasteurization of milk, which became effective in Boston in 1921. Among the gains in infant feeding and milk chemistry achieved on the ships was the development of the first synthetic milk product, known today as Similac.

During the period 1906 to 1927, The Boston Floating operated a

Sick children, accompanied by mothers or grandmothers, being given attention on Boston Floating Hospital when it was a ship that plied the harbor.

small business office in the old *Boston Globe* building at 244 Washington Street. It also maintained a small research building at Huntington and Massachusetts Avenues, and a small "on-shore" hospital with 10 beds at 38–40 Wigglesworth Street, in a renovated house near the Harvard Medical School, whose doctors and students contributed much to the early development and growth of the Floating Hospital.

One of the outstanding physicians aboard the ship was Dr. Henry I. Bowditch, who was in charge from 1906 to 1925. One report stated, "He had an uncanny knack for pediatric diagnosis and an instinct for successful treatment. He taught students and interns in diagnosing the illnesses of children to first look in their ears."

During 1926, the last year The Boston Floating Hospital floated, 255 patients were admitted for bed treatment and 319 were treated on an outpatient basis. The in-hospital mortality rate had been lowered from 40 percent to 12 percent. In addition, the on-shore section treated 594 patients during 2,241 visits. The follow-up work required 3,066 visits. The whooping-cough clinic had grown to such an extent that 1,521 patients were treated.

An even heavier schedule was anticipated for 1927. Workmen were busy getting the ship ready as she was tied up at North End Pier. During the night of June 1, 1927, patrolman Michael Rizzo of the Hanover Street Station made his usual rounds and cleared the pier of "spooners" using the pier as a "lovers' lane." He noted a flicker of flame near the center of the ship. He said the flames then "seemed to explode." Captain William A. Grover was forced to jump over the side and swim ashore. Three crewmen reached safety by lifeboat. Four alarms were rung to call engines and the city's new fireboat. But the flames spread and were reported by the *Globe* to have leaped 300 feet into the sky. Smoke "settled like a fogbank" over Hingham, Hull, and Cohasset. Only the steel hull of the Floating Hospital survived, later to be turned into an oil barge.

Damage was estimated at $200,000. Fortunately, just a few weeks before the blaze (which was believed to have been started by a discarded cigarette) Mr. Ralph Lowell, a newly elected trustee and treasurer of the corporation, had insisted the boat be insured against fire. Despite some discussion about the high cost of premiums, the boat had been insured for $195,000.

Mothers bring children to wharf in Boston for day's outing and treatment aboard the Boston Floating Hospital ship in early 1900s.

For years afterward, the ultrarespectable Mr. Lowell was twitted at board meetings as being an arsonist who had torched the ship so that he could collect insurance toward the cost of a new hospital ashore. The immediate reaction, however, was one of great discouragement at the loss of the ship and the inability to provide free care for the sick children of the poor of the city. A press report quoted residents of Boston as saying, "Too bad! That ends a beautiful philanthropy."

The hospital directors decided not to build another ship, but to base a new hospital on land. The reasons for this were outlined by the president of the corporation, Mr. Edward W. Pope. He said:

"First of all, the diseases of chidren that used to appear in summer have almost vanished. Increased sanitation, education of mothers, better milk, larger use of ice, freer ventilation — all these have acted to reduce summer sickness of babies and small children. But winter diseases are becoming better known and recognized, even if they are not increasing. The Floating Hospital was useless in winter.

"Second, the difficulty of taking care of children on a boat was very great. The ever-present danger of collision, fire or other disaster, the danger of a tumble overboard, the need for constant supervision, the insatiable curiosity of childhood, the inadequate accommodations and shortage of sanitary arrangements, the need of maintaining a full complement of nurses and attendants through a short season continually interrupted by inclement weather with consequent disappointments — these were some of the things with which a ship hospital must cope, and to which a land hospital is not subject." There was another important consideration: it was estimated that a land-based hospital could be operated a year for the cost of operating a ship hospital during the summer months.

The directors of the Boston Floating then joined with Tufts and the Boston Dispensary to form the New England Medical Center, and proceeded to help raise funds for the new center. The main building of the new Boston Floating Hospital, which was built in 1931 after a major fund drive for the New England Medical Center as a whole, was called the Jackson Memorial Building, dedicated to the memory of Henry Clay Jackson and Paul Wilde Jackson.

The Jackson brothers present yet another example of how significant private philanthropy was in the development of the New England Medical Center. Henry Jackson, a bachelor, became wealthy as a leading force in the development of the West End Street Railway Company, an early predecessor of the Boston Elevated and the MBTA. Mr. Jackson made a will, but died before signing it. As a result, his fortune went to his brother, Paul, who became probably the best-known and certainly the wealthiest conductor on the Old Colony and New Haven railroads. When Paul Jackson died in 1928, he left an estate of more than $400,000.

Paul Jackson attempted to carry out, as far as he could, the wishes of his brother as identified in the unsigned will.

Mr. Henry Brainerd, a New England Medical Center trustee, recalls that among provisions of the Jackson will was a trust fund to benefit the families of employees of the Boston transit system after the death of both brothers. Mr. Ralph Lowell was a trustee of this fund, and it was through his influence that $200,000 of it was used to construct the main building of the new land-based Boston Floating Hospital. "According to my recollection," Mr. Brainerd said, "the thinking was that there could be no better memorial to the Jackson brothers than to build the hospital, name the main building after them, and provide care to the children of the transit employees and to all other children of Boston. Remember that, in those days, before Medicare, Medicaid and even Blue Cross and Blue Shield, every child accepted at the Boston Floating Hospital for care was treated free of charge to the family. Nobody was allowed to pay. Some people who had means and whose children were treated in emergency situations made donations and provided volunteer services to compensate the hospital."

As Henry Brainerd explains it, without the Jacksons' bequest, the shore-based Floating Hospital could not have been built in the 1930s. Even with the insurance money from the boat fire, there would not have been enough money to build and equip a new hospital and participate in the development of the New England Medical Center. Henry Brainerd's architect father, William Hungerford Brainerd, who had been a founding trustee of the Floating Hospital Corporation and served as its clerk for 40 years, supervised the construction of the Floating Hospital and much of the New England Medical Center. He was assisted by his son Henry, an MIT graduate engineer.

Mr. Henry Brainerd recalled, too, that there always was a strong bond between the hospital and Jordan Marsh Company, because a child of one of the store's senior executives was once rushed there in an emergency and saved from death. In 1980 Jordan's opened its Far East merchandise exposition with a benefit performance for the Floating Hospital and raised $46,000 for the new building under construction over Washington Street.

# CHAPTER 5

# Tufts Medical and Dental Schools

The fact that Tufts even had a medical school in 1929, to join with the Boston Dispensary and The Boston Floating Hospital in forming the New England Medical Center, was a result of overcoming formidable obstacles. When Tufts College was founded in 1852, in Medford, by the Universalist Church as a non-sectarian institution, it contained a clause in its charter which prohibited the granting of medical degrees. The clause had been requested from the legislature by Harvard, which already had a medical school.

Precedent for such an action was based on a colonial tradition of protecting monopolies. In Massachusetts history, two other colleges were similarly restricted — Amherst at the request of Williams, which once had a medical school, and Holy Cross at the request of Harvard. It should be noted that in the 1960s, when a State medical school was proposed for the University of Massachusetts, underground opposition to it was voiced by many at the medical schools of Tufts, Boston University, and Harvard; but the schools took no formal action, and the State went ahead to build a school and hospital in Worcester.

Fortunately for the future of the New England Medical Center, Tufts College successfully petitioned the legislature for removal of the offensive clause in 1867, 15 years after its founding. Tufts did not envision having a medical school, but chafed under the restriction and fought the ban as a matter of principle.

Harvard again assumed the role of objector in 1867, arguing this time that there already were too many medical schools in New England:

Harvard, Yale, Williams, Vermont, Bowdoin, and Dartmouth. Harvard officials said that Tufts did not have the financial resources of Harvard and that if Tufts did try to start a medical school, it would not be as good as Harvard's. This, they declared, would end up reducing the quality of care to patients.

In citing their resources, Harvard authorities reported that in 1867 their medical school owned real estate worth $100,000 and had an endowment of $80,000. (In 1981 the Harvard Medical School endowment was $142 million. Harvard officials said it was difficult to estimate the value of the quadrangle and land off Longwood Avenue in 1981, but said it included 14 acres of prize land and 1.1 million square feet of floor space. The endowment of Tufts Medical School in 1981 was $4 million. The entire Tufts–New England Medical Center complex (including hospitals, medical and dental schools), comprised only 13 acres of land, one of the most intensely-used areas of any medical center.)

During the 1867 altercations between Tufts and Harvard over the granting of medical degrees, the legislature accepted the views of the Reverend Alonzo A. Miner, then president of Tufts, that it was "intolerable for one college [Harvard] to assume a protectorate over another in this age of freedom." The limitation against granting of medical degrees by Tufts was revoked.

The importance of the legislative victory for Tufts in 1867 was that 25 years later, in 1892, the college trustees were empowered to act when the opportunity actually arose to open a medical school and grant medical degrees.

In that year seven physicians resigned from the College of Physicians and Surgeons of Boston, a medical school they owned and operated in conjunction with a group of doctors. The seven were dissatisfied with the quality of medical education being provided by a school that was run as a private business (a proprietary medical school). They then formed a new non-profit school and asked Tufts to provide academic affiliation, which they believed was essential to quality medical training.

Tufts considered the request, but hesitated for a time in agreeing to it because the trustees feared they might place financial strain on the college. They noted the formidable competition offered by Harvard, and took into consideration the founding about 20 years earlier, in 1873, of the Homeopathic College of Physicians and Surgeons (which was to become Boston University School of Medicine). In addition, several New England medical schools had run into financial difficulties. One example was the Berkshire Medical Institution in Pittsfield, operating in conjunction with Williams College, which had closed in 1867 as a result of high costs and lack of indigent patients for teaching purposes.

The trustees' fears were not unrealistic, as was seen in 1915 when Dartmouth reduced its medical school to two years of preclinical training, also because of financial problems and lack of sufficient patients for teaching. (Dartmouth was able to reopen as a four-year school in 1970, when the Mary Hitchcock Hospital became a major institution.) In 1921 Bowdoin found it necessary to close its medical school altogether.

The Tufts trustees finally agreed to accept the suggestion of the seven physicians, but stipulated that the doctors would have to run the school for a test period of three years at no cost or obligation to the college.

The seven doctors who accepted the challenge were Albert Nott, who became the first dean, William R. Chipman, Walter L. Hall, Charles P. Thayer, John W. Johnson, Henry W. Dudley, and Frank C. Wheatley.

Founders of Tufts University School of Medicine: Front row, left to right, Dr. John W. Johnson, Professor of Obstetrics and Gynecology; Dr. Charles P. Thayer, Professor of Surgical Anatomy; Dr. Albert Nott, Professor of Hygiene and first Dean; Dr. William R. Chipman, Professor of Operative Surgery. Back row: Dr. Henry W. Dudley, Professor of Pathology; Dr. Walter L. Hall, Professor of Medicine; Dr. Frank G. Wheatley, Professor of Materia Medica and Therapeutics.

Doctors Johnson, Dudley, and Wheatley were graduates of Harvard Medical School. The others were graduates of Vermont, Dartmouth, and Bellevue Hospital medical schools.

The new Tufts Medical School attracted 80 students when it opened in the fall of 1893. In 1896, when the test period ended and the college became more actively involved, there were 176 students. The first home of the Medical School was the two upper floors of a retail store building then at 188 Boylston Street, opposite the Public Garden, but since torn down. Tuition for the three-year course (soon increased to four) was $250 when paid in advance. (Tuition in the early 1980s was $9950 a year for the four-year course at the Dental School and $11,950 at the Medical School.)

The original site of the Medical School soon became too small for its rapidly expanding classes, and in 1896, the college leased the old Chauncy Hall School building in Copley Square. A year later, in 1897, a third move was made into an abandoned Baptist church at Rutland Street and Shawmut Avenue in the South End. In 1901, a new building was constructed to house the Medical School at 416 Huntington Avenue.

It was just at the time of the founding of the Medical School that the parent college in Medford made a major policy change. Tufts had always accepted women on a limited basis, but now began enrolling them on the same basis as male students. The policy was carried over to the Medical School, which from its opening day declined to discriminate against women. The very first graduating class, which numbered 22, included eight women. Although Johns Hopkins Medical School also accepted women from the date of its founding in 1893, many medical schools either allowed women to take only special courses or banned their presence altogether until the 1940s.

Commenting on the admission of women to medical schools, President Elmer Capen of Tufts said in a speech on the occasion of the move of the Medical School to the South End in 1897: "The time has gone by for discussing the propriety of women devoting themselves to the practice of medicine. We cannot now raise the question whether women have the requisite qualities for the successful physician, whether the subjects embraced in medical investigation are not too indelicate for the refined instincts and tender sensibilities of women, whether they have the steadiness of nerve, the requisite self-control, and the fertility of resources demanded by great exigencies in both medical and surgical cases."

He concluded: "These questions have all been answered in the most effectual way possible. Women have entered upon the work. They have become both physicians and surgeons. They have shown their ability in the face of prejudice and demonstrated their skill and fitness under circumstances of the gravest difficulty. They have shown that there is a place for them."

In 1980, women made up approximately a third of the entering class in Tufts Medical School.

By 1903, with an enrollment of 403 and a teaching staff of 105, Tufts had become the largest medical school in New England. Ninety-seven percent of the students came from the region and the majority remained to practice in the New England states. Harvard by this time had begun to assume a national role, educating professors and scientists for the nation and the world, but kept classes smaller.

The 1910 report of Abraham Flexner, sponsored by the Carnegie Foundation, was a major turning point for Tufts Medical School. A social scientist, Flexner visited and reported on all 155 medical schools in the United States and Canada at the time. As a result of his appraisals, and with pressure applied by the American Medical Association, 95 schools were closed, leaving 60 in operation. Most of the closed schools had been proprietary, run as private businesses.

Dr. Flexner considered Tufts to be a strong medical school, but he had harsh words about its admission policies (which allowed acceptance, until 1914, of students out of high school). He also criticized the size of the classes, which were reduced from 140 to 100 after his report.

Flexner further criticized the lack of teaching facilities. At the time of his report, Tufts was limited to Boston City Hospital, a Tufts clinic in the South End, Beth Israel Hospital, and Carney Hospital, then in South Boston. A number of specialty hospitals were included later. These were the Evangeline Booth, a maternity hospital conducted by the Salvation Army; the New England Hospital for Women and Children; the Blossom Street Health Center of the City of Boston; and a number of hospitals outside the city.

In 1919 John Albert Cousens became president of Tufts, a post which he was to hold until his death in 1937. He had hoped to be a physician, but had been forced to give up his undergraduate studies at Tufts because of the death of his father. He took over the family coal business, which eventually was merged with the Metropolitan Coal Company. He also was president for many years of the Brookline Savings Bank. Elected a trustee of Tufts, he served so well as an interim president of the college that he was named president.

President Cousens, tall and always erect and dignified in appearance, looked every inch a college president. He was both an intellectual and a good businessman and steered the college successfully through the Depression. He was wholeheartedly in favor of the establishment of the New England Medical Center. There is some evidence that Abraham Flexner, who was a friend of Dr. Pratt, encouraged both Dr. Pratt and President Cousens to join the alliance.

The beginnings of the Tufts School of Dental Medicine bear a striking resemblance to the circumstances surrounding the Tufts Medical School. In 1899, the Boston Dental College, then 30 years old, found that it required an academic affiliation in order to teach advanced physiology to its students. It applied to Tufts for affiliation, which was granted the same year. With university affiliation, the school was able to obtain cadavers for the teaching of anatomy.

Dentistry had been slow to advance in the United States. Colonial dentistry was a technical craft with practitioners who were primarily artisans in gold, silver, and other metals, and who devoted part of their time to constructing prosthetic dental appliances. One of the most eminent of these was Paul Revere, who advertised himself as a "goldsmith who could make false teeth that looked as good as real ones."

By the 1860s, there was a large group of qualified practitioners in Boston who formed the Massachusetts Dental Society in 1864. Within four years they created two outstanding dental schools, Harvard's and the Boston Dental College, which became Tufts Dental School.

The Tufts Dental School was located in the same Huntington Avenue building as the Medical School. Its clinics became so well known in the early 1900s that conductors on the Huntington Avenue streetcar line always sang out the name to let riders know they were near treatment for their ailing jaws. The site of the old dental school is now occupied by Northeastern University. A proud new school building rises at the corner of Kneeland and Washington Streets and is called the Dental

Health Sciences Building of Tufts–New England Medical Center. The school today is the largest source of dental health practitioners in New England. Over the years women students have increased in number constantly; of 246 students at Tufts Dental School in 1980–81, 92 were women. More than half the dentists in Massachusetts have received their degrees from Tufts.

# CHAPTER 6

# Boston and Heidelberg

It was an exciting new world of clinical and scientific medicine into which Dr. Proger was plunged after his arrival in Boston from Atlanta in 1929. He had the opportunity to serve the poorest of the poor in their homes and at the clinics of the Boston Dispensary. He saw at first hand the desperate plight of immigrants crowded into Boston's slums and their devastation when they got sick.

Dr. Proger also had the opportunity to mingle with and learn from some of the best minds in medicine. On Saturdays, for example, when the clinics at the Dispensary were closed, he visited the clinical and research laboratories at Boston City Hospital. There the prominent scientists, physicians, and educators from Harvard, Tufts, and Boston University, who staffed the various services, were making constant progress toward understanding the causes of various diseases and learning better ways to control or cure them.

He also observed medical care programs at the Peter Bent Brigham and Massachusetts General Hospitals and met specialists from the Lahey Clinic and Children's Hospital. He was invited to join a city-wide group of heart specialists organized by Dr. Paul Dudley White to promote the new specialty of cardiology, which still had not been recognized as a major discipline of medicine. In fact the American Heart Association had been organized in 1924, only five years before Dr. Proger came to Boston.

Dr. Proger kept busy, also, with his own research. During his first year in the city he had four papers accepted for publication in the *New*

*England Journal of Medicine,* an unusual honor for a physician still in training as a resident. Two of the papers were on the use of the electro-cardiograph, which had been known in the United States for only 15 years at the time. A third was on psychogenic fever, as observed in a young woman with emotional problems. The fourth paper was a report on studies of kidney function.

During all the activity, young Dr. Proger still missed his fiancée, and returned to Atlanta to marry Evelyn on September 8, the day after her birthday. The couple returned to Boston to establish themselves in an apartment on James Street in Brookline.

The young couple thought their opportunities for getting along finan-cially were pretty good, because the New England Medical Center was to be formally announced as a reality within just a few weeks of their wedding. What they didn't know was that the Great Depression also was due to strike all America in October, little more than a month after their marriage. "In some ways, it was a good time to get started," Dr. Proger said years later. "We all were placed on an equal footing. We were all broke."

The Progers soon gained a wide variety of friends and acquaintances and, despite the Depression, managed to enjoy many of the cultural advantages of Boston. They became enthusiasts of the Boston Symphony Orchestra, which they were to enjoy and support. Maestro Serge Kous-sevitzky would later become one of Dr. Proger's patients.

Among the people he met at the Dispensary was Mr. Arthur G. Rotch, who was president of the board. He was the first of the patrician, service-oriented men the young Dr. Proger was to meet in Boston. Mr. Rotch was indeed the Proper Bostonian in appearance, with his black shoes, conservative ties, dark suits, and black derby, the latter in those days a part of the blue-blood uniform. A descendant of a New Bedford ship-owning family, Mr. Rotch was of medium height and prematurely bald; he had blue eyes and a frequent grin that would bring crinkles around his eyes. For many years concerned about social problems, he had been director of the New England Red Cross before becoming president of the Dispensary. He was later selected by President Roosevelt to be administrator of the Works Progress Administration (WPA) in Massa-chusetts in the 1930s.

A second man of influence at the Dispensary was Frank Wing, a quiet, cautious man who took pride in being a member of the Cape Cod clan of Wings. As director, he efficiently carried out the decrees of his board and guided the Dispensary through the period of alliance and for a number of years after. He served under both Mr. Rotch and, later, Judge Charles C. Cabot, who took over when Mr. Rotch moved to the WPA post. Mr. Wing's assistant was Miss Abbie Dunks, then a young social worker out of Simmons, who was to succeed Mr. Wing and become an eminent director of the Dispensary in later years.

That first year in Boston, so busy and exciting for the Progers, was beginning to draw to a close when Dr. Pratt said he was determined that Dr. Proger should have the opportunity of a year's study in Germany. Dr. Pratt wanted him to work under the same Dr. Ludolf Krehl with whom Pratt had studied years before. In fact Dr. Pratt had been Dr. Krehl's first American student in 1900; and Dr. Proger was to be the last before Dr. Krehl's retirement in 1930.

Dr. Pratt obtained a grant to help finance the year in Germany and the Progers left in July. They went first to Vienna, where Dr. Proger studied pathology for six weeks, and then on to Heidelberg, a city where learning and culture also prevailed. Dr. Proger considered this one of the most important years of his life. He learned a great deal from Dr. Krehl and his associates about research, and began there a lifelong series of research projects involving the function and care of the heart.

One lesson that always remained with him was that patient care deteriorates when doctors (as some of the Germans had) allow science to become predominant over interest in the patient. In later years, as Dr. Proger became the guiding force behind the development of the New England Medical Center Hospital, he was determined to maintain a balance between scientific pursuits and care of the patient. In 1930, when he went to Germany, the balance there had swung so far toward research that he was appalled. "It was not that what they were doing was unimportant," Dr. Proger was to say later. "It was very important; but I felt, even though I was then so young, that they had lost the balance."

When discussing the overemphasis on research to the detriment of patient care, Dr. Proger recalled that the German doctors with whom he worked couldn't get their daily rounds over fast enough. All they wanted was to get back to their laboratories. "One day we saw a patient who had what seemed to me a classical case of myocardial infarction [heart attack due to an arterial blood clot]. I was very much aware of the symptoms because Dr. Samuel Levine at the Peter Bent Brigham had just written a book on coronary thrombosis, as it was then called. I had read the book. The German doctors apparently hadn't, and they insisted the man's condition was due to angina. When the pain did not subside, I spoke to Dr. Krehl again and told him that coronary thrombosis had been recognized in America. But he brushed it aside. I insisted on taking an electrocardiogram, and the evidence of heart attack was there. This was ignored. Then the patient died. I had been telling Dr. Krehl that I would like to attend the autopsy. Again, the evidence was there. This is just one example, of many I can remember, of the lack of concern with clinical medicine in Germany at the time, and how patient care can be neglected when scientific medicine is overemphasized."

Dr. Proger said that he sometimes was embarrassed in Germany when, three years out of medical school, he felt that he was more aware than some of the professors of how to deal with some of the problems of patients. Dr. Proger laid part of the blame for the deterioration of world leadership in medicine in Germany to the imbalanced pursuit of science. He said the deterioration began before Hitler's rise to power, so that the relative decline of German medicine cannot all be blamed on the despotism of Hitler, as is so often assumed.

His observations in Germany made Dr. Proger keenly aware of possible dangers of extremism in medicine in the United States. He emphasized patient care in the 30-year period after 1930, when science held sway in this country and many of the brightest minds in American medicine were to be found in the laboratories and government institutes. Then, in the 1970s, he warned repeatedly against allowing primary care to become such an overriding goal that scientific research would be slighted.

Dr. Proger, since his college days, believed that progress is made only when opposing forces are in proper balance, or seeking to restore balance as a process of nature. When there is too great an imbalance, he said, decline results. In an essay on the subject in 1945, he wrote, "These forces are dynamic and thus there is a constant struggle to achieve balance. A continuing struggle is required, therefore, to maintain a workable range."

In his essay, Dr. Proger said in part: "We accept the naturalness of good and evil, love and hate, right and left, without recognizing the significance of such antagonisms. The concept of the fundamental nature of opposites is as old as philosophy itself. Aristotle's essay on the 'golden mean' was simply a discourse on the virtues of that large, comfortable area within the extremes. Hegel, with his 'thesis, antithesis and synthesis', recognized the importance of opposites. Most people are vaguely aware that somehow or other they are forever involved in the process of resolving conflicts of opposing forces."

He said that "just as Nature abhors a vacuum, so it strives for dynamic equilibrium, a striving that is universal and basic to human physiology as well as matters of the spirit." He said it molds social structures, determines physical reactions, forms the basis for economics, and underlies politics.

"The principle of life itself," Dr. Proger wrote, "appears to be one of antagonistic forces leading to growth, stability or decline, as the case may be. The pupil of the eye is a certain size not because a nerve adjusts it to that size, but rather because of a balanced adjustment between nerves which act antagonistically, one to dilate and one to contract the pupil. The same is true of the caliber of blood vessels, the action of the intestines, the beat of the heart. As we increase our knowledge of some of the more obscure aspects of biological behavior, we find that every phase of such behavior is ultimately dependent upon the satisfactory functioning of the opposing forces within a given range. The wisdom of the body consists essentially of maintaining various states of equilibrium, of functioning within a range consistent with these states of equilibrium and of achieving growth through the orderly development of new equilibria. . . . The whole universe is held together by similar forces. From the macrocosm to the microcosm the energizing force and the source of all vitality is that force generated by the perpetual attempt of opposing forces to achieve some degree of equilibrium."

He concluded that this was a reassuring philosophy because it not only indicates that a struggle is necessary and inevitable, but also that it is, in fact, desirable. Conceding that this philosophy contained a grain of determinism, he said, "There is this important difference; there is a wide range for the operation of the free will within the predetermined area of the struggle."

The year the Progers remained in Germany helped him develop this philosophy, which was to remain a large factor in his life. It also strengthened his own desire for a career in which he could balance research, patient care, and teaching. While in Germany, he received an offer from Dr. Paullin of a post in Atlanta that would satisfy these desires. But Dr. Pratt offered similar opportunities in Boston. Again, there was a need to weigh the balances.

One argument for going back to Atlanta was raised by the same Dr. Councilman who had befriended Dr. Pratt at Harvard and at Boston City Hospital. He told Mrs. Proger that her husband should not opt for an academic career in Boston because prejudice against Jews made it very difficult to rise beyond a certain point in university hospitals and medical schools. They could gain respected positions, he said, but being a chief of medicine or a full professor would be extremely difficult, if not impossible. This impressed the Progers because of their experience in Germany, where discrimination was rampant.

As it turned out, in 1948 Dr. Proger was to become a full professor of medicine and head of a university hopital. By 1980, a considerable number of the chiefs of service at university hospitals in Boston were Jewish. The change in attitude and academic opportunity for Jewish physicians was compared by Dr. Proger to professional sports after the color line was broken and black players, the restraints lifted, emerged into prominence in baseball, football, and basketball.

The decision to remain in Boston was complicated by offers from other cities, but in each of the other offers it would have been necessary to begin by working on research undertaken by other physicians. Dr. Pratt offered Dr. Proger his own laboratory and an opportunity to do his own work. Also influential in the decision to remain in Boston was the academic atmosphere of the city and its surroundings.

Exactly what academic medicine meant in the mind of Dr. Proger was crystallized over the years. Putting his thoughts together on what it was, and on the relationship between laboratory and the bedside, he wrote in the September 9, 1965, *New England Journal of Medicine*:

"If the practice of academic medicine means anything, it means the practice of medicine in an academic environment; that is, an environment of scholarly and creative effort. The talent for such effort may be applied at the bedside as well as in the laboratory, for it is at the bedside that crucial questions are often formulated, a great many of which can still be answered by the prepared and original mind with relatively limited laboratory aids."

He added that "those questions that cannot be answered, or that require further exploration through more advanced studies, can then be passed on to those equipped to carry out such studies. There, too, questions may arise in the laboratory that must ultimately be answered at the bedside. The movement is two-way between the research laboratory and the bedside."

# CHAPTER 7

# Dr. John George Gehring

One of those small coincidences that later turn out to be of major significance to an institution occurred just a few weeks after Dr. Proger returned from Germany in the summer of 1931. A patient named John George Gehring, a physician himself, presented himself to Dr. Pratt for treatment of angina pectoris, chest pains due to insufficient oxygen reaching the heart. Dr. Gehring had been traveling from his home in Bethel, Maine, to Baltimore for treatment by Dr. W. S. Thayer at Johns Hopkins University Hospital. Dr. Thayer told him the travel was a strain for a man of 74 with angina and urged him to go to Dr. Pratt in Boston, an old friend and a recognized authority on heart problems.

Dr. Pratt accepted the patient and instituted a regimen of medication, bed rest, and psychological encouragement. Dr. Gehring knew there was nothing at the time that could really relieve his underlying disease, atherosclerosis (hardening of the arteries). This was long before bypass surgery and modern heart drugs. Somehow, however, he did improve under Dr. Pratt's care and became an enthusiastic supporter of his psychotherapy programs. The two physicians became close friends.

When a young friend of Dr. Gehring's in Bethel developed gall bladder trouble, Dr. Gehring sent him to Dr. Pratt. The young man was William Bingham, 2nd, who was to give millions of dollars over the years to finance the growth of the New England Medical Center Hospital and to support the Bingham Associates Program for development of medical care in Maine.

Mr. Bingham, despite his wealth, was charged a very modest fee by

Dr. Pratt for diagnosis and treatment. He appreciated the fact that he was treated on the same financial basis as other patients. When surgery later became necessary and Mr. Bingham was operated on at a hospital selected by his Cleveland family, he was charged $50,000. This infuriated him. He was told that it was common practice to overcharge the wealthy to help pay for treatment of the sick poor. Mr. Bingham replied that if the hospital needed money it should ask for a gift, not overcharge him. He did not approve of their "Robin Hood" policy. He remained close to the New England Medical Center the rest of his life.

Dr. Gehring's introduction of Mr. Bingham to Dr. Pratt in itself makes him deserving of a footnote in the history of the New England Medical Center Hospital. But he did much more in the 14 months he had left to live after meeting Dr. Pratt, in that he encouraged the founding of the Bingham Associates Program.

Dr. Gehring's presence in Maine had come about in a rather unusual way. He had been a young surgeon in Cleveland, promising enough at age 30 to join with Dr. George Crile in the founding of the famed Crile Clinic there. He suffered a nervous breakdown, however, and moved to tiny Bethel, Maine, where his friends Mr. and Mrs. George Farnsworth lived. The little town on the Androscoggin River, upstream from Rumford and Lewiston, had a population of only 500 when Dr. Gehring arrived there in 1887 and decided to stay.

Within a year Mr. Farnsworth died. Later, Dr. Gehring, a bachelor, married his widow. (Mrs. Gehring was also to play a part in the New England Medical Center Hospital, by approaching Mr. Bingham for his first contribution.) Mrs. Gehring had one son, George Farnsworth, who would become a doctor and for whom the Farnsworth Building at the hospital is named. The young Dr. Farnsworth became a major force in the life of Mr. Bingham and in the development of both the hospital and the Bingham Program.

Dr. Gehring, in the years before he met Dr. Pratt, had become widely known for his programs of psychiatric therapy for business and professional men suffering from overwork and nervous fatigue. The treatment included a stay at the Gehrings' spacious Bethel home, where the patients would swim in the pool, chop wood, weed gardens, feed chickens, and walk in the woods.

Dr. Gehring's patients were free to read what they wanted, with some exceptions. He said that sex stories were decidedly disturbing to the nervous system and banned them. He recommended adventure tales and pirate stories as being good for relaxation.

Everybody at the Gehrings' would dress for dinner in the evening. The conversation would range from politics and religion to art and music. The talk was described by some participants as being "as brilliant as any in the best salons of Europe." Nobody was allowed to talk about his own or anybody else's illness. There was also a list of 17 subjects that were taboo at meals.

It would be nice to have a photograph of one of those dinners, with the Gehrings presiding. He was a jaunty man who wore round, horn-rimmed glasses and a stiff collar. He had a high forehead and parted his hair high on the left side. A smoker of little cigars, he was an elegant dresser and full of verve.

Mrs. Gehring was an imposing woman who wore rimless glasses and piled her white hair high on the top of her head. She was called "the duchess" by other women of Bethel. She was a person of considerable intellect, the patients agreed, and she often tried to impart culture to the students at Gould Academy, where she was a trustee and where her father had been headmaster.

Mrs. Gehring met Dr. Pratt and Dr. Proger through her husband and became a friend and patient of both. Dr. Proger recalled going to Bethel at one time to see Mrs. Gehring: "Evelyn and I were invited to tea. Mrs. Gehring sat there in a high, wired lace collar, looking every bit the duchess. A Mrs. Thurston was her lady-in-waiting. It was just as if you had stepped back into the 19th-century England."

In 1937, when Mrs. Gehring was 87, Dr. Proger was asked to go to Miami where she was ill. She was a widow then, Dr. Gehring having died in 1932 in the middle of a sentence, a typical sudden death from coronary disease. Dr. Proger expected Mrs. Gehring to be concerned about her illness, which was her last. "Instead, I was surprised to learn," he said, "that her first concern was for the British Royal Family. It was the time of King Edward's abdication to marry Mrs. Wallis Warfield Simpson. Even today, years later, it is hard for me to believe. She even asked me if I thought her concern over the king could have caused her illness. She had a strong attachment for the concept of British royalty and all it symbolized."

After Dr. Gehring's death, Dr. Arthur L. Walters of Miami Beach had become Mr. Bingham's personal physician, in that Dr. Farnsworth's main area of expertise was obstetrics. Dr. Walters also became involved in affairs at New England Medical Center. He gave up his practice, as Dr. Gehring had before him, to travel with Mr. Bingham and to be at his call at all times. He became a trustee of the Bingham Program in 1947 and was very active in the Program.

When Mrs. Gehring died, a trust fund of $1 million, which had been established by Mr. Bingham to ensure her freedom from economic worries during her lifetime, became available. Mr. Bingham turned the money over to Dr. Pratt and Dr. Proger for construction of the Farnsworth Building at the New England Medical Center, the building that became the heart of the hospital.

Mr. Bingham, incidentally, also had settled a trust of $1 million on Dr. Gehring during his lifetime. He also donated $200,000 to the Neurological Institute of New York (now part of the Columbia Presbyterian Medical Center) to build an entire floor of four wards and eight rooms in honor of Dr. Gehring and his pioneer work in Maine in group psychotherapy. While Mr. Bingham's first known major gift to medicine was in New York, most of his future contributions were to benefit Boston and New England.

# CHAPTER 8

# William Bingham, 2nd, Philanthropist

William Bingham, 2nd, the financial angel for the early development of the New England Medical Center Hospital, was a shy, reclusive man who dedicated the latter part of his life to medical and educational philanthropy. He obtained the means to help others from a large trust fund established for him by an uncle, Oliver Hazard Payne, who had been one of America's richest men. The lifetime trust is estimated to have amounted eventually to $40 million, thanks to prudent investments and modest living on the part of Mr. Bingham.

William Bingham, 2nd, arrived in New England from Cleveland in 1911, when he was 32. He was a victim of mental depression. He settled in the peaceful town of Bethel, Maine, and placed himself under the care of Dr. John Gehring, hoping that Dr. Gehring's group therapy sessions would improve his health and outlook.

The quiet, withdrawn Mr. Bingham was a sensitive, inward-turning bachelor, very different in personality and makeup from other members of his large and aggressive family. He was quiet and very private; his siblings and other relatives were outgoing and sociable and active in business, politics, and community programs. A sister, Frances Payne Bolton, for example, was a Red Cross nurse in World War I and became one of the early women members of Congress.

William Bingham, 2nd, was born on July 21, 1879, the son of Charles William and Mary Payne Bingham. He was named for his grandfather, who had founded a Cleveland hardware empire and been elected a city councilor and state senator. His mother was a member of the widely known Payne family. His grandfather on the Payne side was United States Senator Henry (Harry) Payne, generally remembered for the Payne-Aldrich tariff legislation of the late 1800s, and because he sought the Presidential nomination at several National Democratic Conventions. The Paynes traced their lineage back to Yarmouth, Massachusetts, and 1639.[1]

The most important member of the family, so far as the history of the New England Medical Center is concerned, was William Bingham's "Uncle Oliver," the brother of William Bingham's mother, Mary, and the man who established the trust fund that made Mr. Bingham's medical philanthropy possible. He was a remarkable character in addition to being one of America's early business tycoons.

After attending high school in Cleveland, Oliver Hazard Payne went to Phillips Academy, Andover, and then on to the traditional family college, Yale. He left Yale after his sophomore year to join the Union Army; he was wounded at Chickamauga, but returned later to lead troops and was commissioned a colonel while he was only in his early twenties.

After the war Colonel Payne returned to Cleveland. There he joined his brother, Nathan Payne, in the oil business, which they entered before John D. Rockefeller (who had gone to high school with Oliver) started the Standard Oil Company. Eventually their company was merged with Standard Oil, of which Oliver became treasurer. He later left, with tremendous stock holdings, and went on to become a founder of the American Tobacco Company, the Great Northern Paper Company, and the Tennessee Coal and Iron Company. He also became involved in railroads.

Oliver Payne owned the *Aphrodite,* the largest steam yacht in the United States, and sailed it around the world; but he didn't spend all his money on yachts. He gave millions to help found Cornell Medical

---

[1] Many Maine people believe that William Bingham, 2nd, was a member of the family for whom the town of Bingham, Maine, is named. Miss Eva Bean, historian of Gould Academy, wrote in her records that she found some evidence of a distant kinship to William Bingham, a pre-Revolutionary resident of Philadelphia who was given vast tracts of land in Maine by King George III. She said it was the Philadelphia family for whom the town was named. William Bingham, 2nd, was descended from the Binghams who came from England in 1642 and settled in Norwich, Connecticut.

College and other millions to Lakeside Hospital in Cleveland, Yale University, and the New York Public Library.

When Colonel Payne died in 1917 at age 78, he left the bulk of his estate, valued in the headlines of the day at $178,898,655, to two nieces and four nephews. Dr. Proger recollected that he was told the estate was divided into 10 shares, with Mr. Bingham's trust consisting of one share. This would have made his trust fund worth more than $17 million, the income from which would be his, as would the income from the trust's growth in value. The money reverted to the family when Mr. Bingham died, as he had no issue.

The others who shared in Colonel Payne's vast fortune included Mr. Bingham's younger brother, Harry Payne Bingham, and his sisters, Frances Payne Bolton and Elizabeth B. Blossom, who each received a share. Two of Mr. Bingham's cousins who benefited from the great fortune were Payne Whitney and Harry Payne Whitney, sons of Mr. Bingham's Aunt Flora. She was the matriarch of the Whitney clan, having married William C. Whitney, a friend of Colonel Payne and Secretary of the Navy under President Cleveland. Between them, the Whitney nephews received the remaining six shares under the will,[2] Col. Payne was reported to be worth $300 million at one period during his long life. He was 79 when he died.

William Bingham, 2nd, was a rather frail child growing up in the midst of intense activity. He knew his Aunt Flora Whitney in Washington was the hostess of presidents and cabinet ministers and a favorite sister of Uncle Oliver. He knew that his father, grandfathers, and uncles were famous men. But even as a boy he was reclusive and preferred to stay in the house and play his violin, abstaining from rough boyhood games. His family considered him a bit of a hypochondriac and chided him for reading so much while his schoolmates played baseball. He did, on a few occasions, go hunting and canoeing with a friend, Gardiner Abbot.

Mr. Bingham's sister, Congresswoman Bolton, told Dr. Jean Curran, a long-time consultant for the Bingham Program, that "Will," as he was called, had no interest in girls in high school; that his manner of life was puritanical and that he was critical of some of the free and easy ways of

---

[2] Two books published in 1980 include further information about Colonel Payne and the Whitneys. One is *Whitney Father, Whitney Heiress,* by W. A. Swanberg, Scribner's; the other is *John D., Father of the Rockefellers,* by John J. Reardon, Harper and Row.

Mr. William Bingham 2nd, playing his violin during a benefit concert for Gould Academy on the campus in Bethel, Maine, during the 1920s. He was a trustee of the school for many years.

his companions at the University School in Cleveland. He was sent to St. Paul's School in Concord, New Hampshire, as an eleventh grader, but didn't care much for preparatory school life. He contracted typhoid fever and was seriously ill for many months. He then went through a great crisis when both his mother, whom he adored, and his older brother Oliver, whom he hero-worshipped, died within a short period. He didn't do much of anything for a time, giving up any ideas of going to college, and staying home to play his violin.

After a time his father urged him to join the family hardware business, but Will was not interested, Mrs. Bolton said. She added that one day their father came home from work after a particularly trying day and saw Will relaxing in the music room, playing his violin. The elder Bingham became so enraged at seeing his son playing the role of dilettante, while he and the rest of the family were engaged in a multitude of activities, that he snatched the violin and smashed it across the corner of the piano.

Dr. Curran wrote afterward in notes he made on the Bingham Program: "That acutely traumatic episode obviously was the final blow to Will's equanimity, and never again did they enjoy a father-son relationship. Apparently his [Will's] reaction was to retreat from the world into a secluded one of his own contriving."

William Bingham left home and traveled to Wyoming, where he rode horses and collected Western paintings. Then he went to Santa Barbara, California, where he spent several winters during his early twenties.

He apparently did not lack for funds during this period, having had money settled on him by various members of his family, including his mother and his Uncle Oliver. He would return to Cleveland from time to time and then travel extensively. But, as time went on, he became convinced that he needed some help and in 1911 he decided to go to Maine and place himself in the Gehring program there.

He became very attached to the Gehrings, living in their home with other patients for a time, then buying a house of his own nearby. As Dr. Gehring's group increased in size and the doctor could not house all those who wanted to join (his limit was 18), Mr. Bingham and a group of Boston and Cleveland men formed a corporation in 1912 to build and operate the Bethel Inn.[3]

Mr. Bingham also became interested, through Mrs. Gehring, in Gould Academy, and began giving financial aid to the school. He even conquered his natural shyness enough to play his violin at a number of benefit concerts for the school, accompanied on the piano by his sister, Mrs. Bolton. Over the years, he donated millions of dollars to Gould, paying for most of the beautiful campus that exists there today. He became a trustee in 1917.

That was the year, also, when Mr. Bingham was able to expand his charities, coming into the trust fund set up by his uncle, Oliver Payne. One of the things he did was to ensure that the water supply of Bethel, famous for its quality, would remain free of contamination: he bought the whole mountainside where the water originated and deeded it to the town, so that nobody could encroach on it.

It was 20 years after Mr. Bingham moved to Bethel that he met Dr. Pratt and, later, Dr. Proger, and began to develop his interest in pro-

---

[3] A plaque in the Bethel Inn reads: "The Bethel Inn stands as a visible expression of appreciation of an unusual physician and of gratitude for the inspiring personality shown in the work of John George Gehring, M.D., and has been made possible through the recognition of Horace Sears, Boston; Robert Winsor, Boston; Charles W. Hubbard, Boston; William J. Upson, Cleveland; William Bingham, Cleveland." Mr. Upson was a friend of Mr. Bingham's who had come with him to Bethel to enroll in the therapy courses.

moting Maine medicine and building the Pratt Clinic and the New England Medical Center Hospital.

Dr. Proger, in 1981, recalled a few of the many meetings he had with Mr. Bingham during the years from 1932 to 1955, the year of Mr. Bingham's death. He described Mr. Bingham as being of medium size, with a prominent brow and sharp blue eyes. "Always neatly groomed, his clothes were conservative and well tailored and ran to dark browns and grays. He was deliberate and unhurried in his movements and he walked with almost military erectness. He changed remarkably little in the 23 years I knew him."

Dr. Proger described Mr. Bingham's lifestyle as unlike any he had ever known. "He created a wall between himself and the rest of the world — a wall through which the outside world could not see or penetrate, but through which he saw clearly and functioned efficiently in the development of his large charities; for he was extremely well informed about what was going on in the world and acutely aware of even the minutest details relating to the affairs that touched his own interests."

Dr. Proger noted that Mr. Bingham's physical health was fairly normal, yet he had a nurse with him at all times. Dr. Proger speculated that at the time of World War I Dr. Gehring, knowing that Mr. Bingham was unfit for military service, had certified him as an invalid. "Mr. Bingham was such a righteous and honorable person that I think he made up his mind, consciously or subconsciously, that he was sick. Because if he became well, he would be living a lie."

Mr. Bingham's attitude toward his health was displayed on one occasion when he came to Boston for a checkup. Everything turned out to be normal. When Dr. Proger went by to tell him the good news, Mr. Bingham's face fell as if he had been told he was going to die. Yet, on another occasion, when hospitalization was recommended for other tests, and the hospital was crowded, Mr. Bingham was concerned that he might be depriving some other patient of a bed.

A very practical side of Mr. Bingham is revealed in a story Dr. Proger often told. It seems that Mr. Bingham never drove a car and paid his chauffeur $7000 a year. Dr. Proger thought that was rather a high salary during the 1930s and asked about it. Mr. Bingham said that the chauffeur was required to own the car and to buy a new Packard whenever one was needed. In this way, if ever there was an accident, the chauffeur would be the person sued. No judge or jury could decide to relieve Mr. Bingham of a chunk of his fortune.

In summing up his thoughts about Mr. Bingham, Dr. Proger said: "He had a mind that was clear and often embarrassingly logical. His questions were penetrating and the answers had to be rational and to the point. His remarkable qualities stand out clearly and strikingly; a concern for human welfare, a special concern for sick people, a gentleness of spirit, a bigness of heart and firmness of conviction, an abiding goodness and warmth, a spirituality, a simplicity of tastes, a wholesomeness, a high integrity, an absolute honesty, an amazing memory, a keen sense of humor, and, to be sure, certain superficial peculiarities. He was as spontaneous and thoughtfully selective in his giving as he was restrained and almost monastic in his living. He was extraordinary in every sense of the word."

# CHAPTER 9

# Birth of the Bingham Program

Rural medicine in Maine was shockingly behind the times in 1930 when Dr. George Bourne Farnsworth, stepson of Dr. Gehring, returned to his boyhood home in Bethel to go into semiretirement at age 50. Accustomed to academic medicine in Cleveland, where he had been an obstetrician for 20 years and an assistant professor of obstetrics at Case Western Reserve University, Dr. Farnsworth told Dr. Gehring he was appalled by the outdated medicine he saw being practiced in Maine.

He noted that many doctors lacked formal training in reading electrocardiograms, and that some older men could not interpret what they saw. Most doctors practicing in rural hospitals at the time had no local pathologists to study tissue samples. Many could not read X-ray films accurately and had nobody available to help them. Most doctors had taken no courses in diet and nutrition, and had no dietitians around to advise them.

Dr. Farnsworth said that a major deficiency was the lack of libraries in local hospitals where doctors could read professional publications and textbooks written by specialists on various diseases.

During a long series of conversations with Dr. Gehring, Dr. Farnsworth pointed out that city doctors obtained the latest information from colleagues, from journals, and from lectures by medical-school professors. Their country cousins, he now realized, lived lonely, isolated lives with few professional contacts and few ways of keeping abreast of rapidly advancing medical knowledge. He did not blame the country doctors as individuals, but saw them rather as victims of circumstances who did the best they could under adverse conditions.

Dr. Farnsworth was not the type to let a problem lie around without trying to do something about it. His own life and medical training had given him an excellent background from which to tackle the situation. Born in Boston on February 16, 1880, during a short period when Mrs. Gehring and her first husband, George Farnsworth, lived in Roxbury, he had graduated with honors from Bowdoin College in 1903 and finished second in his class at Harvard Medical School in 1907. While attending Harvard he had worked at the Boston Dispensary, as his grandfather, a Boston physician, had done before him. After graduation he studied medicine abroad and served a preceptorship under Dr. Joseph Pratt at Massachusetts General Hospital.

Drs. Farnsworth and Gehring came to the conclusion that one possible solution was to send local doctors to the city to attend seminars. The problem, they soon found out, was a lack of substitute physicians to take care of patients while they were gone. They then brought their friend and patient, Mr. William Bingham, 2nd, into their discussions. They knew he was interested in medicine because he had made large gifts to hospitals in Portland, Bangor, and Lewiston, and had made the magnificent gift of $200,000 to establish a wing at the Neurological Institute of New York in honor of Dr. Gehring.

Mr. Bingham was deeply distressed when the doctors told him that physicians in a nearby town, where he had friends, did not possess microscopes. He was horrified when informed that a visiting specialist, called to Maine to consult on a difficult case, had had to drive from Bethel to Rumford to obtain a laboratory examination of urinary sediment.

The three men asked themselves if specialists could be brought to Maine to provide lectures there and to help upgrade local hospitals. Their first step was to confer on this idea with Dr. Pratt and, on his return from Germany in 1931, with Dr. Proger. By this time Dr. Pratt, at the suggestion of Dr. Gehring, had become a consultant on Mr. Bingham's care.

During the period when the discussions were taking place, two events happened that would help crystallize plans for upgrading medicine in Maine. The first one seemed to bear no relation to Maine at the beginning, but was to provide a base for a program in later years. It seemed that there was a 20-bed ward at the Boston Dispensary that was unused because Dr. Pratt lacked funds to equip and staff it. He spoke of the matter to Dr. and Mrs. Gehring.

The two physicians apparently did not want to ask Mr. Bingham for funds to open the ward. Mrs. Gehring, however, was not so shy. According to Joseph E. Garland, in his book *Experiment in Medicine,* Mrs. Gehring approached Mr. Bingham and he donated $50,000 to open the unit. He said he would give another $20,000 for salaries if Tufts would give $5000, an arrangement that was completed. Mr. Bingham then agreed to assume operating deficits, which ran to approximately $2000 per month for some time.

These initial gifts primed Mr. Bingham's long-term interest in what was to grow into the Pratt Clinic and the New England Medical Center Hospital, which would in turn provide the Boston base for the Bingham Program to improve Maine medicine.

The second event related to the future improvement of medicine in Maine was an appeal for help to Mr. Bingham from the 57-bed Rumford, Maine, Community Hospital. The Rumford Hospital had been built in 1924 and served 20,000 persons in Rumford and surrounding towns of Oxford County, including Bethel. It had 11 doctors on the staff.

Many of the weaknesses of the hospital were the same as, or similar to, the ones Dr. Farnsworth, Dr. Gehring, and Mr. Bingham had discussed concerning Maine medicine in general. An inspector from the American College of Surgeons had visited and recommended improvements, but there was no money with which to make them. Mr. Bingham responded with a gift on the stipulation that it not be acknowledged publicly. All his life he was to remain in the background, as much as was possible for a man who gave away millions of dollars.

With funds in place for the upgrading of the Rumford Hospital, and the finances available to open the diagnostic ward at the Boston Dispensary, discussions returned to the plight of Maine doctors.

Now the two events came together. Dr. Pratt suggested that the 20-bed ward at the Boston Dispensary and the Rumford Hospital in Maine be linked together in a project to upgrade the hospital and to provide information for the doctors in Bethel and surrounding towns. Bright young doctors from the Dispensary would be sent to Maine to work for short periods, do some teaching, and give lectures.

The idea was discussed with Dr. Eugene M. McCarty of Rumford Hospital, who approved. Dr. Proger, with his usual sensitivity, suggested that the young doctors, mostly residents, exercise tact to make certain they would not be resented by older physicians. He suggested that the residents say they were reporting what their professors at Tufts had told them and the way their chiefs at the Dispensary did things.

As another feature of the initial program, Mr. Bingham gave Dr. Pratt $1000 to organize teaching clinics at Rumford by specialists from Boston. Beginning in November 1931, eight clinics were held, with Dr. Proger delivering the first one, entitled "Simple Laboratory Tests for the Practitioner."

It soon became apparent that a formal organization would be needed to assure smooth continuity of teaching, clinics, and hospital improvement programs. Dr. Pratt and Dr. Gehring persuaded Mr. Bingham to allow use of his name to the extent of calling a formal organization the Bingham Associates Program, which was formally chartered on June 29, 1932, as a nonprofit corporation in the State of Maine. Its stated purpose was "the advancement of medicine." Drs. Gehring, Pratt, and Farnsworth made up the first board of directors, with Dr. Gehring the first president. Mr. Ellery C. Park of Bethel was elected clerk.

After the organization was formalized, the directors of the Bingham Program decided to go back to their original idea and try to send some doctors from Maine to Boston to work in the diagnostic ward at the Dispensary, attend lectures, and study for a month at a time. Each doctor who went to Boston for a fellowship was paid $250 to cover expenses for himself and his family for the month. Also, whenever possible, a doctor was sent to Maine to cover for the absent physician.

What the program came to mean to Maine physicians was described in an article by Dr. A. J. Fuller of Pemaquid in *Modern Hospital* in 1944. He said that he hadn't even realized, because of being so busy, how much medicine had progressed during the years he had practiced in Maine. He said he had grown complacent over the service he was rendering and that it was an eye-opener to visit the Dispensary and to see how first-class medicine was being practiced.

He wrote that he learned a great deal about improving his diagnostic techniques, studied hematology, took a course in electrocardiography and another in anesthesiology. He learned for the first time about intravenous anesthesia. He also learned laboratory techniques, and found that an intelligent young woman could be trained at the Dispensary to operate an office laboratory for a country doctor practicing miles from a hospital laboratory.

Dr. Farnsworth, commenting on the program after it had been in operation for some time, said that it seemed the better doctors were the ones who grasped the opportunity offered by the Bingham Program. When Dr. Gehring died in September 1932, Dr. Farnsworth was selected to be Mr. Bingham's advisor on medical and financial affairs. As such, he became a major player in the history of the New England Medical Center Hospital and the development of the Bingham Program.

Dr. Farnsworth, like Dr. Gehring, not only guided and advised Mr. Bingham on his medical philanthropies; he also represented him in an academic program designed to help worthy young men and women continue their education when they lacked funds. The program included many graduates of Gould Academy, Colby, Bates, Bowdoin, and the University of Maine. The names were never revealed by Mr. Bingham and the recipients never saw him. They dealt with Dr. Farnsworth after the death of Dr. Gehring. Among these "Bingham Scholars" were such later leaders as Secretary of State Edmund S. Muskie; Dr. Victor Mc-Kusick, chairman of medicine at Johns Hopkins Medical School; his twin brother, Vincent, chief justice of the Maine Supreme Court; Dr. Harold F. Rheinlander, cardiothoracic surgeon at New England Medical Center Hospital; Dr. Leonard S. Gottlieb, director of the Mallory Institute of Pathology and Chairman of the Departments of Pathology at Boston City and University Hospitals in Boston; and Dr. Daniel Hanley, Olympic Games official and physician.

Dr. Hanley, a pleasant, stocky, ruddy-faced man, spoke of his experiences with Dr. Farnsworth in the spring of 1980, just before retiring as Bowdoin College physician. He said, "On my graduation form Bowdoin in 1939, I was offered a job teaching chemistry and hockey at a Boston high school. But I wanted to go to medical school, and had been accepted at Columbia. I spoke to the dean at Bowdoin, and we decided to write to Mr. Bingham and ask for help.

"We both wrote in June and didn't hear a word until September 1. I remember the date because it was the day Hitler marched into Poland. A letter arrived from Dr. Farnsworth telling me to be in Christmas Cove,

Maine, the following day. I borrowed a car from a friend — I was a lifeguard at Salisbury Beach at the time — and got up at four o'clock the next morning to drive to Maine.

"I stopped at the Holly Inn to call Dr. Farnsworth's home and ask directions. When I arrived, he kept me waiting for a half-hour. He finally called me into his office, scowled at me and said that most applicants didn't have the money to stay at the Holly Inn. I explained that I had merely called from there. Then he said most applicants didn't arrive in automobiles. I said I had borrowed this one. He then twitted me about Bowdoin, where he had graduated, and asked me how I thought anybody from a backwoods college like that could succeed at the College of Physicians and Surgeons at Columbia. I said I had been accepted and was determined to go if I had to wash dishes.

"He then got up abruptly and put a check for $1100 in my hand. Declaring himself a Harvard Medical School man, he said he wanted to hear how I did at that school in New York."

Dr. Hanley later discovered that Dr. Farnsworth could be a very pleasant man and that much of the gruffness had been put on for the occasion. During his medical-school days, Hanley was asked twice a year to give Dr. Farnsworth reports on his progress. These reports were made as Mr. Bingham, Dr. Farnsworth, and their entourage stopped in New York in a private railroad car on their way to Florida or home again to Maine every fall and spring.

Dr. Hanley recalled going to the railroad car at seven o'clock in the morning, before classes, to report to Dr. Farnsworth. "He would be wearing a challis robe and a beret, and would be waving a long cigarette holder. He would just walk back and forth as I gave my report and not say a word. Once he took me to the car window and showed me a truck loaded with huge crates. He said it was X-ray equipment being sent by Mr. Bingham to a desert doctor in Egypt."

Mr. Bingham had developed an interest in medicine in the Middle East through his sister, Frances Payne Bolton, who had been a World War I Red Cross nurse. She induced him to become a director for a time of Roberts College in Istanbul, and to participate in the development of a medical center there for the training of nurses.

Mrs. Bolton continued to work for nursing programs at the American Hospital in Istanbul. She also played an important part in developing nursing in the United States, setting up a national committee and helping to develop a school of nursing at the University of Maine. She also founded the Frances Payne Bolton School of Nursing at Case Western Reserve University, the nation's first degree-granting school of nursing.

Dr. Hanley was disappointed that he never was allowed to meet Mr. Bingham to express his appreciation personally. After graduation from medical school and service in World War II, Dr. Hanley tried to repay the scholarship money that had been advanced to him to go to medical school. He was told that he could not. He then established the Farnsworth-Hanley Fund at Bowdoin and paid money into it every month for 25 years to help needy Bowdoin students go to medical school. This fund eventually was absorbed by the Maine Medical Society, expanded and broadened to include all Maine colleges.

Dr. Farnsworth, who was almost exactly the same age as Mr. Bingham, was to continue as advisor and consultant to Mr. Bingham and was to participate in the development of the Pratt Clinic, the New England Medical Center, and the Bingham Program until his death in 1947. The Farnsworth Building at the New England Medical Center is named in his honor.

# CHAPTER 10

# The Boston-Maine Connection

The relationship established in 1931 between the doctors at the Boston Dispensary and the Rumford Hospital began to pay dividends for the two institutions, for the doctors involved, and for their patients, very quickly.

Dr. Pratt explained how patients benefited in an article in the *American Medical Association Bulletin* of June 1932. He cited one case of a woman with anemia and indigestion who was suspected of having cancer of the stomach. The local doctors in Maine sent her to the Boston Dispensary, where it was determined within 24 hours that she was suffering from a rare form of pernicious anemia. Dr. Pratt knew that Harvard's Dr. George R. Minot, at the Thorndike Laboratory of Boston City Hospital, was anxious to treat cases of primary anemia in order to test new forms of liver disease therapy. The patient was given free treatment at the clinic there and returned home within a few weeks, her condition controlled.

Another case was that of a young man from Bethel, who was sent to the Dispensary clinic after suffering recurrent headaches and vomiting spells. Dr. Pratt detected a swelling of the optic discs (where optic nerves enter the eyeball) and sent him to Dr. Harvey Cushing at the Peter Bent Brigham Hospital. Dr. Cushing removed a large cyst from his brain and the young man recovered and went home. He would have died without the surgery, Dr. Pratt said.

The case of the young man encouraged Mr. Bingham in his belief that the New England Medical Center should be an integral part of the Bingham Program. It convinced him that the hospital unit in Boston deserved his support as did the hospital in Rumford and that, indeed, both were essential to upgrading medical care in Maine.

The placing of the two Maine patients with Harvard specialists was typical of Dr. Pratt and Dr. Proger. They both were determined to obtain the best possible physician or surgeon for a particular patient, regardless of hospital or university affiliation. There was no conflict so far as surgery and the Dispensary were concerned, because the Dispensary had no facilities for surgery. But there were some protests from Tufts Medical School surgeons, who thought they should have priority in operating on Dispensary patients. They were always utilized when they were best in their specialties.

Dr. Pratt believed that the most valuable contribution of the Bingham Program during its first year of existence was the placement of the residents in rotation at Rumford Hospital. He wrote in a report of the first year's activities:

"The residents chosen from my staff [at the Dispensary] have proved to be a strong link between the hospital and the local doctors and the medical clinic in Boston. It has made the Rumford Hospital like a branch of a tree of which the main trunk is the New England Medical Center. It is hoped in the near future to extend the system of rotating residents to other hospitals in other parts of Maine."

The first year of the program revealed that the Rumford Hospital suffered seriously from a lack of clinical laboratories and facilities for pathology and radiology. Puzzling X-ray films and tissue specimens, therefore, were sent to Boston for analysis. Pathology proved especially important in establishing good rapport with local doctors. That was an area where they needed help and none had been available. Dr. H. Edward McMahon, Professor of Pathology at Tufts, said that this noncompetitive assistance established goodwill between the doctors in Rumford and those in Boston.

The years 1931 to 1934 saw Dr. Proger's role in the Bingham Program and at the Dispensary grow constantly. He enjoyed the stimulating medical life of the city. One of his happiest memories of those days, he would say later, was of knowing the remarkable group of medical men at the Thorndike Laboratory at Boston City Hospital. "Among them were such famed physicians as George Richards Minot, Soma Weiss, Herrman L. Blumgart, William Castle, Maxwell Finland and Chester Keefer."

Nevertheless, a time came in 1934 when Dr. Proger decided he would have to return to Atlanta. In Boston he was dependent on annual grants for his research, whereas Atlanta's Dr. Paullin had promised long-term support if he would come home. The Dispensary had fallen on hard times during the Depression years. The Progers' first child, Susan, had recently been born, and Dr. Proger told Dr. Pratt that a sense of financial responsibility toward his family was dictating his decision.

In May, just before his planned departure, Dr. Proger went to Atlantic City to attend a meeting of the prestigious American Society for Clinical Investigation, to which he had been elected in 1933 at the age of 27, a signal honor. While there he received a telegram from Dr. Farnsworth, in Maine, who had been told by Dr. Pratt about Dr. Proger's plans to leave. Dr. Farnsworth told Mr. Bingham, and Mr. Bingham responded by offering research support money to keep Dr. Proger in Boston.

Dr. Farnsworth had told Sidney Davidson, Mr. Bingham's attorney in New York, that Dr. Proger was indispensable to Mr. Bingham's medical charities and that nothing should be allowed to sever the connection. He added that Mr. Bingham probably would transfer his principle charitable interests to other institutions if Dr. Proger left.

Mr. Bingham guaranteed $1000 a year for five years, payable in advance each July, to sponsor Dr. Proger's research. "I was rich for a few weeks each year," Dr. Proger said. "Seriously, the offer to finance my research, in addition to my salary, made it possible for me to stay here. I was glad because I was so interested in what we were doing in Maine and in the diagnostic work we were doing at the Dispensary."

The high regard Mr. Bingham had for Dr. Proger was shared by Dr. Farnsworth, Mr. Bingham's adviser, as well as by Dr. Pratt. Once, when Dr. Farnsworth's mother, Mrs. Gehring, was ill in Florida, Dr. Farnsworth telephoned Dr. Proger to fly down to see her. Dr. Pratt had been Mrs. Gehring's doctor, and Dr. Proger didn't know what to say because Dr. Pratt was still active. Dr. Pratt's immediate reaction on being told was that he was proud that Dr. Farnsworth held Dr. Proger in such high regard. It was as if he were pleased by the accomplishment of a son, Dr. Proger later recalled.

The year 1934, during which Dr. Proger almost was forced to leave, was a crisis year all around for the Dispensary. Mr. Arthur G. Rotch, president, finally had to go to City Hall and tell Mayor Frederick W. Mansfield that the Dispensary could no longer be the chief provider of health care for the city's poor. He said this did not mean the Dispensary would close, but that it would have to curtail free care. During 1933, he said, Dispensary doctors had made 27,000 visits to patients in the city, half of them at no charge. Now the deficits were threatening to strangle the institution.

Some of the burden dropped by the Dispensary was taken up by Boston City Hospital. Funds were taken from the George Robert White Fund to support area health stations throughout the city. The easing of the relief burden at the Dispensary gave it a little breathing space and the diagnostic ward a chance to grow.

Despite the financial difficulties of the Dispensary, the relationship between the New England Medical Center and the Rumford Community Hospital continued to flourish, with satisfaction on both sides. There was, however, a limiting factor in that the Dispensary diagnostic ward was too small to handle additional cases; there was also a need to expand the program to other Maine hospitals.

The vital role of the Boston base to the Maine program was spelled out in a tribute to Dr. Pratt by Dr. Proger in 1937. He said that the diagnostic work available through the Boston connection welded and vitalized the administrative, clinical, and pedagogic aspects of the Program. When a desire for better diagnostic work was stimulated, he added, more intelligent and efficient treatment naturally followed.

Dr. Proger also explained how the Bingham Program recognized two factors that more than any others dampen the desire of doctors for professional and diagnostic help. The first is fear that a referring physician may be found to be wrong in his own diagnosis, and thus fall in the estimation of his patients and colleagues. A second fear is that of possibly losing the patient to the referral physician. "That such considerations should not exist is beside the point," Dr. Proger said. "They do exist; they should be recognized and arrangements made accordingly."

To ameliorate these sources of concern, the diagnostic ward in Boston admitted no patients unless they were sent by referring doctors. Once diagnosed, the patients were sent back to their own physicians. Arrangements were made so that the primary physician never lost control of the care of his patient: the Boston diagnosticians sent the referring doctor a complete report and recommendations, and the patient was informed that his own doctor would spell out the diagnosis and treatment. "This gave the doctor an opportunity, if the conclusions differed from his own diagnosis, to present the facts to the patient in a way not to denigrate himself."

These precautions helped influence physicians not to wait too long before seeking consultations and served to benefit the patients by obtaining early second opinions, Dr. Proger said. He added that no policy is justifiable which protects the physician to the detriment of the patient, and this may have appeared to some observers to be the case. "However, there can be no gainsaying the fact that the relationship between the referring doctor and the patient is much more important than the one between an institution and the patient. It is upon the local physician that the responsibility will fall of putting to good use the information which the diagnostic hospital can supply."

For the patient to receive maximum benefits, Dr. Proger wrote, "The application of information, which may involve close supervision and prolonged care, must be made as free of difficulties as possible. It is this point of view which determines the relationship of our institution to patients and physicians. It is the purpose of the diagnostic hospital to help the patient through the physician; the corollary purpose is, therefore, to improve medicine in the small communities by offering to help the physicians."

This kind of help, he added, intends no indictment of the capabilities of general practitioners. "The implication is only that no physician in the 1930s can be wholly self-sufficient, for the simple reason that it is humanly impossible for one person to encompass all medical knowledge. It follows from the recognition of this obvious fact that specialization and the aid of specialists are essential."

He said also that it was his opinion that general practitioners can satisfactorily care for about 80 to 90 percent of patients without the aid of a specialist. This seems true because most illnesses are either self-limited or easily managed. It is the 10 to 20 percent in which help is needed.

He pointed to another example where help may be needed and which points out that there may be a distinction between what sometimes is done and what should be done. "A youngster with a simple sinus arrythmia or a soft systolic murmur does not require a specialist; in fact, he requires no physician at all. But he might be put to bed for several months because of lack of knowledge of what he did not have, namely, heart disease. There are many similar examples."

# CHAPTER 11

# A New Hospital for Boston

The opening of the new Joseph H. Pratt Diagnostic Hospital on December 15, 1938, as the largest diagnostic hospital in the nation, was a major event in the history of the New England Medical Center and in the medical life of Dr. Proger.

Until then, the New England Medical Center had been a medical center in name more than in substance. It had clinics at the Boston Dispensary; a home care program; beds for infants and children at the Boston Floating Hospital; 20 beds for sick adults at the Dispensary; an affiliation with the medical and dental schools of Tufts; but no hospital for adults.

Now, with the Pratt in place, the New England Medical Center still didn't have a general hospital in the modern sense, complete with full surgical as well as medical services; but it did have a hospital for adult patients, and minor surgery could be performed. The complex could truly be called a medical center.

The Pratt Clinic, as the new hospital was popularly known, quickly became recognized for the skill of its doctors in diagnosing diseases, recommending therapy, and providing nursing care. The staff was small but excellent. Led by Dr. Proger, the staff, including doctors, interns, residents, and a number of eminent German physicians who had fled to America, became highly proficient in the difficult art of recognizing symptoms and providing appropriate treatment. Thanks to the fame of the Lahey (founded in 1923) and Pratt Clinics, Boston became known

74

as a center for diagnosis, physical examinations, and pioneering health maintenance programs.

The Pratt differed from the Lahey Clinic in that it had its own hospital for medical care of its patients. Lahey at that time utilized several Boston hospitals, primarily the Baptist and the Deaconess, for its patient care. Pratt doctors sent their surgical patients to other hospitals for appropriate care, selecting the hospital on the basis of its surgeons.

The Pratt assumed special importance to the New England Medical Center because it was one area that was self-supporting almost from the beginning. While doing its share of free care, especially for patients referred from the Dispensary, the Pratt Clinic also encouraged paying patients to come for treatment. It broadened the scope of the New England Medical Center because members of the business community and other persons of means came to obtain diagnostic expertise. Patients at the Dispensary and the Boston Floating were largely paid for by private contributions, with eligibility for care restricted to those who could pay nothing or only part of the cost of their care.

A unit that could maintain itself was extremely important to the Center, especially during those Depression years. Officials at the Dispensary and the Floating Hospital had become more aware than ever of the truth of the old saying that there is no such thing as "free care." Somebody, or some organization, has to pay for all care. Charitable-minded Bostonians had footed the bills at the Dispensary for generations; now money was scarce. There were very few health insurance programs at the time; Blue Cross and Blue Shield were not originated until the late 1930s to provide methods of payment for doctors and hospitals. It was not until after World War II that government programs and government health insurance began to flourish.

The Pratt Diagnostic Hospital was also important for the Bingham Program. Up to the time of the opening of the Pratt, the Bingham Program had been limited by lack of diagnostic beds. Now it would be possible, with a larger base, to expand beyond the one hospital in Rumford and to introduce the concept of regional centers with additional community hospitals.

The idea of regional medical programs, as applied to the Boston-Maine linking, was probably the greatest contribution of the Bingham Program to American medicine. It paved the way for medical schools to move outside their walls; it awakened government attention to medically underserved rural and ghetto areas; and it provided models for future action.

It seems important at this point to go back to the events leading up to the establishment of the Pratt, because these events and the people involved helped to determine the future of the Tufts–New England Medical Center and its continued location in the heart of Boston. The decision to remain in the South Cove area was a major and controversial one, the wisdom of which is still sometimes debated. That it was a wise decision is clear today in light of the new relations being developed with the Chinese community and in view of the development of the entire area through efforts of the Federal government, the city, the hospital, Chinese organizations, and the Boston Chamber of Commerce.

The first step in development of the Pratt Diagnostic Hospital was taken in November 1936, when more than 800 patients per year were being treated in the 20-bed ward at the Boston Dispensary. There also were long waiting lists for admission. Dr. Proger asked Dr. Pratt if they should ask Mr. Bingham for financial aid to expand the ward. Dr. Pratt hesitated, not wanting to push his benefactor for more money. The situation grew so desperate, however, and reached such a critical point that he told Dr. Proger to go ahead if he so desired. A request was made, therefore, for $50,000 to add a floor to the Center building, where the 20-bed ward was located.

Mr. Bingham and his advisor, Dr. Farnsworth, replied quickly that one floor would not be enough. They offered $75,000 with which to build two floors. It was then found that the building could not support two additional floors. The next alternative was to buy the abandoned Franciscan Monastery of St. Clare, across Bennet Street from the Dispensary, and renovate it; but it proved too old for use as a hospital.

Mr. Bingham then offered to finance purchase of the monastery property and erection of a new hospital building on the site at an estimated cost of $750,000. The question arose of whether to use the site or build the hospital away from the slums in a suburban location. Some suggested moving to Brighton; others urged sites outside the city, where there would be room for later expansion. The Route 128 "golden circle" had not yet been developed. One argument against a new location was that the move would destroy the geographical entity of the New England Medical Center. Furthermore, the Pratt was planned as a unit of the Boston Dispensary, whose mission was to serve the people of Boston.

Dr. Proger had much to do with making the decision to stay in Boston. Both supporters and critics of that decision agree that his was the decisive voice. His rank in the official hierarchy of the New England Medical Center was that of physician-in-chief, but his power was much greater because of his close relationship with Mr. Bingham and Dr. Farnsworth. In defending his 1930s choice in the 1980s, Dr. Proger pointed to Columbia Presbyterian Hospital in New York, which was moved to a suburb which has since become a depressed area. He based his decision on hopes the South Cove area would be upgraded, a process that is finally underway, and also on the proximity of the airport, bus terminals, the South Station, and the subway system, all of which he foresaw as bringing patients from Boston and all New England to the hospital. The Eliot Street Garage (now gone) was already in place, and parking was available in the streets.

Transportation and ease of access were bonuses that could not be foreseen, including the express highways that converge on Boston near the hospital and a new subway station under the Medical Center, on Washington Street. Those who still criticize the choice point to giant traffic jams, lack of parking space, pressures for land from the Chinese community, the combat zone, and lack of visibility, all factors that are now being corrected. Dr. Proger calculated that there must be some future in an area which hard-headed businessmen had chosen for their then-new movie palace, the Metropolitan. For years, until the hospital began to achieve a visibility of its own, he had to tell strangers it was located "behind the Met."

When the new hospital was completed, it was Mr. Bingham who insisted that it be named for Dr. Pratt. He declined all suggestions that it be named for him. The only reference to Mr. Bingham in the hospital is a plaque he allowed on the wall of the lobby that reads, "In Grateful Appreciation of the Gift of William Bingham, 2nd, 1937. Solicitude for the Stricken Is the Essence of Altruism."

Judge Charles C. Cabot, president of the Dispensary, agreed that the Dispensary would operate the new hospital, but stipulated that under no circumstances would his institution be responsible financially if anything went wrong. Mr. Bingham agreed that he would meet debts if the hospital should run in the red.

The cornerstone of the Pratt was laid on Dr. Pratt's 65th birthday, December 5, 1937, and it was opened a year and ten days later, on December 15, 1938. The first patients included a woman named Alice King; a member of the medical staff, Dr. Nelson Saphir; and Grace McIntyre, a nurse. Dr. Saphir and Miss McIntyre found the surroundings so congenial that they fell in love and were married after their hospital stay.

The shift from the 20-bed Dispensary ward to the new hospital was a rather simple matter. Dr. Proger, physician-in-chief, simply led his small staff across the street after the patients had been transported. The new building was red brick, modern (at the time) in every detail, and rose six floors.

Doctors at the Pratt were all on salary, receiving their pay from the Dispensary. Placing physicians on salary was a drastic departure from usual procedures, and at the time it aroused the displeasure of the Massachusetts Medical Society. Doctors were supposed to be independent professionals, not wage earners, in the view of the American Medical Association.

Salaries were small, about $3000 a year. Dr. Proger constantly tried to raise them to become somewhat comparable to the fees that could be earned in private practice. Dr. Proger praised the men and women who came to the Pratt and stayed there in the early years as being dedicated to the principles of academic medicine, patient care, and research — not primarily interested in making money. Mrs. Proger said this also was true of her husband. "He had so many prospective patients seeking him as a physician," she said, "that he couldn't accept them all and carry on the work of the hospital and the Bingham Program. He made real financial sacrifices. But we both always were happy that he did what he considered was most important regardless of financial return."

During the construction of the Pratt Clinic, and after, Dr. Proger continued to worry about the future of the hospital because it was dependent to such a large extent on the financial support of one man, Mr. Bingham. No matter how much that support was appreciated, there was always a risk that something might go wrong with the arrangement.

As he looked about him, Dr. Proger saw that the Lahey Clinic, which had been established in 1923 by Dr. Frank Lahey, had great fiscal strength and high-quality diagnostic facilities, but lacked an academic affiliation. On the other hand, the Peter Bent Brigham Hospital had excellent academic affiliations with Harvard, but lacked fiscal strength at the time, because of losses of endowment funds during the Depression. What Dr. Proger wanted to do was to fuse, at the Pratt, the financial stability and quality of care of the Lahey Clinic and the academic excellence of the Brigham. He became convinced that a hospital couldn't have high-quality care in the long run without fiscal strength, although it might have fiscal strength without high quality.

Dr. Lahey had said to Dr. Proger that he was not interested in building hospitals or developing academic affiliations, because these two activities cost money and he wanted to keep costs as low as possible. Similarly, the absence of surgical facilities at the Pratt helped reduce its initial costs of construction and operating budget. Tufts later invited Dr. Lahey to become a trustee, hoping that the Lahey Clinic might become a surgical teaching arm of Tufts Medical School just as the Pratt was a medical teaching arm. Although Dr. Lahey did become a trustee, his clinic did not become affiliated. Dr. Proger said he always had thought that lack of a hospital and an academic affiliation would be a handicap to the Lahey Clinic in the long run. He noted that in November 1980 the Lahey Clinic moved to Burlington, where it had built its own 200-bed hospital under the direction of one of Dr. Lahey's successors, Dr. Robert E. Wise. The new home of the Lahey Clinic, including the hospital and ambulatory care centers, cost $81 million to construct.

As Dr. Proger viewed developments in medical care over the years, he saw the creation of the university hospital and the growth of private group practice as two of the most important facets of American medicine. By group practice, he meant the type utilized at the Pratt, Lahey, Mayo, and Cleveland Clinics. His goal for the New England Medical Center in the long run was to incorporate the best features of all.

Commenting in 1981 on Dr. Proger's decision to stay in South Cove and on the reasons for his success in achieving his goals, Dr. Morton Madoff, assistant to the dean for primary care and public health planning at Tufts Medical School, said:

"Obviously, Dr. Proger had a vision of what might be accomplished in this area of the city, which ought to be called Progerville. There was no need for him to stay with a small, struggling institution. He had endless numbers of opportunities to go elsewhere. But he had a vision of what could be accomplished in this sort of circumstance. Even in the days when the Pratt first became the New England Center Hospital, there really was no medical center here, and certainly no Tufts–New England Medical Center, as such. At that time, the Pratt was generally viewed as an outpatient clinic, along the lines of the Lahey Clinic. It certainly wasn't spoken of in the same breath as the Harvard teaching hospitals such as the Massachusetts General, the Peter Bent Brigham and the Beth Israel.

"President Carmichael [of Tufts] moved the Tufts Medical and Dental Schools down here only because of his faith in Sam Proger. A lot of people have done, and continue to do, things based on their trust in him. This has been true since he was a young man, long before he became an elder statesman. He has seen much of his vision materialize and still participates in its continuing realization."

# CHAPTER 12

# People at the Pratt

One of the factors that would make the Pratt Clinic famous was the extraordinary caliber of the doctors, nurses, volunteers, and administrators who worked there.

Dr. Joseph Pratt, for whom the hospital was named, was a vigorous 66 years old when its doors were opened in 1938. He continued to take an active part as a physician and consultant for many years. His vast experience as a physician and his extensive knowledge of medical literature made him a valuable ally to the staff physicians in diagnosing illness. His empathy with people served to attract large numbers of patients from all walks of life.

Another major contribution of Dr. Pratt had been to attract to the New England Medical Center a group of eminent German doctors, men and women with outstanding reputations for research and clinical care in their own country, but fearful of the rise of Hitler. Despite Germany's decline from the pinnacle of world medical leadership, it still had a great number of outstanding physicians. Some of them came to Boston because of their friendship with Dr. Pratt, joining what later became known as the German scientific brain drain. A number stayed to make major contributions at the Pratt.

One of the brightest of the German stars was a woman, Dr. Alice Ettinger, who actually came to Boston before Hitler's rise, but decided to remain here when she looked at Germany and saw what was happening.

Dr. Ettinger came to the Dispensary in 1932, six years before the Pratt was opened, for a projected stay of six months as a Bingham Fellow. She was 33 at the time and had been working in Germany with Dr. Hans Berg, a radiologist. They had developed a system of viewing gastrointestinal processes with spot films, providing physicians with improved images during examination of the stomach with a fluoroscope. Up to that time, doctors had examined the stomach by first looking at X-ray images on a fluoroscope and then taking films. Now they could take films during the process of fluoroscopy.

Dr. Pratt wrote to Dr. Berg and asked him to send an aide to Boston to teach the use of the new "black box" in the detection of cancer and ulcers. He was very surprised when a young, dynamic woman appeared. She was small and intense, and had such a friendly and outgoing nature she soon became a favorite throughout the Dispensary. In 1981, nearly a half-century after her arrival, Dr. Ettinger still was busy at the New England Medical Center as an extremely popular teacher.

When Dr. Ettinger's six months were up, Dr. Pratt offered her the position of radiologist at the Dispensary. She agreed to remain and became chief of radiology at the Dispensary and also at the Pratt, when it was opened. She became a leading American radiologist, chairman of the Department of Radiology at Tufts Medical School, and chief of radiology at the New England Medical Center. She proved to be a superb teacher, both in the classroom with medical students and in the hospital, as she shared her knowledge of radiology with colleagues.

Dr. Ettinger's natural enthusiasm and excitement over visiting America was somewhat dimmed, as Dr. Proger's had been, when she first saw the area where the Dispensary was located. The neighborhood was so bad that she didn't dare walk out alone at night. If she had engagements, she would take a taxi to Boylston Street to reach the subway. In a 1980 interview she said tartly, "There were whorehouses here!"

Nevertheless, when the time came for a decision as to whether to stay in Boston or go home, she remained, and was glad later that she had. She became friendly with Dr. Proger and with Mrs. Proger, who then worked at the Dispensary as administrative assistant in the diagnostic ward. Dr. Ettinger became very popular with medical students because of her teaching ability and her sparkling personality. Year after year, she was voted "favorite professor."

The same year that Dr. Ettinger joined the staff, Dr. Heinz Magendantz, a German internist of international reputation, also came to the Dispensary. He is remembered by Dr. John Sullivan, emeritus chief of neurology at New England Medical Center, as "an outstanding cardiologist who followed his schedules with typical German punctuality and treated patients with painstaking care . . . a shy person but an excellent teacher of resident doctors." Dr. Magendantz stayed on for years at the Dispensary and the Pratt, working with Dr. Proger.

Another German physician brought to the Pratt was Dr. Siegfried Thannhauser, who was rescued from Germany by the Rockefeller Foundation. He was the son of a wealthy Jewish manufacturer of beer-bottle caps. Initially a bit of a playboy, he had eventually married a beautiful Catholic woman and settled down to being a serious doctor. Dr. Thannhauser had become one of Germany's leading clinicians when he and his wife and three daughters fled to the United States in 1935. He didn't waste any time brooding over the loss of his position in Germany, but settled right in at the Dispensary and the Pratt to become a leading physician in Boston. By 1950 he was considered the world's authority on diseases of fat metabolism. He could have accepted many other appointments in the United States, but preferred to stay with Dr. Proger and Dr. Pratt.

In a eulogy delivered at memorial services for Dr. Thannhauser in 1962, Dr. Proger paid tribute to his friend and colleague. He described him as "A pre-eminent figure in the last glow of brilliance in Germany before the darkness of Hitler set in. Although Dr. Thannhauser had reached the top in medical achievement and acclaim as the chief of one of Germany's greatest university medical clinics in Freiburg, he quickly made himself at home in the modest surroundings of the Boston Dispensary where no task was too menial and no effort too great in his determination to learn the ways of American medicine.

"Dr. Thannhauser was an enormously stimulating teacher," said Dr. Proger. "He was a strong and vibrant personality, whose thoughts and interest always lay chiefly with the patient as a person, as a thinking and feeling human being." He concluded, "The world has lost one of its authentic medical giants."

Another German doctor who joined the Dispensary staff, and later that of the Pratt, was Alfred Hauptmann, who had been director of the Neuropsychiatric Clinic at the University of Halle. He was a pioneer in

Medical Staff of the Boston Dispensary before the Pratt Diagnostic Hospital opened in 1938. Front row, left to right, Drs. Isadore Olef, Samuel Proger, Robert Buck, Joseph Pratt, Siegfried Thannhauser and Katherine Andrews. Among those who remained as long-time members of the staff are Joseph Rosenthal, third from left, second row; Joseph Kaplan, fifth from left, second row; and Robert B. McCombs, extreme right, second row. German doctors who fled from Hitler and joined the Dispensary staff include Dr. Thannhauser, front row; Dr. Heinz Magendantz, sixth from left, second row; Dr. Heinrich Brjgsch, third row, second from right; Dr. Anna J. Reinauer, extreme right, third row; and Dr. Jacob Schloss, extreme right, standing.

the use of phenobarbital in the treatment of epilepsy. Others included Dr. Joseph Igersheimer, who became professor of ophthalmology at Tufts; Dr. Jacob Schloss, a widely known internist; Dr. Heinrich Brjgsch, who later became medical director of the Prudential Insurance Company; and Dr. Martin Nothman, a pioneer in studying the role of the pancreas in diabetes.

Still another doctor from Germany was Dr. Gerhard Schmidt who was dimissed by the Hitler government in 1933 from his post as director of the biochemistry department of the University of Frankfurt. Dr.

Schmidt was a courtly and courteous man and an accomplished cellist; he shared with Dr. Proger a serious interest in classical music. He was a pioneer in the study of nucleic acids and made a significant contribution to the understanding of brain lipids. He received numerous high honors during his many years as a Tufts Medical School professor and as a physician. He died in 1981 at the age of 79.

Among American physicians who contributed much to the Dispensary and the Pratt was Dr. Robert Buck, a friend and colleague of Dr. Pratt, who later became executive director of the Massachusetts Medical Society.

One deeply involved layman was an aide of Mr. Bingham who entered the discussions when the expansion of the 20–bed diagnostic ward was first broached during the 1930s. He was Sidney W. Davidson, a New York attorney. Although a native of Georgia, Mr. Davidson was reared in Pennsylvania; he attended the Lawrenceville School in New Jersey and graduated from Yale, then from Yale Law School in 1918. He served a year in the Naval Reserve in 1919, and received honorary degrees from Tufts in 1952 and Bates in 1960.

As a young attorney Mr. Davidson was sent to Florida by his law firm, Carter, Ledyard and Milburn, to advise Mr. Bingham on some tax matters. He was 36 at the time, and Mr. Bingham 51. The older man developed a great confidence in the younger one. Mr. Bingham did not easily take to newcomers in his life, but in this instance he found a legal adviser in whom he felt he could place great trust and confidence.

Mr. Davidson soon became a close friend and adviser to Mr. Bingham and participated both as attorney and as interested party in the negotiations involving construction of the Pratt Hospital. He could have maintained an aloof legal position concerning both the New England Medical Center and the Bingham Associates Program; but he became personally involved and helped both to grow, serving as a director and trustee as well as a financial supporter the rest of his life. He became involved also in Gould Academy, Mr. Bingham's favorite academic interest in Maine. Mr. Davidson and his family summered at Sebec Lake, Maine, for many years.

One of Mr. Davidson's major involvements in New England was his position as a director of the *Boston Globe* and later of its parent company, Affiliated Publications. The *Globe*, before it became a public corporation in 1973, was owned equally by descendants of the families of General Charles H. Taylor and of the self-made merchant prince, Eben Jordan. General Taylor, the innovative and imaginative editor-publisher, and Mr. Jordan joined forces in 1873 to rescue a recently founded money-losing paper, and to build the *Globe*. They ended up each owning half the paper. The Eben Jordan estate was supervised by three trustees, at least one of whom was to represent the Jordan heirs on the *Globe* board of directors. Mr. Davidson became the trustee and fulfilled this role as Jordan representative for 33 years, from 1946 until his death in 1979. His son, Robert T. H. Davidson, remained a trustee of the New England Medical Center and the *Globe* in 1982.

Another New England interest of Mr. Davidson was Yale University, where a life-size portrait of him, presented by the Yale Law School Association, hangs in the library of the law school to commemorate his many years of service to and interest in Yale.

New England Medical Center Trustees Ralph Lowell and Sidney W. Davidson at meeting in the 1960s.

Mr. Davidson became an associate and close friend to Mr. Ralph Lowell, the famed New England philanthropist and trustee of many organizations. Mr. Lowell was treasurer of the Boston Floating Hospital and a trustee of the Pratt Hospital and the Bingham Program. Mr. Davidson suggested that Mr. Lowell also should become a trustee of the Jordan estate and, with him, represent the Jordan estate interests on the board of directors of Affiliated Publications. Mr. Lowell became a valued director of the *Globe*.

The two men became close despite very different approaches to their duties, according to Davis Taylor, former chairman of Affiliated Publications, and his cousin, John Taylor, chairman of the executive committee. They described Mr. Davidson as a man who prodded for facts, much like a prosecuting attorney, until he had obtained all the information he needed. Once he was satisfied that the facts were all in, he would make a decision and never look back on it, they said. Mr. Lowell was much more reserved. He would show up early for board meetings, ask to see the financial statements, read them quickly and have all the facts in his head when the meeting started.

For many years, directors' meetings at the *Globe* and the New England Medical Center were held on the same day so that Mr. Davidson could attend both without making an additional trip from New York.

Another New Yorker who became involved in the affairs of the New England Medical Center was Joseph R. Barr, a close friend of Mr. Davidson. Head of Barr and Barr, a nationally known construction firm, he served as adviser on the Pratt building construction and helped to keep costs down. He later became a director of the New England Medical Center; and still later his firm was selected to build Posner Hall, the Proger Building, the new Boston Floating Hospital building, and the new Tufts Dental School.

Among others who were involved in construction of the Pratt were President John A. Cousens of Tufts; Dr. Alonzo K. Paine of the Boston Dispensary (known to generations of Tufts medical students as "Achey Paine"); Judge Charles C. Cabot; Dr. Louis Phaneuf; and Dr. H. Edward McMahon, all of whom had great faith in Dr. Proger.

# CHAPTER 13

# The Bingham Program
# Makes History in Maine

If the Joseph H. Pratt Diagnostic Hospital simply added a few beds to those already available for medical care in Boston, it would hardly justify itself, wrote Dr. Samuel Proger in the *New England Journal of Medicine* on May 11, 1939, shortly after the Pratt was opened.

The hospital had been constructed, he wrote, as the focal point in a broad program for better distribution of medical care, so that it could serve a unique and useful purpose in New England medicine. "The hospital was to be the base for the Bingham Program of extending to small community hospitals the medical advantages of a metropolitan center by direct and indirect contacts between those elements, arranged on a permanent working basis."

Conceding that many of the benefits of medical advances ultimately reach small communities under any circumstances, Dr. Proger criticized this natural dissemination, when left to itself, as "haphazard, irregular and slow." He added, "It is our hope to establish regular and directed channels for the transmission of medical developments."

What Dr. Proger spelled out in his article was the new direction in which the Bingham Program would be able to travel when freed of the limitations imposed by the previous small 20-bed ward in the Dispensary. Now the historic step could be taken toward developing regional medical programs in Maine, instead of maintaining direct association only between Boston and Rumford.

"Experience has shown," he wrote, "that when a Bingham-type association is attempted between two hospitals too distant from one another and too greatly separated in relation to size and physical equipment, the relationship becomes one of dependence on the part of the smaller unit and impersonal help on the part of the larger one."

In order to avoid such a problem and in an effort to conduct effective programs which would strengthen the concept of home rule and stimulate greater input by Maine hospital officials, Dr. Proger brought the Central Maine General Hospital in Lewiston and the Eastern Maine General Hospital in Bangor into the program as intermediate centers — middlemen between the community hospitals and the Medical Center in Boston. "Such an arrangement," he said, "tends to enable the units which are graduated according to size and location to be mutually stimulating and effective."

The physicians in Lewiston were generally enthusiastic, but there were some hospital trustees who were at first suspicious. With typical Maine skepticism, they wanted to know "What is the catch?" Some were certain that the Boston group was trying to siphon Mr. Bingham's money into Boston and out of Maine, where they thought it belonged. Dr. Proger went to Lewiston to address the trustees and, with the support of the local physicians, won an agreement for a year's trial. The Lewiston hospital has been an important part of the Bingham Program ever since.

One would think that the Maine Medical Center in Portland might have been a natural regional center for the Bingham Program. Dr. Proger recalled in 1981 that the Portland hospital displayed no interest in joining and that he and his associates thought that two regional centers, in Lewiston and Bangor, were enough to operate the program efficiently. The Maine Medical Center had been a teaching hospital for Bowdoin up to the time when Bowdoin's medical school, the only one in Maine, was closed in 1921. If there was any feeling in Portland that the Maine Medical Center should have been the primary base, instead of Boston, it would not seem to have been justified because the Portland hospital no longer had a university affiliation.

Dartmouth Medical School might have been chosen on geographical grounds, but from 1915 to 1968 it was only a two-year school, sending its students to other medical schools to complete their third and fourth years. Dr. Farnsworth, who was a Harvard graduate, had discussed the idea of the Bingham Program with Harvard Medical School officials; but their reaction had been to suggest endowing a professorial chair for the teaching at Harvard of rural medicine.

In any case, the regional program was initiated by Dr. Proger in 1938 with the Central Maine General Hospital in Lewiston as the hub for hospitals in Rumford, Bath, Brunswick, Rockland, and Skowhegan. During the year, the Augusta General Hospital and the Franklin County Memorial Hospital in Farmington joined that group. That same year, a second regional center was established with the Eastern Maine General Hospital in Bangor as its focal point. Community hospitals initially joining this group were in Bar Harbor, Belfast, Blue Hill, Calais, Caribou, Castine, Dover-Foxcroft, Greenville, Houlton, Island Falls, Machias, and Presque Isle. Later, hospitals in Boothbay Harbor, Camden, Damariscotta, Gardiner, Sanford, and two in Waterville (Sister's and Thayer) joined the Lewiston group. By the end of World War II, 28 hospitals had enrolled in the two regions.

The various ways in which the Bingham Program worked were described in Dr. Proger's *New England Journal of Medicine* article. He began with the plight of laboratory technicians who, he said, gradually lose the ability to do quality work in small hospitals if they are forced to conduct their tests in isolation without supervision or even contact with their peers. Under the Bingham Program, the technician in each participating community hospital spent a month each year in the regional hospital, performing duties under the direction of a full-time pathologist. A second month was spent each year at the New England Medical Center, where instruction was given in new methods and procedures.

The manner in which the Bingham Program helped local hospitals develop their clinical laboratories was described in 1981 by Mr. Eli Dubinsky, for many years director of clinical laboratories at the New England Medical Center Hospital. "I was involved in the Bingham Program for more than 30 years, and in all that time we never went anywhere to offer help in the laboratories unless we were invited." He said the first trip he ever made was in 1950, to Belfast, where the hospital was located in an old mansion overlooking Penobscot Bay. "The lab was in the attic, with the nicest view I ever saw. I helped the pathologist organize the lab."

Mr. Dubinsky said that he would be called to help on a variety of problems. "Someone might have a new instrument that needed calibration to do sugars. Someone else needed to know the proper equipment to buy. Perhaps my most time-consuming project was to help the hospital in Millinocket design a laboratory, which was financed largely by the Great Northern Paper Company."

Every department of the New England Medical Center, from the administrators to the nursing staff, was asked for help at various times. Mr. Dubinsky said that the smaller hospitals came willingly for help because they discovered there were no strings attached. "The goal was solely to improve rural medicine."

He added it was important to tailor the advice to the situation and to consider the limited resources of the local hospitals. "You couldn't be a city slicker, and show how smart you were by telling them to buy a $3500 blood sugar analysis machine when they had only $300; you had to figure out some other answer for them. I think this attitude came right down from Dr. Proger. He and his associates were the least egotistical, most motivated people I saw in the medical profession."

The Bingham Program launched a major drive to promote use of the electrocardiograph. A one-week course was given at the New England Medical Center to representatives of the community hospitals. The course was free of charge, on the condition that the hospital represented purchased an electrocardiograph. After training, the local electrocardiographer would send tracings to Lewiston for confirmation. Tracings too difficult to interpret were sent to Boston, where a whole group of cardiologists consulted when necessary.

In addition, local representatives were eligible to attend a one-month course each year at the Boston Center to learn new methods and procedures.

Under arrangements for X-ray services, the radiologists from the regional centers visited community hospitals for conferences and reviews of films. The Lewiston radiologist frequently attended X-ray conferences at New England Medical Center and Massachusetts General Hospital.

Mrs. Emilie Born, administrator of the Bingham Program, said that an important early part of the effort involved raising the level of nursing in Maine. Frances Ginsberg, R.N., was in charge of this for many years, and in the 1950s traveled the State of Maine to emphasize aseptic practices. She also supervised a surgical technician program in Waterville. Her successor, Phyllis Simmons, established refresher courses for married nurses who wished to return to work.

The Bingham Program also made medical journals available to smaller hospitals, subscribing to 35 journals and circulating them from hospital to hospital for short periods. It also established in Lewiston the Gerrish Memorial Library, in memory of Dr. Frederic H. Gerrish of Portland, an outstanding physician and former Bowdoin Medical School professor, who had treated both Dr. and Mrs. Gehring. The library, with its large number of medical books, periodicals, and reprints, was made available to all members of the Maine Medical Association. The library also helped Maine doctors to obtain material from the Boston Medical Library, now located at the Countway Library of the Harvard Medical School. (The Countway Library itself is a regional facility available to doctors and researchers beyond the Harvard community.)

Spelling out the historical precedents established by the Program during a meeting with Maine hospital administrators in 1944, Dr. Proger said:

"Hospitals until recently have almost scrupulously avoided working with one another. In this sense they have been decidedly isolationist. The days of such medical isolationism are over. The regional grouping of hospitals for the purpose of supplying better medical service is an established fact."

He said that, to his knowledge, the regional organization in Maine was the first in American medical history. He then went on to describe the role of the medical school in such a program, saying that the benefits derived can best be obtained through affiliation of the regional centers with a medical school center. He added that the success of the Bingham Program, affiliated with Tufts, indicated the accuracy of his remarks.

"The entire program," he said, "is fundamentally educational. As such it is only logical to have an educational base. It is a medical program; therefore it needs a medical base. Ideally, then, a clinical center, such as can be organized around a medical school, is best adapted to serve as the nucleus for the program."

He pointed out that there are two types of hospital groupings. One is the type organized under the Bingham Program, in which smaller hospitals are grouped to work with larger, regional hospitals, and the regional centers in turn grouped around the medical school center. The other type is where hospitals are homogeneous in type and size and join together for more efficient and economical utilization of hospital facilities. He said that one group tends to favor more efficient utilization, the other dissemination of advances in knowledge; and that the two functions could and should be complementary.

He urged that any program modeled on the Bingham plan maintain freedom of action by remaining flexible, and that a spirit of inquiry and experimentation be constantly maintained. "The spirit of inquiry which makes the practice of medicine vital, the spirit of humility which makes it great, and the spirit of intellectual controversy which makes it so stimulating are all greatly fostered by the academic atmosphere which a medical school, better than anything else, can effectively instill into a hospital.

"Through Tufts and the Bingham Associates Fund we have tried to extend into even the distant and small hospitals some of the qualities that characterize a teaching hospital. This has been accomplished through a free interchange between the school center and the affiliated hospitals of practicing physicians, teachers, hospital services and patients. Some of these activities, such as teaching ward rounds, had been instituted in only a few of the hospitals before the war."

In the early 1940s Dr. Proger already was looking beyond the war and planning for the time when these programs could be further expanded by a free interchange of students and interns as well. He foresaw extended clinical teaching courses in the regional centers in the community hospitals also. A beginning already had been made by the appointment of Dr. Julius Gottlieb of the Lewiston hospital as an instructor in pathology in the postgraduate division of the Tufts Medical School. Dr. Gottlieb did a great deal of work before he died in his early fifties to aid the Bingham Program. His son, Dr. Leonard Gottlieb, director of Boston's Mallory Institute, remembers such luminaries as Drs. Chester Keefer, William Castle, Maxwell Finland and Samuel Proger staying at his home in Lewiston.

This statement on medical school participation was to have an important influence in future years as the federal government embarked on a series of regional programs. As early as 1944, the same year Dr. Proger made his statement, Dr. Thomas Parran, then the surgeon general of the United States Public Health Service, noted in testimony before a Senate committee the relationship of Tufts College to the Bingham Program, and described the two regional arrangements to the Senate Subcommittee on Education and Labor.

As Dr. Parran described possible future medical programs to be instituted by the United States government, he said, "We believe that in each metropolitan area there should be one or more base hospitals. Our concept of a base hospital is that of a teaching, research and service institution, desirably connected with a medical school, in which all types of care, medical research and teaching will be carried on."

Already, despite the difficulties encountered during the war years, the Bingham Program was beginning to have a national impact, one which was entering into government thinking. It would have still further influence later, when Congress passed the Hill-Burton Hospital Construction Act, the Regional Medical Program, and the Area Health Education Centers program.

# CHAPTER 14

# Surgery Comes to the Pratt

The five-year period after World War II was one of rapid progress in the development of the New England Medical Center and the Bingham Program. Freed of wartime restrictions, Dr. Proger and his associates began to implement long-range plans already formulated.

A major goal, set by a committee comprising Dr. Proger, Sidney W. Davidson, Dr. Farnsworth, and Joseph Barr, was to expand the Pratt Diagnostic Hospital into a general hospital by adding facilities for surgery.

A general hospital, it had been decided, would strengthen the position of the Pratt as a teaching affiliate of Tufts Medical School, attract leading surgeons as well as outstanding physicians, provide improved care for patients, and increase opportunities for research.

Experience during the war had demonstrated that a team approach to patient care, with a single group of doctors and surgeons treating the patient from the beginning to the end of an illness, achieved the best results. Care at the Pratt always had been fragmented when surgery was required, with patients sent to other hospitals for operations. With a general hospital, comprehensive and uninterrupted care could be provided at the one location.

There was some concern among Maine doctors in the Bingham Program when they heard of plans for a general hospital. Some feared they might lose their patients to such a hospital. Dr. Proger and Dr. John C. Leonard, associate medical director of the Bingham Program, reassured them that there were long waiting lists for admission to the Pratt, and that 85 percent of the patients came from Massachusetts and states other than Maine. They said that the expanded hospital would not be dependent upon Maine patients; and that the only Maine patients who would be kept for any length of time would be those who required care or surgery not available at community hospitals.

They said, also, that developing the Pratt into a general hospital would broaden the base of the Boston end of the Bingham Program and thus increase its value to the Maine doctors.

Dr. Proger conceded that any group organized to provide total medical care would to some degree place itself in competition with family doctors. On the other hand, he pointed out, if the group was organized as a reference center, as was the new hospital, it was in a position to support and strengthen the individual family doctor, who must have his own community hospital in which to practice within the limits of his own capacities. He concluded, "The tripod upon which the total program of medical care rests is, therefore, the individual family doctor, his community hospital, and the consultation or reference center, the latter preferably composed of full-time staff specialists."

Mr. Bingham agreed with Dr. Proger's philosophy and was ready to help finance the new hospital. This paved the way for the first step to be taken: selection in 1946 of a chief of surgery to start planning the new department and recruiting surgeons. He would be able to do some surgery even before the new wing was ready, by utilizing one small operating room at the Pratt.

Dr. C. Stuart Welch was selected as first chief of surgery. He was a graduate of Tufts Medical School, and had trained at Boston City Hospital and the Mayo Clinic. Dr. Welch had resigned as professor of surgery at Albany Medical College to become the first full-time surgeon at the Pratt.

Plans for building a surgical wing hit a snag when trustees of the Boston Dispensary, where Dr. Proger had been elected president of the medical staff in 1940, declined to become financially involved. The Dispensary had suffered a $7000 deficit in 1944, and Judge Charles C. Cabot, president of the Dispensary, said that that institution's fiscal problems would not allow participation in any projects that could cost money.

It became obvious that some fundamental change would have to be made in the corporate arrangement linking the Pratt to the Dispensary. Therefore, in January 1946, the Bingham group organized a new non-profit association, which was incorporated on July 1, 1947, as the Bingham Associates Fund of Massachusetts to take title to the Pratt.

Judge Cabot and the Dispensary officers agreed that they would remain affiliated with the new hospital and would temporarily continue to oversee its administration so long as they could not be held financially accountable if anything went wrong.

Members of the incorporating board of the Bingham Associates Fund of Massachusetts were Joseph R. Barr of New York, a close friend of Mr. Davidson; Judge Charles C. Cabot of Dover, president of the Dispensary; Dr. Leonard Carmichael, president of Tufts (chairman); Dr. Jean A. Curran of New York, consultant to the Bingham Program; Sidney W. Davidson of New York (vice-president); John R. Quarles, Boston attorney (secretary); and Arthur G. Rotch of Boston, president of the Boston Floating Hospital.

The incorporators were chosen to represent all areas of the New England Medical Center, as a way of emphasizing that the change was within the family and not a splitting up of it. A major contribution was made by Mr. Quarles, who did all the legal work of setting up the organization and obtaining legal title to the Pratt through a special act of the legislature. The new hospital, in effect, joined Tufts, the Boston Floating Hospital, and the Dispensary as a fourth member of the New England Medical Center.

The wisdom of separating the Pratt from the Dispensary as corporate entities became evident in 1949 when Mr. Carl J. Gilbert, longtime treasurer of the Dispensary and successor in 1946 to Judge Cabot as president, announced that the Dispensary's financial difficulties were so great that its policy of accepting only medically indigent patients would have to be altered.

Mr. Gilbert told a news conference: "We have come to the conclusion that in the Boston Dispensary we must use our equipment and skills to provide service for those of higher income than we have heretofore considered eligible for care; we also intend to offer services of a specialized nature to private physicians." He added that such activities would provide community services for which there was a need and would secure additional income with which to treat the sick poor.

The director of the Dispensary, Frank Wing, noted that part of the necessity for the Dispensary to accept income-producing patients was due to changing social and economic factors. He explained that medical insurance was beginning to become a reality. He also predicted that the government would assume more and more of the cost of medical care for the indigent, a prediction which came true in the 1970s when Medicaid paid medical bills for 22 million low-income people in the United States.

In 1940, nine years before the Dispensary's change in policy, only one in 10 Americans held hospitalization insurance and only four in 100 were covered for doctors' fees. By 1960, a total of 76 percent of all Americans were covered. By 1981, 87.4 percent were covered, leaving 12.6 percent still unprotected.

Patients the Dispensary hoped to attract were those who had group or government coverage, and working people who could afford to pay something for care, but who could not afford visits to private doctors in their offices. They could charge patients at least the cost of rendering the service ($2.90 per visit). In 1948 they had been charging $1.55 to those who could pay. Clinic visits in 1981 vary in charge, but a routine visit to a group practice clinic in Boston hospitals would run in the vicinity of $40.00. Neighborhood health centers charge slightly less, and some provide free physical examinations for senior citizens over 65.

What the Dispensary offered, then, was low-cost quality health care instead of no-cost care except where necessary. It was hoped that people who had been given free care in the past would continue to patronize the Dispensary, utilizing their insurance fees to pay their way. Ironically, however, once patients began receiving government relief funds to pay medical bills, they turned to other health agencies that did not have a stigma of welfare about them. (Something similar happened in the 1970s to Boston City Hospital, after Medicare and Medicaid started to pay bills for people who previously had been dependent upon free care from the hospital.) Medical insurance gradually led to the demise of the Dispensary as a clinic, although its Rehabilitation Institute on Harrison Avenue continues to be very successful.

While the status of the Dispensary was changing, plans for adding a surgical wing to the Pratt continued. It was to be located on the corner of Harrison Avenue and Bennet Street, contiguous to the Pratt, and to be built with interconnecting floors. Dr. Farnsworth, acting as Mr. Bingham's adviser, approved the plans shortly before his death on May 22, 1947. When the new wing was completed Mr. Bingham asked that it be named in honor of Dr. Farnsworth.

The Farnsworth Building cost $3 million, half of which was provided by Mr. Bingham and his Trust for Charity, of which Sidney Davidson and the United States Trust Company of New York were trustees. The balance, $1.5 million, was borrowed from the First National Bank of Boston against collateral loaned by Mr. Bingham. By 1958 this debt had been reduced to $900,000. Mr. Bingham then paid $730,000 of this amount and the hospital paid the remaining $170,000, which rendered the hospital debt-free.

(There were two Bingham charitable funds. One was the Trust for Charity, created on July 5, 1935. The second was the Betterment Fund, created by Mr. Bingham's will and constituting his residuary estate. Trustees of the Betterment Fund were Sidney Davidson, Ralph Lowell, and Dr. Arthur L. Walters of Miami Beach, who was Mr. Bingham's physician during his later years. Dr. Walters also was named a trustee of the Trust for Charity in 1955, shortly before the death of Mr. Bingham.)

Another significant step in the development of the Pratt into a general hospital was the appointment on January 1, 1947, of Mr. Richard T. Viguers as administrator. This marked the transfer of responsibility for day-to-day administration from the Dispensary to the new Bingham Associates Fund of Massachusetts. Mr. Viguers was a quiet, highly competent professional who had been a foreign correspondent, a lawyer, a teacher of economics in China, and an Army hospital administrator during World War II. He had prematurely white hair and a wry and sometimes acerbic sense of humor, and was a constant pipe smoker. He became active in affairs of the Massachusetts Hospital Association and the New England Hospital Assembly.

The name of the Pratt Clinic, with its surgical wing, the Farnsworth Building, was changed in 1948 to New England Center Hospital. (The idea of the trustees was that the name would tie the new hospital in with the New England Medical Center, the overall name for the federation of Tufts, the Boston Floating Hospital, the Dispensary, and the Pratt Clinic.)

By any name, however, the new Farnsworth Building at the corner of Harrison Avenue and Bennet Street was hailed for its many innovative features when it opened formally on May 26, 1949.

Mrs. Frances Burns, then medical writer for the *Boston Globe,* noted that operating rooms were in the basement. Up to that time, surgical suites generally had been on the top floors of hospitals to provide the best natural light. "Modern artificial lighting makes the sun superfluous for operating," Chief of Surgery C. Stuart Welch told Mrs. Burns. The building rose six stories above the street with the main entrance at the corner of Bennet Street and Harrison Avenue.

Reminiscing in 1980 about the opening of the Farnsworth, Dr. Proger recalled that James Michael Curley was mayor of Boston at the time. (He had resumed his post after a prison term for alleged war profiteering and a pardon from President Harry Truman.) Now he was running for reelection and showed up for the dedication ceremonies, expecting to speak, although he had not been invited to do so. Dr. Proger had to tell the mayor as diplomatically as possible that there was no room for him on the primarily medical program. The mayor took it in good grace. He was in his seventies at the time, and lost to John B. Hynes that fall.

Dr. Proger regretted the incident, because Mayor Curley had helped solve some land-taking problems for the hospital. The land along Harrison Avenue, where the Farnsworth Building is located, was occupied by a fire station and some small shops. Mayor Curley offered the fire station, which had been abandoned, to the hospital for a dollar, a not unusual procedure where charitable organizations were involved. The hospital authorities insisted on paying a fair value of $10,000 to the city. They wanted no political debts.

Mr. Quarles, who was handling negotiations, told the mayor that there was one owner of a small shop who had paid $4000 for his property, had upped the price to $35,000 and was raising the price daily. Mayor Curley picked up his phone, called the owner, and said that if the property was so valuable he (the mayor) had better send over an assessor to look at it. The next day the owner appeared at the hospital and agreed to sell for $35,000.

Dr. Proger had an opportunity later to repay Mayor Curley, who showed up at the hospital one day with a young woman in tow, the daughter of a nurse who had looked after Mr. Curley during a serious illness the previous year. The daughter wanted to learn to be an X-ray technician. Dr. Proger sent the young woman to see Dr. Alice Ettinger, who found she had the proper aptitudes. Dr. Proger noted that the mayor remained at the hospital during the entire time the young woman was being interviewed by Dr. Ettinger, and that when the interview was over he drove her home to the South Shore. "He had nothing to gain at the time," Dr. Proger said. "That was a side of Curley that was not always presented."

One of the speakers at the Farnsworth dedicatory exercises was Chester I. Barnard, president of the Rockefeller Foundation, who praised the Bingham Program for its efforts to spread better medical care and postgraduate education of doctors into rural areas. He said that an important feature was that it was being carried out with private funds rather than with public resources.

The Rockefeller Foundation already had put its money where its sentiments were: in 1946 the Foundation had made a grant of $250,000, to be spread over a five-year period, to extend the Bingham Program into Massachusetts. Utilizing the Rockefeller money, the Bingham Associates Fund of Massachusetts extended the Bingham Program to several hospitals in the Connecticut Valley between Greenfield and Springfield. By 1960, hospitals in Massachusetts affiliated with the Bingham Program included Athol Memorial, Franklin County in Greenfield, Holyoke, Cape Cod in Hyannis, Ludlow, Lynn General, Nantucket, Cooley Dickinson in Northhampton, Wing Memorial in Palmer, Springfield and Wesson in Springfield, Mary Lane in Ware, Noble in Westfield, St. Vincent, and Worcester Memorial in Worcester.

Programs similar to those in Maine were instituted, although their beginnings, coming later in time, were at a higher level of sophistication. In following years the Bridgeport Hospital and the Lawrence and Memorial Hospitals in New London, Connecticut, were added.

In Boston, with the Pratt now functioning as a general hospital, the stage was set for further development of both the New England Medical Center and the Bingham Program.

# CHAPTER 15

# A Watershed Period

On July 1, 1949, 20 years to the day after his arrival in Boston, Dr. Samuel Proger, caring for patients at the New England Center Hospital, looked much as he had in 1929. He had the same lean frame and moved with the same deliberate decisiveness. His hairline was beginning to recede, adding to his appearance of quiet dignity. His eyes still sparkled when he told the humorous and pertinent stories for which he was noted.

At 43 he was one of the city's most respected physicians, recognized by patients and colleagues alike as an outstanding diagnostician and internist. He was also widely known for his research in the area of heart disease. As early as the late 1930s he had presented a paper to the Massachusetts Medical Society that spelled out the link between salt intake and congestive heart failure. Up to that time, doctors had prescribed a reduction in fluid intake to reduce fluid retention by patients. Now they would restrict sodium. He had been the first to draw a distinction, important for therapy, between certain acute and chronic phases of coronary heart disease. He had also been first to cite the dangers of prescribing nitroglycerin under certain circumstances for patients with myocardial infarct, a condition in which an area of heart tissue is damaged by interrupted blood supply.

Dr. Proger also had made contributions to knowledge of the beneficial effects on heart function of controlled exercise programs, had elaborated relationships between blood fats and blood coagulation, and had been a pioneer in demonstrating the response to exercise of patients with angina pectoris.

102

As early as his year in Germany, Dr. Proger had studied the relationship between obesity and heart disease. He worked very hard with those patients he diagnosed as obese from overeating or lack of exercise. But for many years he had told certain patients that they appeared to be among a group of people he believed had biochemical traits that turned even normal amounts of calories into fat. He declined to lead such patients into false hopes of becoming lean and trim, but encouraged them instead to restrict calories and increase energy expenditure in order not to become more obese. One of the exciting prospects of the 1980s is the possibility that correctable metabolic defects may be discovered, whose control will help weight reduction. One beginning was a report in the *New England Journal of Medicine* on October 30, 1980, by Beth Israel Hospital investigators who tentatively pointed to deficiency of an enzyme called sodium-potassium-ATPase as reducing activity of the body's sodium "pump," and thus increasing obesity in some people.

Dr. Proger's general rule, as early as the 1930s, was "avoid extremes in daily living and practice moderation in all things." Long before the energy crisis he was telling patients, "Running a car at 50 instead of 70 miles an hour and keeping it in good repair will get more mileage. The same is true of your body." Such advice seems self-evident today, but it was innovative then.

By 1949, Dr. Proger had already received the highest Tufts academic-hospital appointment, having been named professor and chairman of the Department of Medicine at Tufts Medical School, and physician-in-chief at New England Center Hospital. He had been elected president of the Bingham Associates Fund in 1945 and president of the New England Center Hospital in 1946. He also had been elected to the American Academy of Arts and Sciences, and would receive an honorary degree from Tufts in 1952. He also was to be given the American Design Award in New York in 1951, before 1500 business and professional leaders of the nation, for his "inspiring leadership of the Bingham Associates Program."

Dr. Proger had been equally successful in his personal life. He lived in a comfortable and cultured home on Willow Crescent, Brookline, with his wife Evelyn and their then teenage daughters, Susan and Nancy.

During his first 20 years in Boston, Dr. Proger had continued to play his "fiddle," a fine Italian instrument that he had bought during the Depression for $1000. He sold it only when he was in his seventies and realized that none of his children or grandchildren would play it. It was worth $13,000 then. He sold his old English bow to a Boston Symphony violinist.

Dr. Proger had been active in medical and scientific organizations during those first two decades in Boston. He was a member of the American Medical Association and of the Massachusetts Medical Society; a founder of the Massachusetts Heart Association and of the New England Cardiovascular Society. He was a fellow of the American College of Cardiology and the Association of American Physicians. When he was elected a member of the American Society for Clinical Investigation in 1933, he was one of just 25 selected from the nation.

Dr. Proger's holding the dual positions of physician-in-chief and president of the hospital was a highly unusual situation in a teaching hospital. Hearing some comment that he was favoring the medical department over the surgical, he arranged for a secret ballot of the staff. There were no votes against his holding both posts, but there was one abstention. Dr. Proger said in later years that he felt uncomfortable at times, realizing that there was a conflict in a physician-in-chief going to himself as president for decisions. Although the situation would never have worked in the long run, he said, it provided flexibility and helped speed the rate of development while the hospital was small.

During 1949 Dr. Proger could feel satisfaction that another of his dreams for the development of the New England Medical Center was about to come true. He had been assured by President Leonard Carmichael of Tufts that the Tufts Medical and Dental Schools would be moved from Huntington Avenue to Harrison Avenue, across the street from the Farnsworth Building.

Dr. Proger had begun his campaign to link the Tufts schools geographically as early as 1938, soon after Dr. Carmichael took office. In 1940 he wrote to Dr. Farnsworth that Tufts was having difficulty raising $750,000 to move the schools, but argued that for the Bingham Program to achieve its fullest purpose and greatest service, the schools should be located in the New England Medical Center area. "Only then will our work be assured of continuity and permanence." His reasoning was that with the medical school located at the Center, 100 student practitioners a year, chiefly prospective family physicians who would later be settling in New England in considerable numbers, would study at the Pratt at some period and would look upon the Pratt, the Farnsworth, the Boston Floating, and the Dispensary as major links in their medical training.

Emphasizing the importance of Tufts to the Bingham Program, Dr. Proger told Dr. Farnsworth: "Ours [the Bingham Program] is essentially a medical education program. The only really established medical education unit is the medical school. Ours is primarily a Maine, but also a New England program. Tufts is a New England medical school. The BAF [Bingham Associates Fund] is interested in the family doctors. Tufts trains almost exclusively family doctors. If we searched the country we could not find a more ideal medium for the fullest development of our aims than the Tufts Medical School. And very few schools of first rank could be expected to so wholeheartedly adapt themselves to our program as we know Tufts will through President Carmichael and Dean A. Warren Stearns."

Dr. Proger then suggested that Mr. Bingham offer to purchase land for the medical school in the neighborhood of the New England Center Hospital. He urged that three stipulations be imposed: that the school build on the site; that it agree to continue to sponsor the Bingham Program; and that it give preferential consideration to a number of Maine students. Mr. Bingham's response was to provide $100,000 for purchase by Tufts of land across Harrison Avenue from the Farnsworth Building. A number of Tufts medical graduates were unhappy about the whole matter. They did not care for the rough South Cove area and their major loyalty was to Boston City Hospital, where many of them had trained. But President Carmichael stood firm on moving.

It was estimated that construction of a new medical and dental school on the Bingham-gifted land would cost $2.5 million. A fund drive for that sum fell short by $1 million. As a result Dr. Carmichael, who was still convinced that the schools should be located in the New England Medical Center area, purchased an eight-story garment-factory building at 136 Harrison Avenue and converted it into classrooms and laboratories. The building is still in use as part of the Tufts Medical and Dental School complex today, and part of the Bingham land currently is a much-needed parking lot.

The actual move of the medical and dental schools to Harrison Avenue was made in January 1950. It turned out to be as mutually beneficial as Dr. Proger and President Carmichael had thought it would be. It made the Tufts–New England Medical Center an integrated, cohesive unit. Tufts now had a principal teaching affiliation for its exclusive use, not shared with Harvard and Boston University as was Boston City Hospital.

The move meant that teachers, students, and research scientists could cross both ways over Harrison Avenue. The school had easy access to the New England Center Hospital, the Dispensary, and the Boston Floating Hospital for teaching; the hospitals had the benefit of students, interns, residents, and professors in the wards.

Another important development of the 1949 watershed year was the move into the Ziskind Research Building by the general surgical, cancer, and hematology laboratories. The building was the gift of a devoted patient of Dr. Proger named Jacob Ziskind. A native of Lowell, he had become a successful businessman in his early forties, dealing in textile machinery and reviving Depression-closed textile mills throughout New England.

One day in 1943 a Fall River physician, Dr. Samuel Brown, sent Mr. Ziskind to Dr. Proger at the Pratt for a checkup. On his way out Mr. Ziskind asked for his bill and was told by the secretary, Miss Aida Casassa, that it was $25.00, then the standard fee for a diagnostic study. Mr. Ziskind thought that the bill was too small and asked what he could do for Dr. Proger. She suggested asking him.

Dr. Proger's answer was that the hospital suffered from a lack of research funds and that he believed good research was essential for good clinical care of patients. Within a few days, Mr. Ziskind sent a check for $5000 to be spent on clinical research, a gift that he was to repeat annually.

During a subsequent visit, Mr. Ziskind discovered that lack of space for research was a serious handicap for the hospital. There was a small laboratory for Dr. Proger's studies of cardiology; space had been found for Dr. Thannhauser and Dr. Schloss to continue their work in basic metabolic chemistry and gastroenterology. But Dr. William Dameshek, who already had become one of the nation's noted researchers in hematology, was stuck in a small laboratory. He had made immunological discoveries that would, in coming years, allow organ transplantation to develop. He and others deserved room in which to work.

One day, after Mr. Ziskind and Dr. Proger had discussed the need for research space, they walked into a cavernous seven-story building ad-

Mrs. Sol Weltman, sister of Mr. Jacob Ziskind, views portrait of her brother at dedication of Ziskind Building in his name in 1959. Trustee Sidney W. Davidson faces audience in foreground.

jacent to the hospital on the Stuart Street side, owned by the C. E.
Osgood Furniture Company. They agreed that it would make an excellent research center.

The two inquired what the building would cost and were told
$250,000. Mr. Ziskind said, "I'll get it for you and once you have it
you will wonder how you ever got along without it." Before proceeding,
however, Mr. Ziskind asked Mr. Bingham if he would object to someone
else contributing to what up to then had been, in effect, Mr. Bingham's
hospital. Mr. Bingham said he would be delighted to have assistance.
Mr. Ziskind then delivered $100,000 to make a down-payment on the
building.

It turned out that the purchase had to be made through Mr. Joseph
Ford, proprietor of one of the manufacturing concerns housed in the
building, and a friend of the owner. There were problems involved in
the purchase because of long-term leases. Mr. Ford leased the third and
fourth floors to the hospital and later declined to accept payment. Mr.
Ziskind agreed, in view of the situation, to allow his $100,000 gift to
be used to convert the two available floors into laboratories. Other funds
for the conversion came from the Hyams Fund of Boston and a second
gift of $167,000 from Mr. Ziskind. It was 10 years before the purchase
of the building was finally consummated.

Mr. Ziskind became so interested in the development of the hospital
that he was invited to join the board of trustees. On October 18, 1950,
he was in Boston on business when he suffered a fatal heart attack at
age 50. He had been scheduled to attend his first meeting as a trustee
that evening.

Mr. Ziskind's contributions to the New England Center Hospital did
not end with his death. In 1957, the executors of Mr. Ziskind's estate
provided $595,000, as a matching grant to $439,000 received from the
United States Public Health Service, to provide new facilities within the
Ziskind Building. Adding $90,000 from the Ford Foundation, the hos-
pital applied a total of $1.124 million to buy, expand, and modernize
the entire building.

Over the years, Mr. Ziskind and his Charity Trust, administered by
his sister, Mrs. Sol W. Weltman, and attorney Abram Berkowitz, contributed close to $2 million toward research at the hospital. The Ziskind

funds made it possible for the hospital to have research space so that it could participate in the scientific research explosion of the 1960s.

Even before that, however, during the 10 years when the Ziskind Building research area was confined to two floors, important work had been completed.

The Ziskind Building, which is interconnected with the Farnsworth, bears the appropriately inscribed dedicatory tablet: "These Laboratories are the Gift of Jacob Ziskind so that the Welfare of Mankind May Be Advanced through the Continuing Efforts of Medical Research."

Mrs. Weltman, Mr. Ziskind's sister, became a member of the board of trustees; later, her son David Weltman continued the tradition by becoming secretary of the board of governors and of the executive committee of the hospital, performing many valuable services.

# CHAPTER 16

# Recruiting and Paying the Players

By serving in the dual role of president and physician-in-chief during the early years of the New England Center Hospital, Dr. Proger was in a position to move quickly when he spotted an opportunity to recruit top talent. It was almost as if he were the owner, general manager, and chief scout of a baseball team, in terms of flexibility of decision and action. Over the quarter-century from 1940 to 1965, when he was in complete charge, Dr. Proger recruited both rookies and established stars to add to the roster of people already on the team.

He never attempted to raid other hospitals, but always seemed to know when clinicians or researchers were looking around for new positions. He could be very persuasive in his efforts to sign them up for the New England Center Hospital. Commenting in later years on members of the early staff, he said, "These were major figures in American medicine and it was a matter of great gratification to me to have them more or less buried down here on Bennet Street."

If people he wanted were planning to leave the state, Dr. Proger would argue that Boston presented a combination of medical, recreational, and cultural opportunities that could not be found in New York, Baltimore, or Philadelphia. He had come to love the city and the New England life-style and was saying what he really believed. A second approach he took was to pledge considerable freedom of action to outstanding people, telling them that they could pursue their goals in their own way, a freedom that was not always obtainable in larger, older, more regimented institutions. He also pointed out that since the hospital was young and growing, staff members could have a hand in shaping their own departments and developing the institution.

Colleagues of Dr. Proger said that one key to his successful recruiting was that he always sought the best people without fear that he would suffer by comparison. Although low-key and modest in manner, he was aware of his own abilities and possessed sufficient self-confidence to welcome the brightest minds obtainable.

After bringing people aboard, Dr. Proger often went out of his way to include them in decision making. He would ask so many questions, when making major decisions, that one young resident said, "I don't think Dr. Proger is as smart as everybody says. All he does is go around and ask people what to do." His more-experienced elders told the resident that Dr. Proger's questions were intended to obtain varied opinions, and what he mistakenly considered lack of ability was in truth the mark of a thoughtful analytical person with a keen sense of judgment. The staff appreciated the opportunity to contribute their recommendations for major decisons.

It was a tribute to Dr. Proger that once people were in place at the hospital, they tended to remain. If they did leave, it was because more prestigious appointments were offered. Neurologist Raymond Adams and urologist Weyland Leadbetter left, for example, to become chiefs of their specialties at Massachusetts General Hospital and professors at Harvard Medical School.

One reason for the minimal turnover of staff was Dr. Proger's ability to handle prima donnas. He recognized that temperament often goes with brilliance, and he could put up with it if people were good at their jobs. He kept his office door open to the staff at all times and displayed great patience in listening to all complaints. One of the most volatile senior staff members was the famous and popular Dr. Louis Weinstein, a world authority on infectious disease. Gracious and charming one moment, he could stir up a storm the next. Angered by a directive one day, he tore into Dr. Proger's office and demanded to know "what jackass ordered this?" He was completely disarmed when Dr. Proger quietly replied, "I am the jackass, Lou."

Dr. Proger was able to remain calm in the face of ferment partly because of his basic belief that a certain amount of friction is good for every organization. He said once, "I happen to think there is an optimum level of discontent without which you can make no progress. When you fail to reach that level, nothing is happening — there is no creative tension. When there is an abnormal level of discontent, that is when people leave." His attitude in this instance fitted in nicely with his basic belief that progress is made by opposing forces seeking to balance each other.

A feature of working at the New England Center Hospital that appealed to some doctors and repelled others was that all staff members were placed on salary. This was almost unheard-of during the 1930s and 1940s. In effect, it established what in later years would be called an academic group practice. Under the plan, patients were billed by the hospital for the doctors' fees involved in their care. The doctors were hospital employees. This system brought complaints from the American Medical Association, which said it was in violation of its fee-for-service principle. The Massachusetts Medical Society charged the hospital with practicing corporate medicine. The Medical Society later dropped charges, presumably because the group was so small. In Chicago, however, where a similar plan was instituted at Billings Hospital of the University of Chicago, all the salaried doctors were expelled from the American Medical Association.

Group practice and corporate practice of medicine are so common today that it's difficult to realize how innovative the method of payment at the New England Center Hospital was, for its time. It was the forerunner of the way a considerable portion of American medicine is practiced today, with group clinics and Health Maintenance Organizations (HMOs). Dr. Proger considered that one of the advantages in paying salaries was that doctors who were interested primarily in fees would not apply. He said there were variations in salaries, within limits, for doctors who attracted large numbers of patients.

Dr. Proger also obtained grants from Mr. Bingham to help pay the salaries of several basic scientists who worked in the laboratories and did not see patients. Because salaries were paid out of the charges collected by the hospital, he did not want those doctors who cared for patients to feel they were doing all the work, while their colleagues collected pay "for fiddling around in the labs." Dr. Proger equated the institutional handling of fees with a college collecting tuition bills and paying the professors from the proceeds. He said the system simplified the integration of patient care, teaching, and research.

The salary system combined, in his mind, the best features of the traditional university hospital and the private clinic. Patients were listed as patients of the hospital, not of the individual doctors. As such, all were treated in the same way whether they were paying their bills of were charity cases.

Among the stars recruited for the hospital over the years, in addition to the German doctors already mentioned and Dr. Weinstein, a world authority on antimicrobial agents and infectious diseases, were others of great stature as clinicians, investigators, and teachers. Among these was Dr. William Dameshek, honored as a "Leader in American Medicine" during a conference in his honor in 1979 at the Countway Library. Dr. Lauro Cavazos, dean of Tufts Medical School, said at that meeting, "Our doyen of hematology validated the concept of autoimmunity, was among the first to transplant bone marrow, and in 1949, after treating 50 cases of Hodgkin's Disease with nitrogen mustard, predicted the development of chemotherapy." Dean Cavazos noted that Dr. Dameshek was known as the "Father of American Hematology."

One of Dr. Dameshek's proteges, Dr. Robert S. Schwartz, has made the hospital widely known by his work in immunology. He showed that a drug, 6-mercaptopurine, could prevent immunologic rejection of skin transplanted from one animal to another of the same species, an observation that helped speed the transplantation of human organs between nonidentical twins. He also made important discoveries in the treatment of systemic lupus erythematosus (known as lupus or SLE) and other diseases related to the autoimmune system.

In the early 1940s, Dr. Edwin B. Astwood joined the Pratt, coming from the Peter Bent Brigham Hospital, and established the New England Center Hospital as a world resource in endocrinology. He demonstrated that hyperthyroidism could be controlled with drugs, a control previously considered obtainable only through surgery. He also devised a technique of purifying ACTH to arrive at an end product one-quarter the size, 50 times more potent and far cheaper than the product then in clinical use.

In 1946, as already noted, Dr. C. Stuart Welch was named surgeon-in-chief. In 1949, Dr. Benjamin Etsten became chief of anesthesiology, and the same year Dr. George Mitchell began his long and outstanding career as chief of obstetrics and gynecology. In 1950, Dr. William B. Schwartz, then 28 years old, joined the staff with a mandate to develop a major service for the treatment of kidney disorders. He was to become Dr. Proger's successor as physician-in-chief and professor of medicine, and still later was to become the first University Professor in the history of Tufts. Serving also as a Rand Corporation consultant, he became one of the nation's leading specialists in medical economics during the 1970s and early 1980s.

A longtime associate of Dr. Proger was Dr. H. Edward "Ted" McMahon, who for many years was pathologist-in-chief at the hospital and for nearly 40 years chairman of pathology at Tufts. One of the few Americans to be elected to the Royal College of Physicians, he published more than 100 papers on anatomical pathology.

In 1951, Dr. Bertram Selverstone became the first neurosurgeon-in-chief. He and his team perfected a radioactive tool for pinpointing the location of tumors deep inside the brain. They also developed a method of spraying plastic on the walls of ballooning blood vessels in the brain to prevent aneurysms.

Among others who came to the hospital and became leading figures in Boston medicine were Dr. John F. Sullivan in neurology, Dr. Arthur Thibodeau in orthopedics, Dr. B. G. Clarke in urology, Dr. John M. Hope in psychiatry, Dr. Robert P. McCombs in allergy, Dr. Harold F. Rheinlander in surgery, and Dr. Morton Madoff and Dr. Maurice S. Raben in infectious diseases.

Among the first surgeons to join the staff, and still a leading figure at the hospital in the early 1980s, was Dr. Allan D. Callow, a graduate of Tufts College and Harvard Medical School, who joined the New England Center Hospital as a research fellow in surgery when the Farnsworth Building opened. He served as acting surgeon-in-chief in 1958; achieved eminence as a vascular surgeon; became a rear admiral in the Navy Medical Corps; and, in the late seventies, was elected president of the board of trustees of Tufts University.

On a special staff at the hospital during the 1960s were Dr. William H. Fishman, director of cancer research; Dr. Charles V. Robinson, senior biophysicist; and Dr. Gerhard Schmidt, senior biochemist.

All these people served on the Tufts faculty as well, helping to develop the hospital and Tufts School of Medicine into major research centers. The Tufts image was enhanced in the 1960s by Dr. Count Gibson and Dr. Jack Geiger. In addition to serving at the hospital and on the Tufts faculty, these two men established the nation's first neighborhood health center at Boston's Columbia Point Housing Project and, later, the Tufts Delta Health Center in Mound Bayou, Mississippi, where poverty and sickness, especially among blacks, were rampant.

Little public attention was paid to all the activities at the New England Medical Center; so in 1954 the trustees employed Edward M. Friedlander, a Boston public relations consultant and a member of the director's staff of the Community Fund, to be its first public relations director. Up to that time, hospitals generally had not had professional public relations people, but had appointed some member of the staff to be a spokesman. Hospitals had not felt it necessary to promote their identities, and had fended off public notice. One result of this was a strained relationship between the medical profession and the press. Doctors and hospitals cherished privacy and generally considered their activities above public discussion. Newspapers, on the other hand, made no effort to develop specialists in medical writing and generally treated medical stories in the same flamboyant way they approached cops-and-robbers stories, which only increased the tension.

A few leading American papers began trying to break these barriers down in the 1950s, just as a few hospitals began trying to supply information through professional public relations people. Among the progressive papers was the *Boston Globe* which, as early as 1940, had appointed Mrs. Frances Burns as its first medical writer. This middle-aged, motherly-looking, friendly, and intelligent reporter gained the confidence of doctors and hospital directors by eschewing the sensational and by reporting events factually, soberly, and with perspective. She, as much as anyone, brought about a major change in attitude between medicine and the press. Ironically, later there were times (during the 1960s) when scientists sought out the press in efforts to obtain recognition in their pursuit of federal and foundation grants.

One of the most difficult tasks for the New England Medical Center in obtaining good public relations was to establish an easily recognizable identity. Mr. Friedlander said in an interview years later, when he was a special assistant in the Department of Medicine and Surgery of the Veterans Administration in Washington, that he was frustrated by the lack of a single name to exploit.

The confusion in names was due to the complex structure of the New England Medical Center. In 1929, the New England Medical Center was an affiliation consisting of Tufts University, the Boston Floating Hospital, and the Boston Dispensary, all independent though affiliated organizations. Then the Pratt Diagnostic Hospital was built to become a fourth unit in the New England Medical Center. The name of the Pratt was changed to New England Center Hospital when the Farnsworth Building was constructed in 1948 and surgery added to medical care. The similarity between this name and New England Medical Center caused additional confusion, so the name was changed to Pratt Clinic–New England Center Hospital, a cumbersome title.

After merger of the affiliated units was achieved in 1965, the name New England Medical Center Hospitals was given to cover the Dispensary, the Boston Floating, and the New England Center Hospital (formerly the Pratt). In 1981, the name was changed again to New England Medical Center, which recognizes the unity of the components, including the Boston Floating, the Boston Dispensary's Rehabilitation Institute, and the New England Center Hospital.

The confusion, together with the designation of an additional coordinating organization called Tufts–New England Medical Center, has caused real problems for development and public relations officials, the media, and hospital administrators over the years.

The most positive factor in the name has been the constant use of the term, New England. From the beginning this helped establish the image of a regional resource, which is has been, particularly in connection with the Bingham Program. The March of Dimes Birth Defects Center and the Kiwanis Regional Trauma Institute at the Boston Floating Hospital are examples of programs which were attracted to the New England Medical Center because it was a regional hospital, serving much of the Northeast. The Research and Training Center of the Rehabilitation Institute is another regional effort, part of a national network of centers devoted to improving the care of handicapped patients.

The simpler term, New England Medical Center, embracing all the various units, appears to have merit in providing a symbol. Yet there is room for maintaining the name of the Boston Floating Hospital as a unit of the Center. The Dispensary and Pratt names also may be revived if current plans for new ways to deliver medical care through new group practices and HMOs are successful in the 1980s.

# CHAPTER 17

# Dr. Proger's Patients

Mr. Ralph Lowell, chairman of the board of trustees in 1959, highlighted the 20th anniversary celebration of the opening of the New England Center Hospital by describing it as "a recognized part of Boston's world-famous constellation of teaching hospitals."

"I serve on many boards and as director of many organizations," he said, "and I am proud of them all. However, in the field of medical care, medical education and medical research, I have never served on the board of an institution that has come so far so rapidly and yet maintained as solid a foundation of good leaders, good planning, and almost prophetic foresight as the New England Medical Center Hospital and those with whom it works within the framework of the New England Medical Center."

One of the factors that accounted for the advances of the Hospital was the devotion inspired by Dr. Proger in his patients. Fortunately, a number of these not only had financial means, but were ready to provide funds at critical times. They continued the tradition of those charitable-minded Bostonians who had started the Dispensary and the Boston Floating Hospital in earlier times. They set a modern example of the Good Samaritanism of the Dispensary, playing a role that the federal government assumed in part for two decades during the 1960–1980 decades.

The munificent gifts of Mr. Bingham during his lifetime, and of his charitable trusts after his death in 1955, form a distinct chapter in the hospital's history; as do the series of gifts of Mr. Jacob Ziskind while he lived and, after his death, of his charitable trusts managed by his sister, Mrs. Weltman.

Fortunately there were other patients who also gave generously of their time and money. Among these were Mr. and Mrs. Harry Posner of Medford, who first became patients of Dr. Proger in 1938, and who soon afterwards gave the hospital $25,000 to help finance research projects. They provided other gifts over the years, and in 1951 offered $1 million for research. At that time, however, dormitory space for medical students and hospital residents and interns was desperately needed. Dr. Proger persuaded the Posners to let him lend the $1 million to Tufts to build Posner Hall, which is located on Harrison Avenue, on the Medical School side. The plan, as accepted, was for Tufts to pay interest on the loan to the Hospital, the money to be spent for research. The Posners later gave additional funds for research, and Mrs. Posner participated in the formation of the "200 Club" with two other patients, Mrs. David Averback of Lawrence and Mr. John Powers of Brookline. Every member of the club agreed to give $200 a year for research.

Mr. Cameron Biewend of Ogunquit, Maine, who had been born in Roxbury and lived in Wayland before moving to Maine, proved to be a major donor to the Hospital. As a young man in 1935, he became very ill and was advised, as he told the story years later, to go to Boston and see a brilliant young doctor named Proger. "I did," he added, "and it didn't take Sam long to figure out that my basic problem was a thyroid system that wasn't working. I believe that Dr. Proger saved my life and that I have been living on borrowed time ever since. Because Dr. Proger gave me a chance to live, I became interested in health care. As a result, the New England Medical Center and other medical institutions have received the lion's share of whatever I have been able to give."

Mr. Biewend served on the hospital's board of governors for many years and acted as chief financial adviser to the hospital. His profession was investing and he gave freely of his skill and experience to the hospital; he was widely regarded in Boston financial circles as one of the city's most capable people in the area of investments.

In 1962, the hospital trustees were told by one of their members, Robert C. Nordblom, that because of federal legislation limiting the right of film-producing companies to own theaters, the Metropolitan Theatre, the Metropolitan Office Building, and the Wilbur Theatre were for sale.

As Mrs. Biewend watches, Mr. Cameron Biewend toasts his portrait, which hangs in the
Biewend Building, 260 Tremont Street, above the Metropolitan Center. Building was
dedicated in Mr. Biewend's honor in 1980.

He said that these desirable properties near the hospital could be obtained for $1.3 million from American Broadcasting Company–Para-
mount Theatres.

Mr. Biewend immediately offered a gift of $200,000 toward the pur-
chase of all three properties. Mr. Sidney Davidson and Mr. Robert Barry,
as trustees of a charitable trust set up by Mr. Bingham before his death
matched the offer with another $200,000. The hospital borrowed
$900,000 from the Provident Institution for Savings; rentals from the
theatres would help to pay off the loans. The office building, renamed
the Biewend Building in 1980, was turned into a facility housing doctors'
offices and clinics. It will, in the future, become the home for outpatient
care groups. In 1979, arrangements were made to lease the Metropolitan
Theatre to Metropolitan Center, Inc., a nonprofit corporation formed
to foster the performing arts in Boston. In April 1981, the Wilbur
Theatre was sold for $600,000 to Richard E. Bader of New York and
Charles Parker of Connecticut, who were associated with the American
Shakespeare Theatre/Connecticut Center for the Performing Arts. The

two men said they intended to operate the Wilbur in its tradition of distinguished legitimate theatre, including presentation of American Shakespeare Theatre productions, road companies of Broadway productions, pre-broadway tryouts, and music and dance.

The Biewend Building will serve an important role in the future as the location for outpatient treatment by doctors of the New England Medical Center. Purchase and later sale of the old Eliot Street Garage to the state was another important financial gain for the hospital in which Mr. Biewend participated. When other gifts are included, Mr. Biewend's donations to the hospital through 1980 amounted to more than $3 million. About half of this was for the Proger Health Services Building, which was constructed in 1973. Before Mr. Biewend's death on February 5, 1981, at age 77, his wife Lillian and Dr. Proger were named to an advisory committee on the Cameron Biewend Fund.

Mr. and Mrs. Howard Johnson were patients for years, starting long before the restauranteur became widely known. Dr. Proger once flew to Istanbul to treat Mrs. Johnson when she became ill while on a voyage. The Johnsons donated $5000 a year for research while Mr. Johnson lived, and gave more than $100,000 for the Proger Building.

A patient who did not make a contribution to the hospital, but whose fee to Dr. Proger ended up in the hospital's treasury, was Generalissimo Chiang Kai-Shek. True to his belief in privacy for his patients, Dr. Proger did not reveal his visit to Formosa until years later. He was pledged to secrecy at the time, near the end of 1974, because his trip occurred so close to the time when President Nixon and Secretary of State Henry Kissinger were visiting China. Chiang's illness might have complicated matters if it had been known.

Later Dr. Proger was told that to bring in an American physician was the idea of Madame Chiang, who made the point that all kinds of specialists had treated the various conditions of her husband, but nobody had been asked to take an overall view of his medical picture. So a search committee was organized and Dr. Proger was chosen — presumably because he was a skilled internist in addition to being a cardiologist, and because he had headed the Pratt Clinic.

Two Chinese doctors, who had come to the United States to select a physician, accompanied Dr. and Mrs. Proger to Taiwan. The couple were treated royally: given two first-class plane seats each to assure comfort; lodged in the Grand Hotel, owned by Madame Chiang; and provided with a limousine and driver on their arrival. Dr. Proger saw the Generalissimo twice a day every day for a week, and talked with Madame Chiang after each visit. They discussed the case in detail and conversed about Wellesley College, which she had attended and for which Dr. Proger served as a trustee.

There were 12 Chinese physicians attending Chiang, with two on duty at a time in 24-hour shifts. Dr. Proger met with each pair separately and with the entire group. He recommended medication, but told Madame Chiang that treatment was difficult because of a very weak and irregular heart beat. He suggested a pacemaker, but the Chinese physicians feared that the surgery involved would prove fatal in itself.

When the time came for Dr. Proger to return home, Madame Chiang asked him his fee. He said he was unaccustomed to calculating fees of this nature, but suggested $10,000. He was paid with 100 crisp $100 bills, American money. "I was impressed," he said later, "that you could put 100 $100 bills in a single envelope. Madame Chiang paid cash so there would be no record of the illness."

When Dr. Proger arrived home, he turned the $10,000 fee over to Mr. David Everhart, the hospital administrator, for the pool from which doctors were paid. Mr. Everhart said that the hospital had recently discharged a patient, an illegal immigrant from China, who had no money and had cost the hospital $90,000 to treat. Madame Chiang never knew that her payment helped to pay the cost of free care for one of her countrymen, possibly a mainland sympathizer.

Dr. Proger recalled that among other widely known patients he was asked to see was Pablo Casals, who had had a heart attack in Puerto Rico. Casals was a fan of Boston, partly because he had once been given a very valuable cello by Mrs. Jack Gardner during a visit to the city. He also had been treated by Dr. Paul Dudley White. When Dr. Proger left, Mr. Casals said, "Give my regards to Pablo Blanco."

Not all of Dr. Proger's patients were statesmen or financiers or even upright characters. A legend around the hospital is that one was a member of the Mafia who later ended up in prison. The story is that a secretary of Dr. Proger was given unsolicited tips on horse races by the patient. Dr. Proger remembers the patient well, but said he had never heard of the horse-race incident.

Another early patient who gave the hospital a great deal of support over the years, especially for research, was Mr. Earl Tupper, the inventor of Tupperware. In addition to money, he gave the hospital a tract of forest land in Maine. When he offered a boat, Dr. Proger called attorney and board member John Quarles to ask what he should do. Mr. Quarles said to accept the boat and figure out later what to do with it. (It was sold.) Mr. Tupper not only gave money, but became a trustee in 1958, joining the board the same year that Robert T. H. Davidson, son of Sidney Davidson, became a trustee. Robert Davidson, a trustee of Mr. Bingham's Trust for Charity, also became a trustee of the Bingham Program and the *Boston Globe*.

Maestro Arthur Fiedler was another longtime friend and patient of Dr. Proger. Mr. and Mrs. Fiedler both became interested in the hospital and peformed a number of services for it over the years. During his last years, when he was in and out of the hospital on numerous occasions, Arthur Fiedler kept insisting that Dr. Proger stand with him when news photographers took his picture. But his overwhelming sense of the privacy of the patient-physician relationship would not allow Dr. Proger to pose.

Mr. Fiedler was far from being a passive patient, anxious always to get back to Symphony Hall to lead his beloved Pops Orchestra. Neither was he one to follow strictly the rules of daily living laid down for him, such as regular hours and careful diet. He may well have been a good example, however, of the value of exercise, as anyone can testify who ever saw him wielding his baton.

Dr. Proger, thanks to his own love of music and acquaintance with musicians, had many as patients for years. Among them was Serge Koussevitzky, the colorful leader of the Boston Symphony Orchestra from 1924 to 1949.

Some hospital people believed that Dr. Proger was too strict in refusing to acknowledge publicly that he was a physician for famous patients. These critics said that association in the public mind of widely known patients with the hospital would have helped to raise the hospital's image. But Dr. Proger would have none of it, although he admitted to this writer that Dr. Paul Dudley White had achieved much constructive publicity for the Massachusetts General Hospital by public appearances with noted patients. Dr. White also used his own eventual public status to further one of his more ambitious goals, the fostering of peace through international medicine.

Two people, not patients but very close to Dr. Proger, who came to contribute a great deal to the hospital are his two sons-in-law. One is Dr. Marshall M. Kaplan, chief of gastroenterology at the hospital, and married to daughter Nancy; the other is Edward LaVine, Boston attorney, member of the board of governors and chairman of the hospital's finance committee, who is married to daughter Susan. During 1977, Mr. LaVine participated in the reorganization of the financial structure of the institution and helped to pull it out of a difficult fiscal period.

Dr. Kaplan, a graduate of Harvard Medical School and well-known in his specialty of gastroenterology, was asked during an interview to explain the close relationship between Dr. Proger and his patients, and what made them so anxious to contribute to the hospital. Dr. Kaplan said there are several aspects. "In the first place, Sam Proger is very gracious, a personally charming person. Add to that that he is one of the brightest people you could hope to meet. You don't realize it at first because he is so soft-spoken and he does not push his brilliance on anyone. He is an exceptionally good conversationalist and raconteur, a great after-dinner speaker with a photographic memory for appropriate stories.

"In terms of his success, there are two other qualities which impress me. One is his ability to look into the future and predict what is going to happen, particularly in regard to medicine and government's impact on it. He has been 10 to 20 years ahead of everybody else in literally predicting what is going to happen. I think this has to be impressive, especially if you stay around him long enough to see his predictions come true. I remember seeing speeches by Sam on how medical departments would be organized in the future. This is the way they are now."

Dr. Kaplan said that other institutions often got credit for innovations instituted years earlier at the New England Center Hospital. One was the introduction of basic scientists into departments of medicine. Another hospital in Boston received an avalanche of publicity in the 1970s, he recalled, for appointing a female chief resident in surgery. "We'd had women chief residents in surgery for years."

Dr. Proger's unflappability was another quality cited by Dr. Kaplan. "He never loses his cool. Back in the 1950s, it was discovered that he had a large tumor in his groin, which by all criteria appeared to be cancer. He came into the hospital the night before surgery and everybody was absolutely terrified. It looked like the end. Sam got into bed and calmly started reading a book. He was the only one who kept his calm. Fortunately, the tumor turned out to be benign. The only two times I ever saw him upset was once when my wife was sick, and another when my daughter, Susan, was waiting for her admission acceptance to Harvard. He called me three or four times a day until the affirmative answer came."

Dr. Kaplan said the only criticism he had heard of Dr. Proger was the old charge that he favored the medical department over surgery. Dr. Kaplan noted, however, that practically every building, except the new Floating, was built with money from Proger patients; and that surgeons use those buildings too.

Asked about this in 1980, Dr. Proger said: "I tried, and I tried desperately, as president of the hospital not to favor the Department of Medicine over Surgery. But the surgeons have been unhappy at times and maybe they are right. Yet, the first laboratories we opened were surgical labs. We did add the Farnsworth as soon as we could. It was delayed by the war years. If money had been given to me for use of the Department of Surgery, we would have used it there."

He said that, despite the slow start, the Department of Surgery, as developed by Dr. Ralph A. Deterling and later by Dr. Richard J. Cleveland, is one of the strongest surgical departments in Boston. Dr. Deterling recruited an able staff and led them wisely, Dr. Proger said. Dr. Cleveland a graduate of Tufts Medical School and the Medical College of Virginia, was named director of surgical services and chairman of the department of surgery at New England Medical Center in 1972. He also is director of cardiothoracic surgery programs at St. Elizabeth's Hospital and the Boston Veterans Administration Medical Center. He is professor and chairman of the Departments of both Surgery and Cardiothoracic Surgery at Tufts University School of Medicine. He has done outstanding work in surgery since returning to Boston, and also has accomplished a great deal in tying together the surgical departments of the teaching and community hospitals associated with Tufts and the New England Medical Center.

Commenting in 1980 on relationships between physician and patient,

Dr. Proger said: "One of the most delightful aspects of medicine is that you get to know a lot of people, different types of people. You get to know them awfully well. You get to know them in a way you never would in ordinary relationships. If they have anything that they use as a cover, it all melts away. It makes no difference how important people may be, they are all pretty much alike when you see them in the doctor-patient relationship. You see their underlying character. You sense, without being aware of it, the internal elementary qualities of people. In this kind of relationship, you can't put on anything. You have to, in a sense, undrape. Some people you are disillusioned by under these circumstances. Others impress you. I don't suppose anybody has a better opportunity to get to know well a greater number of personalities. Some of the most remarkable are those nobody ever heard of."

The regard and affection Dr. Proger had always displayed for patients and colleagues was returned in a tangible way when he retired as physician-in-chief and chairman of the Department of Medicine in 1972. A sum of $1 million was raised to endow a chair in his name. Dr. Proger declined the honor and insisted that the fund be established for the use of future chairmen of the Department of Medicine. Dr. Sheldon Wolff, a successor to Dr. Proger, said that this typical gesture can be utilized to enrich the department in ways that the chairman considers wise and helpful. The fund cannot be used to pay the chairman's salary, but rather to enhance the Department of Medicine.

# CHAPTER 18

# The Parts Finally Come Together

For 35 years, from 1930 to 1965, the New England Medical Center existed as a federation of independent clinical units affiliated with a medical school. The public didn't refer to the New England Medical Center, but to its component parts — the Boston Floating Hospital for Infants and Children, the New England Center Hospital, the Boston Dispensary, or Tufts Medical and Dental Schools. The name, New England Medical Center, stood only for a corporation which purchased real estate, supplies, and equipment, and performed some maintenance and accounting services for the individual hospitals and for Tufts.

It really was a very loose federation with each clinical unit going pretty much its own way. The major unifying factor was Tufts, which moved its Medical and Dental Schools from Huntington Avenue to Harrison Avenue in 1950. It was the Tufts connection that gave the New England Center Hospital, the Dispensary, and the Floating status as university teaching hospitals. They, in turn, helped Tufts by supplying the Medical and Dental Schools with teaching facilities in pediatrics, adult care, and clinical care.

A valuable addition to the complex was added in 1958 when the Dispensary built the Rehabilitation Institute on Harrison Avenue. This five-story building, with clinics and beds, was constructed with the aid of federal funds, the Junior League of Boston, and a successful $450,000 fund drive headed by Mr. Weston Howland, a trustee and Boston businessman. The Institute gave the Center and Boston an important pioneering resource in the rehabilitation of patients with temporary or chronic disabilities.

From time to time, over the years following the establishment of the New England Medical Center in 1930, various people suggested that the loose federation be replaced by a true merger of the clinical units, so that the Floating, the Dispensary, and the New England Center Hospital would be an entity with one set of governors, one board of trustees, and a single executive head. Each time such a suggestion was made, the idea was knocked on the head. There was just too much competition, jealousy and suspicion among the three boards, and between them and Tufts University, to allow such a move.

Mr. John Quarles, an able attorney and a member of both the Center Hospital and Boston Floating Hospital boards, described the problems once during a meeting of trustees as "a crippling lack of mutual confidence and cooperation among the clinical units and also between the university and the hospitals, especially the Center Hospital." He added that Dean Joseph Hayman and Hospital Director Richard Viguers "argued interminably over which institution needed the other most and which contributed most to the other."

He went on, "Each unit seems to approach all issues solely from a partisan point of view with little regard for the effect on the other units. No real decision-making authority has been delegated to the New England Medical Center. All decisions have to be referred back to the units for approval."

An effort to obtain some relief from the conditions described by Mr. Quarles was made in 1960, when the name of the umbrella organization was changed from New England Medical Center to Tufts–New England Medical Center. The name change brought Tufts into the organization in a public way and gave recognition to the academic involvement.

A second step was to employ Dr. George A. Wolf, Jr., dean of the University of Vermont Medical School, an accomplished administrator and a man skilled in hospital politics, to be executive director of the Tufts–New England Medical Center. He also was given the title of vice-president for medical and dental affairs of Tufts University.

Dr. Wolf soon discovered that, instead of being executive manager of the four units that made up the Tufts–New England Medical Center, he had four bosses. He did manage to coordinate urban planning, public relations, and some administrative functions, but the arrangement was no substitute for integration. Mr. Quarles said later, "Dr. Wolf worked with sincerity and devotion, but his efforts were doomed from the start."

Because others agreed with Mr. Quarles's opinion that Dr. Wolf's efforts would fail, the boards of the three clinical units selected an Integration Committee in 1960 to study and recommend possible approaches to consolidation. The committee comprised Dr. Nils Y. Wessell, president of Tufts (chairman); Mr. Robert W. Meserve, president of the Floating Hospital and a trustee of Tufts; Mr. Augustin H. Parker, Jr., president of the Boston Dispensary and a member of the board of the Floating; and Mr. Quarles.

A Subcommittee on Legal Affairs, headed by Judge Charles C. Cabot, was appointed, as were a Subcommittee on Finance chaired by Mr. John Q. Adams and a Subcommittee on Organization headed by Mr. John M. Wood, Jr.

After lengthy deliberations, the Integration Committee suggested in 1963 that a feasible first step toward complete integration, including Tufts, might be integration of the three clinical units. The governing boards of the three units approved in principle before the year was up.

During this period, however, the chairman of the Integration Committee, President Wessell, suggested an additional step. He urged that when the clinical units were united into a single hospital, the unified hospital be turned over to Tufts so that the university would own and operate it. Commenting on this idea, in an address to the trustees after Dr. Wessell's proposal was rejected, Mr. Quarles went into the matter in some detail. He noted that ownership of teaching hospitals by medical schools remains a matter of controversy in American medicine.

Mr. Quarles said in his address: "There is in this country what lawyers would call a 'clear split of authority' on the issue of whether in a univerisity medical center the principal teaching hospital should be run by the university or a separate board of trustees." He said that both President Wessell and Dr. Wolf felt strongly that in order to have a real university teaching hospital, Tufts should own and operate the New England Medical Center hospitals. Mr. Quarles continued: "To them this means that our hospital board should resign and turn the hospital over to the university so that it could be operated primarily in the interest of education rather than patient care — for example, that patients should be admitted on the basis of their value as teaching material rather than on their need for medical care."

Mr. Quarles added that "the hospital representatives disagreed in principle and were firm in their conviction that, regardless of the theoretical answer, the express purpose for which these hospitals were established requires us to continue to make patient care our primary purpose."

Dr. Proger, discussing the issue years later, noted that this debate goes on. The University of Massachusetts owns its own teaching hospital, built by the state. University Hospital, on the other hand, is an independent corporation, not owned by Boston University. Dr. Proger argued at the time of Dr. Wessell's proposal that Harvard, Yale, Columbia, and Cornell did not own their teaching hospitals. Harvard, however, was criticized in the Flexner Report for not owning a teaching hospital, a criticism with which Harvard administrations disagreed.

Dr. Proger said that the New England Center Hospital could not abrogate its commitment to the community by placing education first and patients second, even if doing so did not diminish patient care. He agreed that some patients are more suitable for teaching purposes than others, but said that in all cases the needs of the patient must receive top priority.

Neither would Dr. Proger have agreed with President Wessell's contention that a teaching hospital was logically a subordinate part of a university. He noted that the budget of a teaching hospital could be as great, or greater, than that of a university. The arguments on both sides are long and complex and include such items as costs of teaching, research grants and expenses, rents for laboratories, and patient charges. In the Tufts case, Dr. Wessell accepted the vote of the majority against his recommendation of university ownership, and continued to work generously for the consolidation of the clinical units.

In a recent interview, Dr. Allan D. Callow, chief of general and vascular surgery at New England Medical Center, also (at the time) chairman of the Tufts University board of trustees, said that in his opinion the degree of cooperation between the heads of the teaching hospital on the one hand and the university and medical school on the other is more important than who owns the hospital.

On March 1, 1965, after five years of work, all parties involved having given final approval, a certificate of merger was filed with Secretary of State Kevin White. Perhaps the one thing, more than any other, that finally brought unity was the realization that without merger the whole complex might disintegrate. With merger, the trustees of the new organization, called New England Medical Center Hospitals, could present a united front in dealing with city, state, and federal officials in an urban renewal program, just getting under way, included in its plans the redevelopment of the South Cove area.

All others concerned agreed that merger probably could not have been accomplished without Mr. Quarles. Dr. Proger said, "John is a wonderful person, fine, clear-thinking, absolutely fair. Nobody could ever question his integrity and nobody would ever accuse him of scheming. I think the Dispensary would have dropped out without him." Mr. Quarles was given an honorary degree by Tufts in 1967.

Under the merger agreement, ownership of the hospitals was given over to a new charitable corporation called New England Medical Center Hospitals. First the "s" was dropped to emphasize the unity, and then in 1981 "Hospital" was dropped to recognize the institution's broader range of health care delivery. It is well to keep in mind, if all this seems a bit confusing, that Tufts was not part of the merger, but gained greatly because it now was affiliated with a major teaching hospital with pediatric, adult care, and clinical care facilities, instead of three separate units.

Mr. Quarles was elected president of the board of governors, which contained 18 members elected in equal numbers from the three units to actively govern the hospitals. Dr. Samuel Proger, Mr. Robert W. Meserve, and Mr. Augustin H. Parker, who had been presidents of the Center Hospital, the Floating Hospital, and the Dispensary, respectively, were elected vice-presidents. Others elected were Mr. John M. Wood, Jr., treasurer; Mr. Paul F. Perkins, Jr., secretary; Mrs. Frederick N. Blodgett, Mr. Cameron Biewend, Judge Charles C. Cabot, Mr. Sidney W. Davidson, Mrs. Henry E. Foley, Mr. James Garfield, Mr. Oscar W. Haussermann, Jr., Mr. Harold U. Johnson, Mr. Ralph Lowell, Mr. Alan R. Morse, Mrs. Sol W. Weltman, and Dr. Nils Y. Wessell.

A board of trustees was also organized, with Mr. Sidney Davidson as honorary chairman and Mr. James Garfield as chairman. Other officers of the trustees were Judge Cabot, Dr. Wessell, Mr. Lowell, and Mr.

Attorney John R. Quarles, first president of the board of governors of the New England Medical Center Hospital, relinquishes his post to Mrs. George L. Sargent in 1974. Mr. Quarles, who guided the merger of the clinical units of the New England Medical Center, served as president from 1965. Mrs. Sargent, at the time, became one of the few women in the nation to head a major university teaching hospital.

Perkins. All officers and members of the board of governors and the corporation were also members of the board of trustees.

All factions agreed that Mr. Richard Viguers, administrator of the New England Center Hospital, should be administrator of the merged hospitals. Miss Abbie Dunks, administrator of the Dispensary, and Miss Geneva Katz, administrator of the Floating, were named assistant administrators. Miss Dunks (who had fought the merger vigorously for fear her institution would lose its identity) retired shortly thereafter. Ellwyn D. Spiker, associate administrator of the Center Hospital, and Edmund J. McTernan, who succeeded Miss Dunks, were also named assistant administrators.

Dr. Nils Wessell, who had said on assuming the position of president of Tufts in 1953 that he thought a college president should serve not more than a decade, retired in 1966 to become president of the Alfred T. Sloan Foundation in New York. Dr. Proger and President Wessell remained on excellent personal terms despite their differing views on ownership of the hospital, and Dr. Proger remained as physician to the Wessell family.

Shortly after the merger of the hospitals, Dr. George Wolf, who had been executive director of the Tufts–New England Medical Center, resigned his position to become vice-president of the University of Kansas. It was decided that, instead of a new director, an administrative committee would be established to operate the umbrella organization, which had been given the acronym T-NEMC, pronounced "Tea-Nemick." The committee comprised the deans of the Tufts Schools of Medicine and Dental Medicine and the executive director of the Hospital. The committee agreed to meet weekly and rotate the positions of chairman, vice-chairman, and secretary.

T-NEMC was organized as a separate corporation, whose members included all members of the board of trustees of Tufts and all members of the board of governors of the Hospital who were willing to serve. If representation became unequal, additional individuals were selected. An administrative board also was organized to provide general supervision and control over the affairs of the corporation and its property.

The Tufts–New England Medical Center's powers and influence were expanded to include government grants, medical service contracts, health insurance programs, and community health programs in Chinatown,

South Boston, and North Dorchester; also, mental health services in various sections of the city, laboratory animal care, medical engineering, and many other activities.

As time went on, an administrative office was organized which eventually was staffed by more than 200 people and had responsibility for an annual budget of $10 million. It served to bring Tufts and the hospitals much closer together.

The Tufts–New England Medical Center drew praise from Dr. Burton C. Hallowell, the ninth president of Tufts, who succeeded Dr. Wessell. He said cooperation was reaching a point where personnel and activities "are becoming so entwined, they are as one." He said, "The hospital's first concern is with patient care. The university's first concern is with education. Both are concerned with research. But what needs to be recognized is that to retain first-rate quality in any of these objectives — medical-dental education, related research and patient care — requires a fusion of all these functions."

Mr. Quarles said in an interview in 1980 that, in the years after the merger, the hospital and the university were getting along well because each agreed that neither could attain its highest goals without the other, and because both freely admitted they were mutually dependent. In 1976, the T-NEMC Corporation voted a commendation to President Hallowell for his "significant and unique contribution to the improvement of mutual understanding and cooperation among the several segments of the Center and to the advancement of their joint plans and programs." The resolution said that Dr. Hallowell had come on the scene at a time when relations between the hospital and the university were at a particularly low ebb and that he had given top priority to resolving differences and developing an atmosphere of mutual trust. It concluded, "If T-NEMC now moves rapidly and steadily forward, as we confidently expect it to do, he will be entitled to a major part of the credit."

# CHAPTER 19

# A Tribute in Glass and Stone

The period following merger of the clinical units of the New England Medical Center proved to be one of unprecedented progress. Despite the fact that scars remained from the years of rivalry, there was a new spirit of cooperation. Mr. Richard Viguers, administrator of the combined hospitals, was able to say, nine months after consolidation, that services to patients, teaching, and research all had been strengthened.

He noted that 20 important appointments had been made jointly by Tufts and the New England Medical Center Hospitals in less than a year, including three new chiefs of service: Dr. Sydney S. Gellis, pediatrician-in-chief and chairman of the Department of Pediatrics at Tufts; Dr. William H. Crosby, Jr., chief of hematology and professor of medicine; and Dr. Robert H. Paul, Jr., radiologist-in-chief and chairman of the Department of Radiology.

He also reported that service to patients during 1965 had been double that of 1950, with the hospital providing 113,000 days of bed care and 104,000 days of clinic care. The total number of employees had doubled, numbering 1800 with a payroll of $8 million. He said there were 440 physicians and surgeons on the staff, with 85 of these full-time. The education program involved 212 interns, residents, and fellows.

One result of the growth, Mr. Viguers said, was that space for patient care, research, and teaching was again becoming a problem. He said the Boston Floating Hospital needed a new building, not only because of cramped quarters but because its main building, though only 35 years old, was not designed for modern pediatric care. There was no room for

135

the diagnostic and therapeutic electronic equipment that had been developed. The New England Center Hospital unit required additional space for radiology, clinics, and additional beds.

The Pratt Hospital building was beginning to show signs of wear and tear from excessive use, and the Farnsworth Building was crowded. The operating rooms of the latter, hailed as innovative and modern in 1949, were proving inefficient and outmoded in 1966. Advances of medical technology had raced ahead so rapidly that obsolescence had speeded up also.

Fortunately, even before the merger, the Tufts–New England Medical Center had employed Mr. Hermann H. Field, an urban planner, to draw up a phased expansion program for the Medical Center and to work with the Boston Redevelopment Authority on any plans it might have for the renewal of the South Cove area. Mr. Field, in association with The Architects Collaborative of Cambridge, had prepared a master plan for physical development.

Two major projects under the Field plan were a new building for adult medicine and a new building for the Boston Floating Hospital. The question was, which should come first. Dr. Gellis (pediatrician-in-chief) and Miss Geneva Katz worked hard to seek priority for the Floating. The adult care project, however, finally won out. Needless to say, there was great disappointment among the staff at the Floating.

Priority was given to the adult care unit for several reasons, Dr. Proger said later. One was that Tufts School of Dental Medicine was moving rapidly in its plans to build a $16.5 million Dental Health Sciences Building at the corner of Kneeland and Washington Streets; in effect, a new Dental School. This presented an opportunity to build the new hospital adult care center right next door, on Washington Street, and connect it with the Dental School. For the floors of the two buildings to open into one another, it was advisable to build both at the same time.

Integration of a hospital building with a dental school would pioneer a number of innovations. It would give emphasis to the progress in dental care from the old concept of tooth repair to the new one of total oral health. It would make it possible to provide preventive dental as well as surgical care to patients, and it would enhance the possibilities for teaching dental students. In addition to these considerations was the probability that Dr. Proger could raise money more quickly for an adult care building, and that aid might be obtained more easily from the federal government for such a structure.

When plans were announced for the adult care building, many of Dr. Proger's patients and friends did come forward with donations for what was to be labeled the Health Services Building. Mr. Sidney Davidson, acting as trustee for Mr. Bingham's charitable trusts, provided $2 million and arranged for another gift of $250,000 near the end of the drive as matching funds to stimulate giving by others.

The Jacob Ziskind Charity Trust contributed $1 million, carrying on the support that Mr. Ziskind had begun in the 1940s. Mr. Ziskind's sister, Mrs. Sol Weltman, had proved to be a good friend to the hospital on her own behalf and as her brother's trustee.

Mr. Cameron Biewend also gave $1 million. Toward the end of the fund drive, he gave another $700,000 to build a badly-needed dining area on the seventh floor, which serves as a large cafeteria for much of the Medical Center.

Many patients of Dr. Proger gave sizable donations; and the American Cancer Society Massachusetts Division, Inc., gave $500,000 for the purchase and installation of one of the world's most powerful betatrons, a 45-million-volt unit, to be used in the radiotherapy center in the Health Services building.

Despite the excellent start to the fund-raising drive, there was disappointment that as the months went by no word came from Washington on a request for a share of special hospital construction funds that had been voted by Congress. Dr. Proger and Mr. Viguers had made a request for a share of these funds. Dr. Proger investigated and learned that the money had almost all been allocated; the Boston request has been approved as "worthy," but no funding action had been taken.

Dr. Proger also learned that $16 million remained in the fund and that 13 institutions that had been designated "worthy" of help were vying for it. He decided that, on that basis, he should make a personal plea for a share of the money. He went to Washington to see Speaker of the House John W. McCormack, who had long been a personal friend and who had a deep commitment to the hospital. His interest traced back to the Dispensary Home Service, which had cared for many generations of sick people in South Boston, Congressman McCormack's home district. The Speaker also knew that the New England Center

Hospital was the favorite of many South Boston residents. (And it remains so into the 1980s.)

Mr. McCormack, in a letter to Mr. Elliot Richardson, then the secretary of health, education and welfare, said he believed the hospital deserved a share of the money because of its dedication to community health, and also because of its service to New England through the Bingham Program. "This project is not just locally important, but important to the nation," he wrote.

The result was word from Washington to update the application and to resubmit it. Within a few weeks, notification of approval was received. Altogether, $6 million was received from the federal government to add to the $11 million that had been raised from foundations and other private sources. A mortgage loan for $4 million was obtained to reach the total expenditure, which amounted to $21.5 million.

Mr. Quarles suggested that the new building be named the Samuel H. Proger Health Services Building "for obvious reasons." The motion was voted enthusiastically by governing officials, who also voted to name individual floors for people who had made major contributions. Floors were named to honor Mr. Davidson, Mr. Biewend, Mr. Ziskind, Mr. Lowell, and Mr. Joseph Barr, the New York builder and Bingham trustee whose firm, Barr and Barr, constructed the building.

When Mr. Quarles retired as president of the board of governors of the Hospital in December 1974, a floor in the Proger Building was also named for him.

Dr. Proger never referred to the new structure as the Proger Building, calling it either the Health Services Building, or Building 1-A. The latter designation indicates that it is the first new building in the long-range development program of the Hospital. The second, or 1-B, is the new Boston Floating Hospital.

The Proger Building contains many special features. For example, each supporting column sits on a two-inch pad of lead and asbestos designed to eliminate vibration throughout the structure. Built in is a kind of electric miniature railroad that carries supplies in cars throughout the building on aluminum tracks. The building has through-wall supply stations that allow linens to be stocked without anyone's entering patient rooms. There are modern devices that sense smoke and automatically close fire doors, as well as direct alarms connected electronically with the Boston Fire Department.

Photographs of nurses and doctors working in the old clinics of the Boston Dispensary and the old Boston Floating Hospital at the turn of the century present a graphic contrast between the way medicine was practiced then and today. The most important tools for treating the majority of patients 80 years ago were kindness, attention, crude drugs, rough surgery, and a few primitive vaccines.

The development of X-rays, antibiotics, electron microscopes, electronic monitoring, microsurgery, sophisticated drugs, open-heart surgery, organ transplantation, radiotherapy, and genetic engineering are just a few of the changes that have forced a revolution in hospital design and construction.

The Proger Building added 90 beds to the capacity of the New England Medical Center, raising the total of 470. The hospital gained additional clinic space to the extent that it can now care for 250,000 ambulatory patients a year. The basement is used for therapeutic radiology, where the betatron, linear accelerator, and cobalt units are housed for the treatment of cancer patients. The ambulatory care center occupies the first floor, general services the second, multi-purpose clinics the third, and diagnostic radiology and nuclear medicine the fourth. The fifth and sixth floors are used for adult acute care and coronary care beds. The seventh floor contains the dining facilities, and the eighth floor the blood bank.

The combination of the two buildings — the Proger and the Dental Health Sciences — provides new visibility for the Tufts–New England Medical Center. The Dental Building rises above the busy corner of Kneeland and Washington Streets. The Proger Building adjoins it on Washington Street. Construction of the new Boston Floating Hospital building over Washington Street provides still another and identifiable landmark for the Medical Center.

At the time when the Proger Building was dedicated in 1973, Dr. Proger had been officially "retired" for two years from his positions as physician-in-chief of the hospital and professor of medicine at Tufts. But he still taught students and consulted with his successor, Dr. William B. Schwartz — only the second physician-in-chief ever. Dr. Proger was still president of the Bingham Program, vice-president of the joint administrative board of the Tufts–New England Medical Center, vice-president of the board of governors of the New England Medical Center Hospital, and a trustee of Wellesley College — posts he continued to hold into the

1980s. He also continued to see patients and do research.

In a tribute to Dr. Proger on May 13, 1973, the day of the dedication of the Proger Building, the editor of the *New England Journal of Medicine*, Dr. Franz Ingelfinger, wrote in an editorial: "Dr. Proger eschews the cult of personality and lets his accomplishments speak for themselves. Unobtrusively, without fanfare and shunning the contrivances of showmanship, he has led his Department of Medicine and his Medical School to a position of eminence. Moreover, since his leadership has been based on inspirational rather than disciplinarian measures, loyalty and high morale mark the spirit of his staff."

Mr. Sidney Davidson, speaking at the dedicatory exercises, recalled that President Carmichael of Tufts once described Dr. Proger as "as close to a genius as any really nice fellow you have ever met."

# CHAPTER 20

# The Bingham Program at Age Fifty

A half-century ago, when The Bingham Program was incorporated on June 29, 1932, hospitals still were battling a widely held assumption that they were places people entered to die. Since then, medical care and technology have advanced to the point where hospitals often can keep people "alive" indefinitely, raising questions as to when they should be allowed to die.

In the early 1930s, surgeons did not know how to operate within the human heart, how to rejoin amputated limbs, how to transplant major organs. Physicians did not have antibiotics to stem infections; they lacked chemicals to kill cancer cells, drugs to lower blood pressure, tranquilizers to ease mental distress.

The past half-century has experienced greater medical progress than had been made in the entire previous history of mankind. Changes have been so rapid and widespread that postgraduate education of doctors and allied health workers has become a necessity, enforced by licensing laws. While many saw early the need for postgraduate education to keep physicians abreast of changing knowledge, Dr. Proger and his associates in the Bingham Program were pioneers in putting these thoughts into action, particularly in rural areas.

A goal of the Bingham Program from its inception was to help hospitals and doctors to help themselves, so that eventually they could carry on their own programs of professional development and postgraduate education. Over the years, the Bingham directors have seen this happen in hospital after hospital and town after town throughout Maine.

But sole credit for Maine's medical progress cannot be given to the Bingham Program. During the 1960s and 1970s there was a great infusion of federal money into Maine under programs generally conceded to have been based on Bingham Program principles. The government programs, much greater in scope than the financially limited Bingham efforts, appeared to be drying up as the 1980s began. The new decade presented new challenges to the people of Maine and the Bingham Program as it continued into its second half-century of existence.

The Bingham Program, from a New England point of view, may be looked at as containing two parts: the hospital in Boston and the program in Maine. It seems fair to say that the New England Medical Center could not have been brought to its present eminence without the help given by Mr. Bingham and the Bingham Program. It was Bingham money, more than $7 million over the years, that financed the early bed ward in the Boston Dispensary, that built the Pratt Hospital and the Farnsworth Building, that helped finance the Proger Health Services Building and purchase the Metropolitan and Wilbur Theatres and the Biewend Building on Tremont Street. It also helped develop the hospital into an important medical research center.

Mr. Bingham was convinced that an academic medical center was essential as a base for the activities in Maine. He considered that money spent for development of the New England Medical Center was being spent for the Program as a whole. Crossing state lines from Maine to Massachusetts for his philanthropy didn't bother him, although it did bother some people in Maine, who resented what they considered to be Maine money being used to build a hospital in Boston.

It has gradually become accepted that the money was Mr. Bingham's; that it came from Cleveland and not Maine; and that, in the long run, the Boston base benefited Maine greatly. Furthermore, activities of the Bingham Program in Maine have cost approximately $200,000 a year — which, although admittedly limited in relation to the total range of Maine's medical needs, did amount to $10 million spent in Maine over a half-century.

Financial support to continue the Bingham Program has been arranged by the trustees of Mr. Bingham's two trusts, which are turning over $3 million over a period of several years to the New England Medical Center, the earnings from which are to be used to finance the program.[1]

From a national point of view, there is no question but that the pioneering efforts of the Bingham Program in New England have influenced other groups, governmental and private, to work toward similar goals. The experience gained by the Bingham Program as a nongovernmental agency may prove to be even more valuable to the private sector if federal funds for social programs continue to decrease.

The influence of the Bingham Program on a national scale was indicated as early as 1944, when United States Surgeon-General Thomas Parran recommended to Congress that it adopt a nationwide plan based on the Bingham model of regional medical programs. Congress decided that hospital construction, interrupted by World War II, was a more immediate problem. It therefore passed the Hill-Burton Hospital Construction Act instead, and voted $75 million a year from 1946 to 1951 for matching grants to help build hundreds of hospital buildings in the nation. Dr. Proger was asked to testify during the congressional hearings.

In 1946, Dr. Proger was asked to serve on a national committee recruited by the North Carolina Medical Care Commission, to make recommendations for a medical-school and health-education plan for that state. As a result of the committee's recommendations, a four-year medical school and a hospital were built at the University of North Carolina at Chapel Hill.

The school and hospital operate a program similar in many ways to the Bingham Program; but, being generously financed by state funds, it has grown into a much larger and more extensive operation than the privately funded Bingham Program could become. In the 1970s, the North Carolina program, thanks to its roots in the Bingham Program and the infusion of state funds, was to become the flagship of the federal government's Area Health Education Centers (AHEC) programs.

---

[1] Current trustees of Mr. Bingham's Trust for Charity are Robert T. H. Davidson, Robert T. Barr, and the United States Trust Company. Trustees of Mr. Bingham's Betterment Fund are William M. Throop, William B. Winship, Carolyn S. Wollen, and the United States Trust Company. Both trusts are based in New York City. Generally, funds for use in Maine under the Bingham Program have come from the Trust for Charity; while money for hospital development has come from Mr. Bingham personally and, later, from his Betterment Fund.

In 1950, the United States State Department presented a lengthy account of the Bingham Program in the magazine *Amerika,* distributed in the Soviet Union. It noted the link between the Bingham Program and the Hill-Burton Hospital Construction Act, and it described in detail how the Program helped doctors and hospitals in Maine.

In 1967, Congress passed the Regional Medical Program (RMP) first suggested by Dr. Parran. The law provided millions of dollars to develop plans similar to that of the Bingham Program, which by that time had been in operation for 26 years.

Maine, thanks to its Bingham experience, was ready for RMP and jumped ahead of Massachusetts and other states to implement activity. Maine succeeded in gaining $6 million in RMP funds during the years when money was available — 1967 to 1974. The state also obtained another $2 million in impounded RMP funds in 1975, making a total of $8 million. In addition the state received another $1 million a year for several years under various federal programs for medical education and other health care programs.

In 1970, the Carnegie Commission on Higher Education described the American health-care system as "85 islands of excellence rising above inadequate medical and dental care in much of the nation." The "islands" referred to were the major medical and teaching-hospital centers such as Boston, which provided first-class care by faculty, interns, and residents, as well as by private and group practitioners.

The commission noted that doctors and dentists often remain in practice in the areas where they were trained. It suggested that university centers send students to medically underdeveloped areas for part of their training, in the hope they would remain to practice. The long-run results of such decentralized education, it was hoped, would be better distribution of doctors and improved care for millions of people.

Congress thought the idea was a good one and, in 1971, voted funding for 11 programs in the nation to be called Area Health Education Centers (AHEC). Tufts was selected as the only university in the Northeast to be given a program, largely on the basis of its experience with the Bingham Program, on which the idea of AHEC was based. Tufts was given a $4.8-million federal contract in October 1972, to administer an AHEC program for five years in the State of Maine. (Because Maine did not have a medical school of its own, it seemed reasonable to the federal authorities to turn to Tufts.) The contract called for close collaboration with Maine Medical Center in Portland, the Eastern Maine Medical Center in Bangor, and the University of Maine; the goal was to implement decentralized education and to organize medical and dental care delivery systems in Maine.

The AHEC program made possible a greater flow of interns, residents, and fellows into Maine hospitals — particularly the Maine Medical Center in Portland, where the Bingham Program had helped to establish a third-year teaching program for Tufts Medical School students the year before AHEC started. Under AHEC, larger numbers of medical and dental students were sent to Maine hospitals and clinics to work and study. In addition, family-practice residency programs were established, community health centers opened, and the biological science department at the University of Maine strengthened — all with AHEC assistance.

Tufts was the only medical school in the nation located in one state and conducting an AHEC program in another. Much of the credit for the progress that was achieved under this awkward situation was due to Dr. George J. Robertson, medical director of the Bingham Program for years, who had practiced in Maine before joining the Bingham Program and was well known and respected in that state. He was named project director of the AHEC program, in addition to serving as medical director of the Bingham Program. He was able to involve doctors, hospital directors, and officials of other health groups in Maine in the program.

As a result of the flow of RMP and AHEC funds over a period of more than a decade, Maine developed several regional projects, coordinated by an area organization called Medical Care Development, Inc., in Augusta. One of these, the Kennebec Valley Regional Medical Care Development Agency, opened 11 health-care centers over a wide area.

While much progress was made in Maine during the decade, it was not as great as it might have been. The federal plans required sophisticated community groups to plan and sponsor programs. Such leadership required time to develop. Like many out-of-staters, Tufts encountered some local antagonisms, which were exacerbated at times because of a belief among proponents of a Maine medical school that Tufts was opposing formation of such a school.

Dr. Proger said suspicions that Tufts opposed a Maine medical school were completely unwarranted. Dr. Daniel Hanley of Bowdoin recalled in an interview that he was in the office of the late Governor James B. Longley at the Maine State House when Longley, who had been weighing pro and con arguments concerning a medical school, called Governor Michael Dukakis of Massachusetts on the phone to ask him how much the University of Massachusetts Medical School in Worcester had cost. When Dukakis said $200 million just to build the school and its teaching hospital, plus millions more to operate it, Governor Longley decided to block the school in Maine. He realized, of course, that proposals for the Maine school included use of existing school and hospital buildings, with very little in the way of new construction. But he worried about the cost of maintenance of a school and questioned whether a "medical school without walls," as it had been billed, would be first class.

During the first half-century of the Bingham Program, an effort was made at all times to maintain close personal contacts with Maine health and hospital officials. For example, Dr. George Robertson, who was Bingham Program medical director from 1963 to 1977, had gone to Maine from Massachusetts in 1944 as the second teaching fellow in the Bingham Program at the Eastern Maine General Hospital in Bangor. After that, he went into private practice in Waterville and served as the first director of medical education at Thayer Hospital. He was called to become medical director of the Bingham Program both because of his skills and because he would be accepted by Maine physicians.

Dr. Robertson, one of those physicians who always placed service before personal gain, devoted much of his life to postgraduate education. Dean Lauro Cavazos of Tufts Medical School, in a eulogy delivered in 1979 after Dr. Robertson died of cancer, praised him for his pioneering efforts in medical educational television. The Bingham Program, in co-operation with the Postgraduate Medical Institute of the Massachusetts Medical Society, for several years broadcast daily programs for Maine doctors over public television networks.

Dr. Richard T. Chamberlin, who became medical director of the Bingham Program in 1977, has even closer ties to Maine than did Dr. Robertson. Although born in Vermont, Dr. Chamberlin lived in Maine from the time he was a year old, making him almost a complete Mainer. He attended Waterville schools and Colby College before moving on to Tufts Medical School. After serving his residency at Boston City Hospital and the Boston Veterans Administration Hospital, he returned to Maine to practice. For the next 15 years he held a number of posts in continuing medical education in Maine, taught at the University of Maine in Gorham, joined the medical staffs of several Maine hospitals, and became a member of the Maine Medical Association. He has been instrumental in launching several family-practice residency programs in Maine hospitals.

Mr. George Nilson, field director for the Bingham Program for many years, has performed a vital role in coordinating activity between the Boston base and Maine doctors and hospitals. He is a graduate of Harvard School of Public Health and has taken active roles in both the RMP and AHEC programs in Maine, as well as serving as executive director of the Maine Lung Association.

Another key person in the Bingham Program is Mrs. Emilie Born, who joined the administration in 1966. She is administrator of the Bingham Program, an assistant to the director of the Tufts-Maine AHEC, and registrar for continuing education at Tufts. She has spent much time working in Maine over the years and is a summer resident of that state. Mrs. Born emphasized in an interview that the Bingham Program always depended on a Maine advisory committee in evaluating pleas for help. Thus decisions have not been made in Boston and handed down from afar, even though final approval of expenditures had to come from the Bingham trustees.

Dr. Morton Madoff, director of the then-dwindling Maine AHEC program, said in 1981 that responsibility for developments in the early 1980s was being shifted over to the University of Maine, which would work with a statewide advisory committee.

Incidentally, the Commonwealth of Massachusetts eventually benefited from an AHEC program. Pleased with the success of the first 11 contracts, Congress approved a second group of programs in 1978. The University of Massachusetts Medical School in Worcester obtained one. The program is currently being carried on in both rural and urban areas of Massachusetts.

At Tufts, efforts toward postgraduate education, through the Bingham Program and through regular university channels, continue to be a major endeavor. Dr. Norman Stearns, formerly medical director of the Postgraduate Medical Institute of the Massachusetts Medical Society and director of the Tufts Medical Service at Boston City Hospital, is associate dean for continuing education at Tufts. He has praised Dr. Proger for his early recognition of the need for postgraduate education and his foresight in extending it to Maine under the Bingham Program.

Dr. Chamberlin and Mrs. Born said that postgraduate education was not limited to physicians under the Bingham Program. For a number of years, some Bingham money was used for scholarships to help send Maine students to medical school. There also were extensive programs that were designed to upgrade the quality of nursing in Maine, both by working with students and by helping hospitals train their nurses in various specialties.

A major project initiated by the Bingham Program in 1965 was called the Guest Residency Program. This is a continuing-education project under which senior residents or fellows are sent by the New England Medical Center to work for a week at a time with doctors in rural hospitals. This allows doctors in communities to find out the procedures followed in teaching hospitals under specific conditions. The approach is similar to the problem-solving method of disseminating knowledge. The guest residents attempt to identify problem areas in the local hospitals, as well as to help doctors update diagnostic techniques and clinical practices. They may do this through one-on-one discussions, by lectures, or by example.

Needless to say, residents must practice tact in order to be successful. The residents who have done best have approached their experience with the attitude that they also had something to learn in seeing how experienced doctors care for patients under oftentimes difficult circumstances. Where mutual respect is evident, the program works very well, a study indicated.

The federal government has sponsored a number of guest residencies under the AHEC program in Maine, basing its support for such efforts on the Bingham Program. It would appear that the Guest Residency Program will continue to be a feature of the Bingham Program in the future.

Health care in Maine today is much better organized than it was before 1970. But progress has been slow and painful, and there still is a long way to go. A survey by Medical Care Development, Inc., at the end of 1979 indicated the following among many problems:

— Maine ranked 50th among the states in per-capita income, when the expense of living in that cold northern state was taken into consideration.

— Maine had the worst dental-health record in the nation, with 800 decayed teeth for every 100 children aged 6 to 14. Very few city water supplies were fluoridated and well water in the State was low in natural fluorides.

— Alcoholism affected about 60,000 people — one out of every ten adults. About 11,000 of the problem drinkers were women and another 2500 were youths under 19.

— Doctors were in short supply and badly distributed, in that two-thirds of them practiced in urban areas, whereas two-thirds of the people lived in fishing, farming, or lumbering towns and villages.

Improvements in Maine included development of 40 ambulatory-care centers (before 1970 the state had only four); 20 certified home health agencies; an emergency medical-care network; and the creation of a corps of pediatric and family nurse associates.

Another survey by Medical Care Development in 1980 indicated that the state still remained short by 350 physicians; and that a large number of those practicing were approaching retirement age. The average age of the general population also was increasing and required increased medical attention. Maine was obtaining some primary-care reinforcements through nurse practitioners, midwives, physician assistants, and National Health Service Corps doctors (who work off medical education loans from the government by serving in areas where they are needed). .

The new family residency programs also appeared to be paying off, but more time would be needed to determine if the graduates stayed permanently in Maine. One other factor in the primary-care picture is the new New England College of Osteopathic Medicine (NECOM) in Biddeford, which graduated its first classes in the early 1980s.

In Boston, Mr. Nilson and Mrs. Born meet frequently with Dr. Chamberlin and Dr. Proger to discuss medical progress in Maine and to consider ideas for future projects. The era of helping hospitals directly appeared to be pretty much over. One study of Maine hospital needs said "the baby has grown up and gone off on his own." In recent years, the Bingham Program has aided a number of education and training programs. Some of these include the Knox County Emergency Medical Services, the Maine Interagency Council on Smoking and Health, Maine

Medical Center's medical student teaching, the training of pediatric nurse associates, and respiratory therapy programs. Other groups given assistance include the Maine Medical Education Foundation, the Medical Education Consortium, the North New England Branch of the American Psychiatric Association, the Nutrition Program in Washington County, the University of Maine dental hygiene program, the Westbrook College nursing program, the Arthritis Foundation of Maine, the Kennebec Valley Regional Health Agency blood banks, the Mid-Coast Mental Health Agency, the Primary Medical Care Center, Eastern Maine Medical Center Rural Health Associates, and others seeking to deliver health care in creative ways.

The emphasis today, in short, is more on supporting residency programs, helping to establish community health centers, and meeting some public health needs, than in helping hospitals directly. For example, Bingham officials are involved in making a study of nutrition in Washington County, Maine, where food stamps have been widely distributed. They are trying to discover whether stamps are used to provide nutritious foods, whether they have had an impact on health, and what the people are going to do as the program is cut back, as planned by the federal government.

Nutrition may soon play a major role in Bingham activities as the U.S. Human Nutrition Research Center at Tufts–New England Medical Center develops, and as Tufts assumes a leading role in that area through the Frances Stern Nutrition Center and the University's own Nutrition Institute in Medford, and with nutritionist Dr. Jean Mayer, president of Tufts, supporting such efforts.

One of the factors that makes the Bingham Program important, despite its limited funds, is that it is small and flexible, so that it can experiment and change direction when necessary to meet new conditions and challenges.

An innovative idea Bingham directors have come up with is the possible use of government-sponsored medical "consensus findings" to promote medical education and at the same time to help reduce medical costs. Consensus findings are made by groups of medical specialists who get together in meetings and hammer out procedures they believe most appropriate for treating various illnesses.

The Bingham directors are seeking to obtain consensus data on the most common group of illnesses for which patients are admitted to hospitals. They would then send residents to community hospitals to explain the consensus findings. Doctors would thus obtain education on the consensus opinion on the best modes of treatment, and could even gain continuing-education credits for attending the lectures.

The cost-saving aspect of the plan lies in the possible reduction in the number of tests or other procedures a physician might feel compelled to order to protect himself against malpractice charges. If he followed the accepted procedure outlined for treating a particular illness, he would have a strong defense in that he had acted according to the expert wisdom of the consensus specialists. On the other hand, if doctors did not follow consensus findings, they might well be subject to criticism by their peers.

An example of how consensus opinion can save costs is indicated by the Canadian Task Force Study of 1973 on hysterectomies. When criteria for performing hysterectomies were established by the task force and sent to Canadian hospitals, the number of hysterectomies performed dropped by 50 percent. Nobody told doctors to lower the rate of hysterectomies, but, when they studied a consensus of the opinions of the best specialists, they had guidelines with which they could feel comfortable and they stopped doing operations in marginal cases.

Innovative thinking, such as the use of consensus opinions, appears to make the future of the Bingham Program continue to be important medically to Maine. The challenge remains great, but along different roads from those traveled in the past.

# CHAPTER 21

# Doctors and Their Patients

Asked in 1980 to discuss physicians and patients from the vantage point of 75 years of life and 55 years in medical environments, Dr. Proger began by saying: "I shall assume that the physician is first of all a decent person. Without such human qualities as integrity, kindness, courtesy, high ethical standards, and deep concern for people, there is no substance on which to build a career as a physician, nor for that matter any other worthy career."

Asked about medical education, he said: "If the medical school does nothing actually to stifle the student's interest in problems outside the human body, it certainly does little to stimulate or enhance such interests. But the medical student has had four years of undergraduate work in a liberal arts college and should, therefore, have acquired sufficient background in the humanities and social sciences to meet his future needs. This is theoretically true, but unfortunately there is a sharp break between the cultural environment of the liberal-arts college and the professional scientific environment of the medical school; and this break can suffice to snuff out any smoldering nonscientific interests on the part of the hard-pressed medical student. The liberal-arts courses come to be something which one has been through and with which one is finished. The break usually has a finality about it so that few are inclined to clamber back to Mount Parnassus at a later time."

Dr. Proger suggested, during the Sixth Dr. Aaron Thurman Lecture, which he delivered in November 1980 at Beth Israel Hospital, that integration of scientific medical and more general educational training might be begun in the first year of college and continued throughout an eight-year period in such a manner as to make the two types of educational experience inevitably and naturally correlative.

Drawing on his academic experiences as a professor of medicine and a trustee of Gould Academy and Wellesley College, Dr. Proger provided, during the Thurman Lecture, his definition of an education in the liberal arts: "It is, through a continuous process of learning, to expand and discipline the mind, giving it improved perspective, understanding and judgment, along with a power and clarity of expression. Such a mind should enable one to recognize more clearly one's role in the human order of things, adjust with grace to time's inevitable changes, govern more adequately life's unreasoned passions, meet more effectively its recurring problems, and savor more fully its varied gifts. A mind so molded becomes a fitting instrument for the realization of man's active and abiding concern for the betterment of the human condition. Clearly, I might add, a mind so fashioned also becomes a fitting instrument for the medical care of people."

Addressing the problems of medical school admissions, Dr. Proger said that most admission committees look primarily for the kind of intellectual attainment measured by high grades, which mainly reflect study habits and the ability to absorb and retain masses of information, and to test well on examinations. He said that for such factors as personality, character, motivation, and social values, committees rely on personal interviews, which might seem to be useful instruments. "However," he added, "since those interviewed tend to be bright and opportunistic, they are quite capable of slanting their responses away from negative values of self-interest, such as a drive for money, rank and prestige. Investigators generally regard the interview as an unreliable indicator. The interviewer's judgment is by nature subjective, and skeptics suspect interviewers of selecting in their own self-images. The important fact is that there seems to be little correlation between the interview and predicted outcome in a career in clinical medicine."

Among other observations of Dr. Proger, made during formal lectures and discussions in the early 1980s, are the following:

— Let us remember that science without service is rather like a superstructure without a foundation. On the other hand, we must be equally aware that service without science is little more than a foundation without a superstructure.

— We must never lose sight of the central position of the individual; not just the patient as a person, but the person who is at the same time a unique individual. It is both wholeness and uniqueness that concern us.

— The good physician is one who recognizes limitations. Advancing knowledge is often accompanied by expanding ignorance. It is the unawareness of that vast expanse of ignorance that has led to so much iatrogenic, i.e., doctor-induced illness. It is this unawareness that led to the aphorism, *"primum non nocere"*: first, do no harm. The admonition to do no harm was what Benjamin Franklin must have had in mind when he said, "There is very little difference between a good doctor and no doctor." In his day, the 18th century, there were practically no curative drugs or procedures. All illness then was, with respect to treatment, analogous to the common cold today. In treating the common cold, there is, as Franklin would have put it, very little difference between the greatest virologist in the world and no doctor. But it is important to note that Franklin went on to say, "There is a great deal of difference between a good doctor and a bad doctor."

As dramatic an example of what Franklin had in mind was George Washington's experience with his last illness, a severe sore throat. Among other remedies endured by the robust 67-year-old man were: A blister-producing powder of cantharides beetles and flannels soaked with a variety of compounds applied to the neck; a gargle of ammonia preparation which "caused severe irritation to the already inflamed tissue"; wheat and bran poultices on his legs; calomel to induce diarrhea; antimony tartrate to induce vomiting; and particularly, bloodletting. Over a period of 18 hours, the former president was relieved of 82 ounces of blood — about half the total volume of blood in his body.

— Not only is the physician today necessarily limited as to his knowedge, he is remarkably dependent upon a host of other health practitioners. In 1900, physicians constituted 35 percent of all health workers; by 1975, physicians constituted only 4 percent of those employed in health services. For these allied health workers, there are now 125 titles. Thus, while we may be the virtuosos of the health professions, it is clear that we do not function without all sorts of help.

— There are fashions in concepts, in drugs, and in procedures; and they need not be rational or sound to become fashionable. Indeed, fashion often prevails over reason. With respect to concepts, we need only recall the common belief in the theory of auto-intoxication that led shortly after the First World War to the widespread use of purging and colonic irrigations. Then there was the theory of "foci of infection" that led to the irrational removal of teeth and tonsils among other valueless procedures.

— We need to understand the effects on biological behavior of differences in patients' personalities. It is because of these effects that the symptoms and signs of illness often seem so capricious, unpredictable, and infinitely varied. Not only are the evidences of a particular disease dissimilar from patient to patient, but the accounts of the symptoms are also likely to be diverse. There are those who have a high threshold for symptoms. They minimize or even deny them. On the other hand, there are those with a constant overflow of disturbing sensations, many of which are unrelated to recognizable diseases. Some patients are voluble, some laconic. Some are histrionic, some are reserved. Some come quickly to the point, others circumnavigate it.

The closemouthed patient may give the questioner only what is demanded, the agreeable patient what he or she thinks the questioner wants, the loquacious, assertive patient what he or she thinks the examiner should have. The physician's questions may be parried by irrelevant interjections which are likely to take the interviewer far afield. On the other hand, an occasional, apparently irrelevant remark by a patient may provide the essential clue to a diagnosis.

Such variations in the patients' descriptions of their illness, as well as their responses to it, may create intellectual distortions. The basic difficulty, I suppose, is that human beings so often seem irrational, and their behavior quixotic. There is a limit to logical responses. There is no limit to illogical ones.

— No physician can be effective if he or she is not persuasive. To be kind and considerate, to know all about the biological mechanisms that are associated with hypertension, to know all about the effective treatment for hypertension, are to little avail if the physician cannot persuade the patient to follow carefully detailed therapeutic measures. Ultimately, what the physician can achieve as a therapist is what he or she can persuade the patient to do. . . . Persuasiveness appears to be directly related to the degree of a patient's confidence in the physician; the greater the confidence, the greater the compliance.

Throughout his more than half a century in New England medicine, Dr. Proger guided himself with a number of principles. One is the motto he devised for his autobiography in *Who's Who in America*: "To succeed is to learn from failures and successes, and to be unafraid of new failures in seeking new successes."

Three questions he asked himself when considering new steps at the hospital were: "Is this step in and of itself worthwhile? Does it fit into the overall program? Is it reversible?" Commenting on the third question, he added, "A good general always prepares a line of retreat."

In defining medical practice, Dr. Proger said in an interview: "It is both a science and an art. It is a science in that it deals with biological mechanisms. It is an art since it involves the application of human skills. But it is more than science and art. For medical practice reaches its loftiest peak when it ripens into the supreme blend of science, art, and compassion — a blend that may be peculiar to the practice of medicine."

On striking a balance, he said: "To me, one of the most pernicious of intellectual traps is the either-or trap. We often find ourselves in a spot where it seems it has to be one or the other. What we really need is a balance between the two, or a combination of the two. In American medicine, we went all out on the scientific trend, to the neglect of clinical medicine. Now we are going whole-hog the other way, and I am afraid it may be to the neglect of scientific medicine. It is going to be very difficult to maintain the sense of balance that we need. The trick is to recognize these trends early as they are developing and to see that they are properly balanced."

Another of his thoughts about medicine: "Things are never as bad as they might be or as good as they should be. Much of what we think we know is still uncertain, while most of what we need to know is still unknown."

Addressing the role of the New England Medical Center and, in a sense, the role of the medical-school hospital in American medicine, Dr. Proger said: "The two major advances contributing to the present high level of medical practice in this country are, first, the creation of the university hospital and, second, the development of group clinic practice. The university hospital was inherited from German medicine. Group clinic practice, on the other hand, is a peculiarly American phenomenon. The university hospital has created our high standards, while group clinical practice has provided the best means for applying these standards. The prototypes of these two great developments are the Johns Hopkins Hospital and the Mayo Clinic. I like to believe that the two movements will in time be coordinated and fused. I like to believe, furthermore, that both the university hospital and the group clinic will be stronger and more useful when combined than either can be separately. It is a principal goal of the New England Medical Center to achieve such a fusion in the most nearly ideal manner possible."

Speaking on the "God complex" in medicine, Dr. Proger said: "I sometimes think that no other career is better than that of the physician for anyone hankering to be appreciated and admired. I have sometimes said in lectures to students that it is difficult for a patient not to like his doctor and that, therefore, they might do well not to allow the 'God complex' to develop."

On heart attacks: "Perhaps the greatest contribution of President Eisenhower to American life was to show that a person did not have to be permanently disabled after a heart attack. Up to the time that Ike decided to run again, with the backing of Dr. Paul Dudley White, people generally thought that a heart attack necessarily meant the end of productive living. Dr. White's approval meant that he expected President Eisenhower could endure at least five more years of the presidency."

Dr. Proger's syllogism on the inflexible person: "You begin with the minor premise that a person is inflexible. Then take as a major premise that everybody is occasionally wrong. It follows therefore that the inflexible person will occasionally be inflexibly wrong. And that at times can be serious."

On academic medicine: "We hear much about academic medicine and it seems to be variously defined. It is well to remember that a chief goal of all academic medical activities is the highest possible standard of medical practice. If academic medicine is not a means to this goal, it loses its reason for existence. It may be that academic medicine is nothing more than the model teaching of medicine in an environment that prizes and encourages creative achievement and scholarship along with a human concern for the patient as a person. Students, house officers, and staff learn to practice medicine in an academic environment. They do not learn to practice academic medicine."

A favorite aphorism of Dr. Proger is one he has tried to follow in his own thinking: "Nothing is so valuable or rewarding as to be able to distinguish form from substance, to recognize readily the unimportance of unimportant things."

When asked recently to address the Tufts Alumni Association on what medicine might be like in the year 2000, Dr. Proger suggested that some progress will have been made in retarding the degenerative processes such as atherosclerosis. He said he was not sanguine about cancer, except in prevention, or the inflammatory diseases, such as rheumatoid arthritis and ulcerative colitis.

"As for mental illness," he said, "drugs are destined to replace much of psychotherapy. We may hope, as Freud himself hoped, that drugs will make much of the time-consuming and often unsatisfactory psychotherapy less necessary."

He said that environmental pollution may become the social antigen that will produce a rejection response in the eighties and nineties comparable to what Vietnam produced in the sixties. "The battle lines are being drawn. The stage is set for a titanic battle between industrial and human needs, between carcinogens and human life. We shall be facing the questions of how many lives and how much suffering we are willing to pay, in return for material comforts. . . . As I look ahead, I see the pollution fighters winning their battles. I believe that just as the beginning of this century witnessed a sharp decrease in preventable man-made bacterial spread, so the beginning of the next century will witness a sharp decrease in man-made illness due to pollutants."

He warned that when the health problems he reviewed have been finally conquered, "we shall be left with the biological breakdowns that result from self-indulgence. I refer to the illnesses resulting from such pursuits as gluttony, indolence, tobacco, alcohol, drug abuse, sexual promiscuity, reckless driving, and perhaps I may include wars. In attacking these problems, we shall be shifting our concerns to problems of human behavior. The outlook for illnesses relating to behavioral problems appears grim. We need only glance back at the end of the first millennium and measure the progress in this area through the entire second millenium. In this area we have not moved far ahead of Galen or even Hippocrates." Dr. Proger said he expects diagnosis and therapy to be greatly advanced by technology, but cautioned that technology can be exploited and its hardware overused. "To avoid this will require a rational approach to proper evaluation. When we enter the twenty-first century, the primary physician will be as far advanced over today's family physician as the latter is advanced over his nineteenth-century predecessor."

Touching on world leadership in medicine, Dr. Proger said: "It is often easier to achieve eminence than to retain it. Minerva Medica, having moved her temple in the past five centuries from Italy to England, to France, to Germany, and finally to America, will not hesitate to move it on to Russia, to Japan, to China, or to some other country if any one of them provides a more felicitous environment. As we enter the third millenium, the temple, I believe, will still be in America. Where it will be at the end of the millenium, no one can say."

# CHAPTER 22

# A Modern Berth
# for the Floating Hospital

A new, land-based Boston Floating Hospital, construction of which was begun in 1980, is moored today crosswise over Washington Street, adjacent to the theatre district and Chinatown. The superstructure sits atop a bridge spanning the busy roadway, which allows traffic to flow freely underneath. Below the street surface lies another form of transportation, the subway system of the MBTA, with a new station, called Chinatown/Medical Center, opening into the hospital.

The building, which rises eight stories into air rights granted by the city, serves as a flagship for the entire Medical Center, providing high visibility, enlarged main entrances, and a central core that physically links hospital buildings on both sides of Washington Street.

The new Boston Floating Hospital, pediatric unit of the New England Medical Center, was built about 30 years after the need for a new structure was first realized. The old hospital on Ash Street, built in 1931 after fire destroyed the ship hospital in 1927, became overcrowded and outmoded within a quarter-century of its construction. It was only through dedicated service by a humane and skilled crew of doctors, nurses, aides, volunteers, and trustees that patient care was kept first-class despite obsolete facilities. As the years went by, the doctors and nurses brought many very sick children through crises; surgeons reconstructed broken bones and bodies; psychiatrists provided assistance to emotionally disturbed children — all under difficult physical circumstances.

The troubles of the first land-based Floating Hospital began as early as they did for several reasons. One was that pediatric care changed enormously after World War II, with new equipment and techniques requiring additional space. A major flaw was that the hospital was built too small in the first place, containing space for only 57 beds and too few areas that could be used for outpatient clinics. There was no money available in the Depression year of 1931 with which to build a larger structure. Had it not been for the money in the trust fund of brothers Henry Clay Jackson and Paul Wilde Jackson, and the insurance payments from the fire that destroyed the hospital ship, there might not have been any land-based Floating Hospital at all.

The original land-based Boston Floating Hospital had also encountered severe financial and staffing problems during World War II. It was a period of strict economy, of recruitment of young physicians into the armed forces, and of inability on the part of civilian medical facilities to obtain the best-trained and most desirable residents. Maintenance work was deferred, nursing staffs overworked, and donations reduced.

The difficulties continued after the war ended and culminated in a request from the trustees in 1950 for a survey by Director Frank Wing to determine if the hospital could weather the storm. He reported that it could with reorganized administration, an improvement in the economy, the institution of realistic charges for services rendered patients, and the addition of beds to increase the hospital's size.

Mr. Wing then retired as director on December 31, 1950, turning administration over to his assistant, Geneva Katz, RN, a dynamic young nurse who, on New Year's Day 1951, started making fresh approaches. She was joined by Dr. Orvar Swenson, who recently had been appointed the first surgeon-in-chief at the Floating. Dr. Swenson attracted a number of new patients and helped to increase financial support for the hospital. Miss Katz enlarged the institution to 101 beds by refurbishing a fourth floor in the Jackson Building and adding 24 beds there. Then she took over a floor of the Center Building, installing an additional 20 beds. This was a major step because it had become generally accepted that, to be economically viable, a hospital should contain at least 100 beds.

When the Boston Floating Hospital was a ship, and for its first seven years on land, there was never a charge for patient care. If this system had been in effect in 1951, adding beds would only have increased the size of the deficits. In 1938, however, a nominal charge of $5.00 a day had been assessed. By 1951, when the beds were added, the charge had been raised to $11.00 a day for a ward bed and $13.00 a day for a semiprivate room. A great deal of free care still was being given, supported by gifts from the United Fund and private donors. The fee scales helped save the hospital.

In order to cope with inflation, to allow purchases of complex and costly electronic equipment, and to allow employment of skilled technicians to operate it, fees have been raised over the years. By 1980, charges were up to $224.00 per day. Free care still is given when there is no third-party insurance coverage or where the family just cannot pay. Asked about the 30-fold increase in costs over a 20-year period, Dr. Sydney Gellis, pediatrician-in-chief in 1980, said that new diagnostic tools, new drugs and chemicals, and modern radiotherapy equipment cost a great deal of money; but that every year they allow the hospital to save the lives of hundreds of children who would have died within a few days after admission in the years before these tools existed.

Miss Katz, the former administrator, said during a recent interview that it was most fortunate the hospital survived in 1950 because it was inundated with patients during the polio epidemic of 1954. Before summer was over that year, there were 60 polio patients at the Floating. Beds were in such demand that some children with less serious illnesses were sent home or transferred to the adult wards at the New England Center Hospital.

Incidentally, a young Boston city councilor named John Collins was a polio patient at the Rehabilitation Institute of the Boston Dispensary that summer. He was persuaded to continue his political career from a wheelchair and played a role, while mayor of Boston, in developing the urban renewal program of which the new Boston Floating Hospital is a part.

Despite its small size and persistent financial straits, the hospital built a national reputation on its pediatric research and teaching, as well as its medical care. Half of all the pediatricians practicing in New England today were trained at the Floating. One of the reasons for continued eminence was selection of a series of outstanding physicians for the post of pediatrician-in-chief. During the first half-century ashore, they included Dr. Elmer W. Barron, Dr. James Marvin Baty, and Dr. Sydney S. Gellis.

By 1960, twenty years before construction of the new Boston Floating was started, the hospital had become seriously overcrowded. Some additional space for clinics was obtained by taking over floors at the Boston Dispensary, whose clinical needs had grown smaller. This gave slight relief, but the only real hope for the future was a new building. The problem was that the money could not be found.

In 1965, as plans proceeded for merger of the Floating with the Dispensary and the New England Center Hospital, the Floating Hospital trustees invited Dr. Gellis to become pediatrician-in-chief. He leaned toward acceptance, partly because he feared for the future of Boston City Hospital; but he hesitated because of the need for a new building at the Floating and lack of guarantees that one would be built. On the morning of the day on which Dr. Gellis had to make his decision, Dr. Samuel Proger took a taxi to Boston City Hospital and met with him. When Dr. Proger returned, he had Dr. Gellis's acceptance in his pocket. Dr. Gellis noted later that Dr. Proger said he would do everything in his power to obtain a new Boston Floating Hospital and that he would support Dr. Gellis in every way he could.

As it turned out, the Proger Health Services Building was given priority over a new Boston Floating Hospital building by the trustees of the merged hospitals. There were a number of reasons, including the availability of federal funds, the promised gift of a betatron by the American Cancer Society, Massachusetts Division, Inc., and the necessity of integrating construction of the building with the new Tufts Dental School.

Dr. Gellis and Miss Katz swallowed their disappointment and continued to work hard for the Floating Hospital. Among other things, they promoted the "whole child" approach to hospitalization, a concept which recognized the need to treat not just the child's illness but the child as an individual person. They also advanced the Family Participation Unit, under which parents are encouraged to remain with hospitalized children, help with meals and medications, and be present to give reassurance. Dr. Gellis and Dr. Murray Feingold, the latter widely known for his television reports on medicine, were instrumental in establishing the Birth Defects Center at the Hospital, sponsored by the March of Dimes Birth Defects Foundation. This center carries on patient care, research, and teaching in the treatment of congenital diseases and defects. They also helped establish the Tufts–New England Medical Center's Birth Defects Information Service. This valuable service, also supported by the March of Dimes Birth Defects Foundation, provides a world clearinghouse of information concerning birth defects for doctors and hospitals everywhere.

In 1973, with the Proger Building and the new Dental School in place, plans were pushed for a new Boston Floating Hospital building. By that time, the Massachusetts legislature had established a system under which major construction programs by hospitals required issuance of a Certificate of Need from the State Public Health Council before they could proceed.

In September 1974, therefore, the New England Medical Center Hospitals applied for permission to proceed. The application submitted to the Massachusetts Public Health Council asked for a Determination of Need certificate for a $51 million project, which included construction of a new Boston Floating Hospital and renovation of the Boston Dispensary, the Biewend Building, and the old Boston Floating Hospital building. After prolonged hearings, the application was denied in 1976. Following appeals and the dropping of proposals for revamping the Dispensary and Floating buildings, the project was resubmitted. The new application was for a total of $38 million, a reduction of 25 percent from the original request. Reductions had been made by cutting the planned cost of renovation of the shell of the Biewend Building from $2 million to $1 million; by downgrading the basic quality of the exterior siding and interior finishes of the Floating building; and by changing the anticipated financing mechanism. Space was not sacrificed, according to Director of Planning Roger T. Block.

The great need for the new Boston Floating Hospital, and the merits of allowing the construction, were spelled out before the Public Health Council on October 11, 1977, by Dr. Proger. He emphasized that every forward move ever made at the New England Medical Center had been the result of clearly demonstrated need, never just in anticipation of future prospects. He urged the council to make certain that a socially and economically justified project was not smothered during what he described as "the necessary and admirable process of controlling unwise and wasteful expansion of health facilities." He said that "need for a new building at the Boston Floating had never been more urgent or essential."

The Public Health Council approved the $38 million project in November of 1977, with the stipulation that construction begin by November 25, 1979, a deadline that was met. Unfortunately for the hospital, however, inflation by that time had raised the cost of the total project to an estimated $55 million, more than the cost of the several projects included in the 1974 application.

The Boston Redevelopment Authority made available a small parcel of land next to the Proger Building and granted air rights over Washington Street for construction of the new hospital. Financing was arranged by obtaining a mortgage loan insured by the Federal Housing Administration and a Government National Mortgage Association collateralized revenue bond issue through the Massachusetts Health and Educational Facilities Authority, to pay for a major portion of the costs. A major fund drive was under way in the early 1980s to raise money from private sources and public subscription to help meet the costs of mortgages and loans.

While the new eight-story structure over Washington Street is called The Boston Floating Hospital for Infants and Children, only half of it is devoted exclusively to the care of children. The building also contains operating rooms for adults. This allows the Medical Center as a whole to centralize its surgical area, and to put to other uses outmoded surgical suites in the Farnsworth Building.

The new building, with about 280,000 square feet of space, was designed to replace the old Floating Hospital with a more cost-effective, technologically modern, and space-efficient pediatric facility. It also provided large ambulatory clinics and space to expand the concept of family participation in the care of sick children. It permitted replacement of outdated radiologic facilities for both adult and pediatric therapy, and centralized laboratories for the entire hospital.

The Public Health Council would allow no additional pediatric beds in the new Floating, actually restricting the number to 96, with 12 of these for intensive care. Although this is four beds under the generally accepted figure of 100 for financial viability, that standard does not

Breaking ground for new Floating building in 1979. From left, William L. Saltonstall, chairman of Board of Governors, New England Medical Center; Franklin P. Parker, a member of the board; Marvin Siflinger, U.S. Departments of Health, Education and Welfare and Department of Housing and Urban Development; Dr. Samuel Proger; Dr. Jean Mayer, President of Tufts University; Dr. Sydney S. Gellis, pediatrician-in-chief; Miss Geneva Katz, former Floating Hospital administrator; Dr. Jerome H. Grossman, President of New England Medical Center; Mayor Kevin White of Boston. In front of Mayor White are April Murphy and Lee Stimson, former patients. Lee underwent a 17-hour operation which rebuilt his legs, crushed in a sledding accident involving a freight train. April was treated before birth to lower her organic acid levels, which had accumulated due to a hereditary disorder.

necessarily apply because half the hospital structure is being used for purposes associated with the adult units of the New England Medical Center.

Dr. Gellis said that he was not particularly concerned about bed numbers, so long as large clinic areas were provided. He said that he believed ambulatory care would be a very important part of pediatric hospital medicine in the future. The reason for this is that children with serious defects, who previously would not have survived, are living nearly normal lives but require periodic outpatient follow-up treatments by specialists.

The beds, he said, are needed for initial treatment of very sick children who need care beyond what can be delivered at community hospitals — which, in turn, have grown more sophisticated. Dr. Gellis said a policy of the Floating has been to reserve beds for severely ill or injured patients, except where children who live in the immediate neighborhood are concerned.

When Dr. Gellis, who had served as pediatrician-in-chief since 1965, reached retirement age in 1980, he was succeeded by Dr. Richard C. Talamo, formerly professor of pediatrics at Johns Hopkins Medical School and a pediatrician at Johns Hopkins Hospital. Dr. Talamo became seriously ill shortly after his appointment, and Dr. Marshall B. Kreidberg, associate pediatrician-in-chief, was named acting chief to head the medical staff and to supervise the detailed preparations for the move to the new hospital structure.

Dr. Gellis said in an interview at the time of his retirement that he expects to be active at the hospital for years to come, free to continue teaching and to practice in the area of ambulatory pediatrics. He also will work with Dr. Murray Feingold, chief of the Birth Defects Center, and with Dr. Lucian L. Leape, the outstanding surgeon who was named surgeon-in-chief at the Floating in 1973 — after graduating from Harvard Medical School and serving at Massachusetts General Hospital, Children's Hospital Medical Center in Boston, Alder Hey Children's Hospital in Liverpool, England, and the University of Kansas School of Medicine. Dr. Leape said that the new facility, with its modern operating areas and centralized laboratory services, provides what is needed for the type of major surgical procedures undertaken today.

Dr. Leape said, in an interview with medical writer Loretta McLaughlin in the *Boston Globe* in 1980, that the new building will provide an excellent setting for the New England Pediatric Trauma Institute, sponsored by the Kiwanis Foundation of New England. "Trauma is the major cause of death in children, far ahead of cancer," he pointed out. "Among New England's 3.4 million children under 18, some 250 deaths occur each year from about 8,000 accidents, excluding poisonings, drownings, and burns." He added that children require a very different type of care from adults, with disability and death often prevented when proper equipment and specially trained personnel are available. He cited as an example the case of a South Boston boy, Lee Stimson, whose legs, nearly amputated by a train, were saved after many hours of surgery. "That boy might have died in a non-specialized hospital," Dr. Leape said. "That is the kind of thing we want to make available for all children in New England." The New England Kiwanis district has 12,500 members in 250 clubs, and favors carrying out service projects that help young people. The goal of this project is to improve the care and survival of children who have suffered severe injury, through stepped-up research, education, and specialized care. Under the program, whenever a child is injured beyond the capacity of a local hospital to provide care, the child may be rushed to the Boston Floating Hospital. Training in the handling of trauma victims by the Institute also will help to disseminate this specialized knowledge.

Everyone concerned with the New England Medical Center is acutely aware that, with the new Floating Hospital, opportunities for service will be far greater in scope than was possible either aboard ship or in the cramped previous quarters.

# CHAPTER 23

# New England Medical Center Today

A visitor returning to the New England Medical Center today, a half-century after incorporation of the alliance linking Tufts, the Boston Floating Hospital, and the Boston Dispensary, might paraphrase Winston Churchill to ask, "How could so few do so much with so little in so short a time?"

Lack of money was a problem during the entire time period. Tufts, always struggling for funds, did not have endowments to lavish on its medical and dental schools; the Boston Dispensary, never self-sustaining, had given its substance to aid the needy sick since George Washington's time; the Boston Floating Hospital, begun as a ship to provide aid to the poor, had been giving costly care to children since the 1890s. Institutions which raise money to nurse the needy may be following the example of the Good Samaritan depicted over the door of the Dispensary building, but they don't build cash reserves.

As a result, Tufts University School of Medicine remains housed in renovated garment-industry buildings on Harrison Avenue and lacks a suitable medical library, for which a fund drive now is underway. Tufts University School of Dental Medicine does have a new building, partly financed by the federal government. The Medical Center does have the new Proger Health Services Building and the new Boston Floating; but the Farnsworth, Pratt, Dispensary, and old Floating Hospital buildings are now obsolete.

The foundations for the current New England Medical Center were designed and built over the years by a few dedicated people of means,

as described in previous chapters. With basic structures in place, the
Medical Center was able to benefit in the 1960s and 1970s by obtaining
a share of the grants for education, research, and construction made
available by the federal government. In the 1980s, as federal assistance
wanes, continued support for the center appears to be dependent again
upon the willingness of the private sector to resume the tradition of
private giving that persisted in Boston for so many generations.

New leaders were chosen at New England Medical Center during the
late 1970s and early 1980s to wrestle with rapidly changing health care
systems in a world of rising costs. Dr. Samuel Proger was still active as
president of the Bingham Program, as chairman of the trustees of the
Medical Center, and as a physician. He also served as elder statesman
when the new chiefs asked for advice. In July 1979, Dr. Jerome H.
Grossman was chosen to become president, executive director and chairman of the executive committee of the New England Medical Center.
The three appointments mean that he is president of the corporation
that owns the Hospital, chairman of the executive committee of the
board of governors that runs it, and chief executive for operations. This
was the first time since the merger that such a large measure of authority
was lodged in one person. Several other hospitals were also pursuing
this trend at the time in an effort to see if tighter control could achieve
more efficient and less costly operation.

Dr. Grossman is the first physician-administrator of the hospital since
the merger of the clinical units in 1965. Only 39 years old at the time
of his appointment, he already had held major positions at Massachusetts General Hospital in directing ambulatory care services, emergency
ward areas, group practices, and neighborhood health centers. Among
his other duties, he had the responsibility for planning the new $26
million ambulatory care health center at the MGH.

In addition to being a physician and administrator, Dr. Grossman is
an economist and historian who lectures at the Harvard Business School
and the Sloan School of Management at Massachusetts Insitition of
Technology. He is a computer expert, who studied electrical engineering
at MIT and served as associate director of the Laboratory for Computer
Science at Massachusetts General Hospital.

Dr. Grossman was born in Newark, New Jersey, on September 23,
1939. He received a B.S. degree in the Humanities from MIT in 1961,

and his M.D. degree from the University of Pennsylvania in 1965. Since 1967, he has been a consultant for a number of national and local organizations, including the Harvard Community Health Plan, the National Center for Health Services Research and Development, and United States Department of Health and Welfare, and the President's Advisory Council for Management Improvement. He served in the United States Air Force for two years from 1972 to 1974.

Dr. Grossman's initial major tasks after joining the Hospital included reorganizing of a number of administrative areas, strengthening the financial system, and supervising construction and financing programs for the new Boston Floating Hospital.

His early successes caused Chairman William Saltonstall of the board of governors to report at the annual meeting in January 1981: "Our auditors have told us we are in the black. Our patients are getting the best of care. Everything about the institution seems to be upbeat. Much of this is due to our president, Dr. Jerome Grossman. There is no question that Jerry's activities and optimistic attitude have made their mark on the New England Medical Center and almost everything with which it comes in contact."

Another key figure in recent activities of the hospital, Dr. Sheldon M. Wolff, came to Boston in 1977 from the National Institutes of Health to become the third physician-in-chief, Endicott Professor and chairman of medicine at Tufts Medical School. He succeeded Dr. William B. Schwartz, a kidney specialist and authority on computer use in medicine, who resigned in 1977 to become the first University Professor in the history of Tufts. Dr. Schwartz had succeeded Dr. Proger as physician-in-chief when the latter retired in 1971.

Before coming to Boston, Dr. Wolff was for eight years clinical director of the Institute of Allergy and Infectious Diseases at the National Institutes of Health. He also was that institute's chief of clinical investigation. He is a consultant in immunology at the World Health Organization and the Pan American Health Organization and, in the Proger tradition, carries on research programs in addition to seeing patients and administering his department. Among many varied activities, he teaches international health at the Fletcher School of Law and Diplomacy on the Tufts campus.

In 1977, Dr. Wolff obtained an eight-year grant from the Rockefeller

Foundation to support research on tropical diseases, making Tufts and the New England Medical Center a part of the "Great Neglected Diseases" network supported by the Rockefeller Foundation. His Geographical Medicine Division has attracted outstanding specialists such as Dr. Gerald Keusch (an international authority on diarrheal diseases, particularly in young children) and Dr. David Wyler (a major figure in infectious diseases), among others.

Dr. Wolff, in cooperation with Dr. Grossman, himself a primary care internist, also established a new Division of General Medicine within his department, and named Dr. John Harrington, who in 1980 was president of the medical staff, as its first chief. A major new service of the division was the establishment, in July 1981, of a new group practice called General Medical Associates (GMA), to serve adults. This organization, set up under an $800,000 grant from the Robert Wood Johnson Foundation, is designed to deliver personalized primary medical care in a teaching hospital. It uses a team approach, comprising physicians, nurse practitioners, registered nurses, social workers, and nutritionists. Each patient is assigned to one physician, who assumes primary responsibility in a private practice fashion. By being a group practice, however, GMA can provide seven-day-a-week, 24-hour response to patients, even if the physican with primary responsibility is not available. The service provides referrals to appropriate specialists when required, and has all the facilities of the Medical Center as backup in providing patient care.

The GMA offers preventive medicine, geriatric care, telephone consultations, and inpatient care; it also provides a method of entry into the hospital, other than via the emergency room, for people working or living in Boston who do not have a family physician. The emergency room at the New England Medical Center is one of the busiest in the city, but (like all emergency rooms) it is costly to use, and many people who go there for help need not just emergency treatment but continuing care. The new outpatient service, according to Dr. Wolff, is designed to offer this.

Dr. Wolff said that the primary care practice does not alter the main character of the hospital as a tertiary care institution, but provides a setting where a teaching hospital can be responsive to the daily needs of people in the community, a setting where high-quality care can be given at reasonable cost by first-rate generalists. The setting also provides opportunities for teaching and research. He noted that Dr. Grossman's success in organizing a similar outpatient department under a Johnson Foundation grant at the Massachusetts General Hospital had convinced him of the need and value of such organizations in Boston. Dr. David R. Rogers, Robert Wood Johnson Foundation president, said that 25 percent of all visits to physicians in the United States in 1979 were made in hospital outpatient settings, a 50 percent increase in 10 years.

Outpatient services, with their emphasis on diagnosis and health maintenance, could lead to revival of the name and character of the original Pratt Clinic at the New England Medical Center. Many people believe that much was lost when the Pratt name was allowed to fall into disuse, and that it may be possible to utilize it in the future in providing modern diagnostic services.

A major patient care development under way at Tufts Medical School in 1981, in conjunction with the New England Medical Center and a group of Tufts Associated Hospitals, was the organization of the Tufts Associated Health Plan. It consists of individual Health Maintenance Organizations (HMOs) to function autonomously at the start at seven hospitals, with others to be added later. The original group comprised Emerson Hospital (Concord), Faulkner Hospital (Jamaica Plain), Lawrence Memorial Hospital (Medford), Newton-Wellesley Hospital (Newton Lower Falls), New England Medical Center (Central Boston), St. Elizabeth's Hospital (Brighton), and St. Margaret's Hospital for Women and Carney Hospital (Dorchester).

An HMO provides prepaid health services and offers a continuity of patient-doctor relationships wherever possible. Usually, there is one physician responsible for the long-term care of the patient, whether ambulatory or hospitalized. This primary physician calls in appropriate specialists from the HMO staff whenever he considers consultations necessary.

Benefits to the patient include ability to budget for health care, often with the assistance of employers. An HMO often can result in better care, because the primary physician has consultants and a hospital at hand. In the Tufts Associated Health Plan, a patient also could be moved to another of the cooperating hospitals if there were a need for some specialized care or equipment.

The Tufts HMO differs from the Harvard Community Health Plan in that there is no central headquarters in Boston or Cambridge to which patients go and where staff doctors are on call. In the Tufts plan, the HMO doctors will be working at their own home bases, under the umbrella of an overall organization which will set and collect fees, pay the doctors on a fee-for-service basis, work out contracts with Blue Cross and other health insurance agencies, and monitor costs and the quality of care. This type of HMO program is called an Independent Practice Association–Health Maintenance Organization.

Dr. Morton A. Madoff, assistant to the dean for primary care and public health planning, and Dr. Arthur R. Jacobs, associate professor of community health, Tufts Medical School, organized the program.

Because of the tie-in with the Medical School and with the New England Medical Center, Dr. Jerome Grossman sees the new HMO plan as a modern-day version of the Dispensary, sending out its physicians to care for sections of Boston and surrounding areas. In this instance, large numbers of physicians in a number of cities and towns will be formalizing the HMO effort that was started by the Dispensary in 1796.

The nucleus of people to be served by the HMO at the New England Medical Center itself is seen by Dr. Grossman as those who live in Chinatown and its surrounding areas, as well as residents of the South Cove, the South End, South Boston, and North Dorchester, who traditionally have comprised the Hospital's primary care area. People who work in downtown Boston also may decide to join. He said he believes the system affords the widest possible spectrum of free choice of a health care delivery plan by patients.

As the New England Medical Center entered its fifty-second year in 1981, Dr. Jean Mayer, noted educator and nutritionist, was in his fifth year as the tenth president of Tufts. Among his accomplishments during the period was a strengthening of nutrition programs at both the Liberal Arts College and the Medical and Dental Schools. He also was instrumental in bringing to New England the Human Nutrition Research Center, sponsored by the United States Department of Agriculture, and located adjacent to the new Boston Floating Hospital building, at the corner of Stuart and Washington Streets.

During ground-breaking ceremonies for the 14-story, $23 million Human Nutrition Research Center building in 1979, Dr. Mayer said, "Like the Lincoln Labs at MIT, the Argonne Laboratory at the University of

Chicago, and the Jet Propulsion Lab at Cal Tech, the Human Nutrition Research Center has a mission mandated by Congress: long-term research to determine and clarify human nutrition requirements with a special emphasis on adulthood and aging.

"Here," he continued, "some 50 of the nation's foremost nutritionists and 150 to 200 support staff, together with visiting scientists from the nation and the world, will try to answer two simple and very complex questions: What roles do nutrition and diet play in the normal aging process? What are the optimal nutrient requirements that, combined with other factors, will contribute to an alert, healthy, vigorous, and perhaps extended lifespan for all men and women?" He added that the goal of the Center is the one Hippocrates set for his patients almost 2500 years ago: "That they may die young, as late as possible."

Dr. Mayer said that Boston provides an ideal location for the Center because the population contains representatives of every ethnic group, living in many different social and economic environments. He described the Tufts–New England Medical Center as being especially appropriate as a site because of the support it provides through its existing Hospital, Medical and Dental Schools, Veterinary School, and other units.

The School of Veterinary Medicine is a new school for which Dr. Mayer fought long and hard. It opened in 1979, with Dr. Albert M. Jonas as dean, and already is contributing to animal care in New England. Clinics and a hospital for large animals, under construction in 1981 at a campus in Grafton (site of a former state school an hour's drive west of Boston), are the main clinical facilities. Science courses are conducted at the Medical and Dental Schools in Boston.

Another development at Tufts is the formation of the Sackler School of Graduate Biomedical Sciences, of which Dr. Murray R. Blair, Jr., is dean. The school was made possible by three brothers, Dr. Arthur M. Sackler, Dr. Mortimer D. Sackler, and Dr. Raymond S. Sackler, all noted psychiatrists and philanthropists, of New York, who have made major contributions to education and research in the health sciences. The school, established July 1, 1980, obtains faculty and students from existing departments, including biochemistry and pharmacology.

The Sackler School serves as a major center for research and teaching of complex biomedical issues. Dean Blair served for several months in 1980–81 as acting dean of the Tufts Medical School after Dr. Lauro

Cavazos, an outstanding teacher and researcher, resigned as dean to become president of his alma mater, Texas Tech University, and of its Health Sciences Center in Lubbock, Texas.

Selected in February 1981 as Medical School dean to succeed Dr. Cavazos, and named at the same time to a new post as vice-president for health sciences at Tufts University, was Dr. Robert I. Levy, who had served as director of the National Heart, Lung and Blood Institute (NHLBI) of the National Institutes of Health from 1975 to 1981. Before becoming NHLBI director, he was director of the Division of Heart and Vascular Disease of the Institute, and directed programs attacking atherosclerosis, high blood pressure, rheumatic heart disease, heart failure, shock, and various kidney disorders.

As vice-president for health sciences, Dr. Levy was instructed to coordinate the work of the health science deans. These include Dr. Erling Johansen of the Dental School, an internationally known researcher, particularly in the area of dental care for cancer patients undergoing radiation treatments. A native of Norway, he graduated from Tufts School of Dental Medicine and is a specialist in pathology.

In 1981, the Dental School reverted from a three-year to a four-year curriculum. The three-year educational program had been initiated in 1972 when the federal government perceived a severe shortage of dentists and offered grants to schools that would expand and speed up their educational programs. Dean Johansen said in November 1980 that "the dental profession and the government now share the opinion that the nation's dental needs of those years have been met."

Reversion to the four-year course, 17 weeks longer than the abbreviated course, will allow increases in science instruction, preclinical instruction, and clinical requirements; also, it will provide a reduction in class size and thus greater research opportunities for students and faculty, Dean Johansen said.

Surgery, as has been noted, came late to the New England Medical Center, arriving only with the opening of the Farnsworth Building in 1949. A rapid turnover in chiefs did not help at the beginning. Dr. C. Stuart Welch, the first chief of surgery, left in 1952, to be succeeded by Dr. Weyland Leadbetter as acting chief. He left after one year to become chief of urology at Massachusetts General Hospital. Then Dr. Charles G. Child, III, came for a single year. During the succeeding five years, surgery was overseen by the competent Dr. Arthur Thibodeau, as acting chief. Within this system, the chief of each of the surgical services rotated as administrative head of the general surgical services. These chiefs were Dr. Allan D. Callow in vascular surgery, Dr. Harold F. Rheinlander in thoracic surgery, and Dr. Harry Miller in tumor surgery and surgical research.

The man who brought long-term leadership and stability to surgery was Dr. Ralph Deterling, who served for 16 years as surgeon-in-chief at the hospital and also as chairman of the Department of Surgery at Tufts Medical School. Looking back over his period of stewardship, Dr. Deterling cited orthopedic surgery — first under Dr. Thibodeau, then under Dr. Henry H. Banks — as the pacesetter for the surgical divisions. Dr. Banks, a Tufts Medical School graduate, came to the Center after having developed Harvard's orthopedic program between Children's Hospital and the Peter Bent Brigham Hospital. In addition to developing an outstanding orthopedic service at Tufts, Dr. Banks has built a highly regarded training program in that specialty.

In 1975 Dr. Deterling retired as chairman of surgery in order to devote more time to his practice and research. The Search Committee for his successor, after interviewing candidates throughout the nation, selected Dr. Richard Cleveland. He was given the joint title of director of the surgical service and chief of general surgery at New England Medical Center and chairman of the Department of Surgery at Tufts University School of Medicine. He also retained his title as cardiothoracic surgeon-in-chief. Dr. Cleveland has continued to strengthen the surgical staff and has helped foster improved relations between the New England Medical Center and the Tufts Associated Hospitals. Under his direction, the New England Medical Center has developed into a major cardiac surgery center.

Psychiatry is an area in which the New England Medical Center has excelled, thanks in large part to Dr. Paul G. Myerson, chief of the department from 1963 until his retirement in 1979. The current chief is Dr. Richard I. Shader, who previously was associate professor of psychiatry at Harvard Medical School and director of the Psychopharmacology Research Laboratory at Massachusetts Mental Health Center.

The Department of Psychiatry has been and continues to be deeply involved in community outreach programs that treat the families of psychiatric patients in addition to the patients themselves. Activities span a wide range of mental health programs, including operation of the Bay Cove Mental Health Center. The center encompasses more than 30 different programs serving more than 7500 individuals a year. The Bay Cove service area covers part of downtown Boston (the South Cove, theater district, and Chinatown), Columbia Point, South Boston, and parts of North Dorchester. The department is geared to provide both outpatient and in-hospital services for patients.

The New England Medical Center since 1976 has unified all its aspects of cancer treatment under a single office called Office of Cancer Control (OCC), headed by Dr. Douglas J. Marchant, senior gynecologist and director of gynecology at New England Medical Center. OCC was organized to coordinate efforts in cancer management, to prevent duplication, and to make certain that patients always receive the best therapy available for each particular case.

By 1981, 50 years after the first beds were available at the Boston Dispensary in 1931, Dr. John Harrington, president of the medical staff, reported during an annual meeting of the hospital that 250 full-time physicians and 475 associate physicians were on the staff at New England Medical Center. (A list of the names of the full-time physicians and those of the current chiefs of service is in the Appendix.)

Dr. Harrington reported that in 1981 the hospital provided a full range of diagnostic and treatment services for patients of all ages, except for maternity inpatient services. He said that, during 1980, a total of 13,650 patients were admitted and 144,200 days of care provided. Approximately 250,000 outpatient visits were made to the hospital and approximately 10,000 operations performed. He said that 745,000 X-rays were taken and 1.6 million laboratory tests made. Dr. Harrington noted that the number of ancillary services such as X-rays and laboratory tests had not increased over 1979, and said that this could be accounted for by greater awareness on the part of physicians of rising hospital costs and a need for eliminating marginal tests in the interest of controlling costs.

An important element added to the hospital's resources during 1980 was a five-year grant of more than $700,000 from the National Library of Medicine, for the establishment of a program in clinical decision making. The grant is the first to emphasize the application of decision theory to patient care and is training physicians to act as consultants in both patient care and research by applying the tools of logic, analysis, and computer science. The program is under the direction of Dr. Steven Pauker, a cardiologist and associate professor of medicine at Tufts, with Dr. Jerome Kassirer, associate physician-in-chief, and Dr. Jane Desforges, senior physician in hematology and oncology, involved.

Another important development in 1980 was the establishment of a memory disorder clinic in the Department of Neurology, directed by Dr. John Growdon, assistant neurologist. Special emphasis is being placed on research into Alzheimer's Disease, which affects approximately 15 percent of the population over 65. The clinic offers specific programs to deal with medical, social, and economic consequences of memory loss.

A part of the Tufts–New England Medical Center system that has grown in importance over the years is T-NEMC, the umbrella organization described earlier. It is a separate corporation today, with its trustees, administrative boards, and committees selected in equal numbers from representatives of the university and the hospital. Mr. Franklin Parker was chairman of the corporation in 1981. The executive committee, which meets monthly, is composed of President Jean Mayer of Tufts and Tufts trustees Dr. Allan Callow and Mr. Warren Carley. The hospital members are Chairman William Saltonstall, President Jerome Grossman, and Mr. Parker. Beyond this group is a management committee that meets weekly, comprising Dr. Grossman and the deans of the Medical, Dental, and Veterinary Schools. With Dr. Levy's appointment as coordinator of the deans, a large measure of responsibility for the smooth working of this management committee, which seeks to achieve unity between the university and the hospital and to remedy any conflicts while they are small, rests on the shoulders of Dr. Levy and Dr. Grossman. The T-NEMC corporation conducts about $15 million in business a year for the allied institutions, according to Mr. Edward Ehrlich, its administrative officer. The works includes overall planning and property management.

As a result of their planning and property responsibilities, Medical Center officials have for many years been involved in discussions with various representatives in the Chinese community.

Various committees on which Dr. Grossman served in 1981 began making long-range plans for the development of new residential communities in the South Cove–Chinatown area. Goals included preserving an improved Chinatown, providing better housing throughout the area, building on land that was unoccupied, rehabilitating some existing housing, and providing additional space for the medical complex. Dr. Grossman said that the time for cooperation between the Chinese community and the New England Medical Center was overdue, and that he would work hard to try to build a spirit of cooperation under which both would benefit in the future. This would signal a different approach from that during the 1960s after the Central Artery and the Massachusetts Turnpike had been built and reduced the acreage of the area. The Chinese, faced with old buildings in a narrow space and with increased immigration, suffered from overcrowding. The Medical Center, containing the smallest land mass of any major university teaching center and hospital in the nation, felt that it, too, was fighting for space in which to survive.

This produced a paradoxical situation. The Medical Center provided increasing numbers of jobs for the Chinese, tended to their health care needs, and supported the South Cove (Chinese) Community Health Center to the extent of more than $1 million in support funds in less than a decade. Yet the housing problems of the Chinese community were so intense that friction between the community and the Medical Center was inevitable. The work of the various special committees and task forces and the move of Wang Laboratories into the area in 1981 were a significant first step in easing the housing and employment problems of the Chinese community.

Another step taken by the Medical Center was to give employment preference, when possible, to neighbors from the Chinese community. Although admittedly starting with a small group, the hospital steadily increased the hiring of Asians (mostly Chinese), and during a six-year period in the 1970s was able to report that the number of men and women of Chinese background working at the center had increased by 154 percent, whereas total employment during the same period had increased only 35 percent. In 1981, minorities totaled 20 percent of total technical and clerical employment of 3459, with Chinese constituting 5 percent of all employees.

Still another important ingredient of the New England Medical Center

since its establishment, and one which dates back to the founding of the
Dispensary, is the assistance of volunteers, whether they are trustees,
members of the Ladies Committee, or people who assist patients or work
in staff hospitality areas. The Saltonstall family, for example, has been
involved in the Dispensary and the Medical Center from the beginnings
of these institutions. Mr. William Saltonstall, who was elected chairman
of the board of governors in January 1979, and who has served as a
governor since 1972, is currently carrying on the family tradition. One
of his forebears was among the original 74 founders of the Dispensary
in 1796. His grandmother, Mrs. Eleanor Brooks Saltonstall, served 27
years on the Dispensary's board of governors. An uncle, Richard Saltonstall, served 33 years on the Dispensary board, 26 of them as treasurer.

William Saltonstall, former state senator and aide to his father, Senator
Leverett Saltonstall, in Washington, is the first head of the board of
governors to be designated chairman. A change in the by-laws in 1979
designated Dr. Grossman as president. (Earlier presidents had been Mr.
John Quarles; his successor, Mrs. George L. Sargent; and Mr. Paul F.
Perkins, Jr.) The move is not unusual in teaching hospitals today, in
efforts to provide extra strength to the executive in charge of operating
such hospitals. All those elected as president or chairman of the New
England Medical Center have had distinguished records of service in one
or more clinical units or, since the merger, in the combined units. Mrs.
Sargent had 35 years of service to various units of the Medical Center,
and Mr. Perkins 25 years. The current number of trustees of the New
England Medical Center is 95 (list in Appendix).

Membership lists of the board of governors and the board of trustees
are sprinkled with names of several generations of certain families,
indicating the strong attachment those families have to the Medical
Center. There is general agreement that in the years ahead the voluntary
efforts of private citizens will be as great in importance to the future of
the Medical Center as such efforts have been in its past.

# CHAPTER 24

# A View of the Future

Dr. Jerome Harvey Grossman, who became president, executive director, and chairman of the executive committee of the New England Medical Center in July 1979, displayed on his arrival a keen interest in the history of the various institutions that made up the center, as well as in the activities of Dr. Proger during the half-century since 1929. He considered that knowledge of the strengths demonstrated since 1796 would provide him the background needed to plan for the future. "I wanted to know," he said, "how this center was different, in which areas it had excelled, what its missions had been, and figure out where to go from here."

Dr. Grossman was particularly well suited to take both the short and long views because of the variety of his educational and professional pursuits. He had received training in medicine, engineering, economics, and history. He was a specialist in internal medicine, business management systems, computer sciences, and health care delivery programs. It was this variety of training and expertise that impressed the trustees and prompted them to give him the comprehensive controls embodied in the three posts they devised. They anticipated that he would tighten administrative systems throughout the center, carry on long-range planning programs, and provide day-to-day administrative procedures to meet the new challenges of the 1980s.

In his first report to the trustees, only six months after joining the New England Medical Center, Dr. Grossman said: "It doesn't take long to recognize the things that make this hospital special — the qualities that set it apart and contribute to its fine reputation and success. There

182

is an extremely close and productive relationship among medical staff members — all working together smoothly for the good of the patient. There is an unusually high degree of concern, shown by professional and support staff alike, for patients and their families. The quality of nursing care is outstanding — despite the difficult conditions imposed by inadequate facilities — and there is a warm, friendly, informal atmosphere in which all patients, as well as their families, feel welcome."

Dr. Grossman added that there is a clear history of scholarship at the New England Medical Center. "Many advances in medicine and many of the great figures in American medicine were and are part of this institution. There is a close cooperative relationship with Tufts University School of Medicine, mutually supportive and with a shared goal of excellence in education and research. Finally, there is an energy and excitement here that looks to building on these traditions."

Partly in order to maintain a direct and unbroken line between the physicians of the past and those of today and tomorrow, Dr. Grossman became a senior physician on the hospital staff. He continued to make rounds and to see a limited number of patients, believing such a procedure was also important in helping him administer the Medical Center.

Discussing the care of the patient in the future, Dr. Grossman said, "The previous generation of medical leaders did a superb job in research, tertiary care, training, and academic medicine, much of it sponsored by the National Institutes of Health. Now we face a set of new problems which a new generation of us have to tackle. These problems are different, but no less intellectually stimulating. We must go forward with biomedical research to understand the underlying problems of disease. We are suited by our history here at the New England Medical Center to continue along these ways. We also are suited by tradition to emphasize compassion in the care of patients. The compassion for children, for example, for which the Boston Floating Hospital has become so widely known, provides one model on which to build. The balance between science and compassion that such people as Dr. Proger and Dr. Gellis have personified, and which our doctors and nurses have displayed, is part of our unique strength.

"But, it is a different world in which we do these things today. It is a world of limitations. For medicine, it means that quality and compassion in their traditional sense are no longer enough. We must redefine them to include economy and efficiency. Are we using too much technology? No longer is there a shortage of medical resources; there may be a surplus. No longer are we sure that government can grow and take on ever-increasing responsibilities for human services for the country.

"We in the private sector are, after a respite of just 30 years, increasingly responsible for the activities we relegated to the government. But we cannot simply go back 30 years. It is an enormously more complicated world, more expensive and more demanding. We must now take the lead in the effort to find new ways to make the best use of our limited resources."

Discussing the future of the New England Medical Center and of American hospitals in general, Dr. Grossman said that economic conditions were forcing an end to hospitals operating as "a cottage industry." "We are being forced to move on into the industrial world," he said. In order to survive, he predicted, "doctors and hospitals will have to be organized in formal ways to deliver health care. Doctors will have to work more closely with other doctors and with hospitals. Hospitals will have to work more closely among themselves. Relations between hospitals and medical schools will have to be meshed. The whole system will have to be more highly organized. It will be in many ways similar to industry and less like the voluntary, often inefficient efforts of the past."

Dr. Grossman said that bringing industrial systems into medicine means that there will have to be research and development programs to find out how management of health-care delivery efforts can be improved. He said that if the New England Medical Center can provide one model of doing this, it will have performed its part in the effort. Once specific studies of industrial ways of doing things were completed, he said, then it would be time to install new systems and by example to teach younger people how to put them into effect. "One does not attempt to alter a system of medical care delivery until there is understanding of why things cost what they do and how that affects quality." He said that up to 1980 there had been no encouragement to do the research on such matters, but that economic changes had brought about a situation where economists, scientists, managers, and physicians needed to work together to set standards for change and to put changes into practice.

Under Dr. Grossman's leadership, answers were being sought for these and many other questions. It was apparent to all that vast changes were on the horizon so far as hospital care was concerned. What was difficult to see in 1981 was just what those changes would be and how to adjust to them. Tufts–New England Medical Center trustees, with their new teams in place at the hospital and at the Medical and Dental Schools, appeared to be in a good position to study trends, anticipate changes, and help to influence them for the benefit of both the patient and the Medical Center.

During the half-century after 1929, Dr. Samuel Proger had been the leader in anticipating trends, preparing to meet them, and successfully, in many instances, devising systems and ways of doing things to adjust to changing conditions. He was ably assisted by his team of doctors, trustees, administrators, advisers, social planners, and architects. Dr. Grossman, with a similar team of players, but attuned to different times and new situations, was working, planning, driving, to meet the problems of the '80s with the same hopes for success that Dr. Proger and his group felt in the past.

Convinced, as was Dr. Proger, that a hospital must be financially sound in order to provide high quality care, Dr. Grossman devoted much of his attention his first year to solving financial problems that had arisen from slow bill collections, bad debts, inflation, and extra expenses involved in complying with numerous federal regulations. He strengthened management, installed more efficient computer systems, and speeded collections. In view of the Medical Center's lack of large endowments, he said, it was essential that the center maintain great efficiency in financial areas in order to pay its way as it went along.

With the financial situation under control and his senior management team in place, Dr. Grossman turned during his second year to the future. He held a number of conferences to discuss the role of the academic medical center in American medicine, and the role of New England Medical Center in the medical care systems of Boston and New England. In his annual report to the trustees in January 1981, Dr. Grossman outlined the future direction of the hospital. He emphasized that specialty (tertiary) care would continue to be the central mission of the center, but that primary care should also be provided to the people in the community. He said that this is one way to maintain flexibility in the radically changing external world. He compared the center to a corporation with separate divisions performing different services (producing various products), seeing such diversity as a strength for the hospital as a whole and as a strong supporting base for the traditional tripod of patient care, teaching and research. Development of diversity would continue the center's tradition of adaptability by introducing new methods of accomplishing established goals. Thus, Dr. Grossman said, "Our principal work is referral and tertiary. In the 1980s this will continue to be our central mission. However, we will not lose sight of the patient as a whole human being, nor will we forget that our humaneness and compassion are strengths equal to our sciences. These are qualities of our institution that will be nurtured.

"Our second mission is to serve as a catalyst in the creation of a model system of care. This continues our historical mission to organize, coordinate and provide care to a large segment of the people of Boston. This model builds on the existing relationships with Tufts' University School of Medicine and the more than 30 different health care institutions with which we are associated. We are part of a fully integrated system of care, from community health, to individual private practices, through community hospitals, to the center, for specialty referral care. In some ways this is a modern version of the Dispensary system, for it reaches out to every district of Greater Boston through the newly created Tufts Associated Health Plan. Our referral care also extends beyond Boston as exemplified by the newly founded Kiwanis–New England Medical Center Regional Pediatric Trauma Institute and the Bingham Program. A part of this mission will be to provide primary care to our immediate community. We have discovered that large numbers of people come to us not only from Chinatown, but from the South End, South Boston, North Dorchester, and people who work in downtown Boston as well."

Dr. Grossman said that he thinks tiered levels of care, as exemplified in the Tufts–New England Medical Center system, could be a model for medical systems anywhere in the country. "I think it is a model that well might be applied to other places. In some ways, we are the only medical school in Boston with that kind of a mission. Harvard is a national institution; its focus is national and international, and it does mainly tertiary care. I think we can be more regionally minded and do more primary care. We also, however, are not neglecting the world picture, as witness our tropical medical programs, the Human Nutrition Research

Center, and other programs which benefit others, but also New Englanders.

"Our third mission is to continue our special relationship with the people and physicians of New England. The Tufts Medical School has reaffirmed its dedication to the training of physicians for New England, and our hospital has reaffirmed a commitment to train them in its graduate programs and to continue a relationship with them throughout their careers."

Elaborating on care throughout the region, Dr. Grossman said: "The history of the New England Medical Center is a history of service to New England. It is devoted to the people of this area. I believe this is a unique strength, of which we are kept aware constantly because of our wide distribution of teaching resources, and by the fact that most of our graduates of the Medical School and of the hospital's residency programs practice in New England. With the new Kiwanis program, we are reiterating, in a way, the mission of the Bingham Program. Now we are talking about a system of care that is integrated, through which a child can be moved up vertically from hospital to hospital, depending upon the extent of his injuries. This vertical care system, in which we are associated with 38 hospitals throughout New England, is what differentiates our center from other local medical centers. Patients can be moved vertically through tiered levels of care when the situation requires it.

"Our final mission is continued participation in the redevelopment of downtown Boston. Just as we are at the center of an emerging new medical care system, we are at the center of a massive urban revitalization. Within four blocks of the Medical Center, construction is under way for Lafayette Place, a new subway station, the State Transportation Building, the newly renovated Metropolitan Center — which, with the Human Nutrition Center and the Floating Hospital, total nearly $250 million of new construction."

Dr. Grossman said that he is enormously excited to be a participant in the revival of the South Cove area as a part of downtown Boston. "The hospital is almost the stone which, when dropped in the water, spreads ripples in circles," he said. "We developed a master plan for the area under the direction of architect Hermann Field in the 1960's, and that, in conjunction with the work of Mayor John B. Hynes, Mayor

John Collins and Mr. Edward Logue, then Boston Redevelopment director, began revitalization of the South Cove area, including the theater district. I am cochairman of a special task force of the Boston Chamber of Commerce which is committed to eradicating the combat zone."

In concluding his look into the future of the Medical Center, Dr. Grossman said: "Our vision places our four missions within the context of a model system which can be viewed as three concentric circles radiating from the central core — the New England Medical Center — bringing its traditions in patient care, research and education to the communities of Boston, the Commonwealth and the six-state New England region."

But the Medical Center extended itself beyond provision of health care to and relations with the local and regional communities. It was also strongly dedicated to research and teaching, not only in the traditional medical sense but in terms of improving systems of health care delivery in the broader context. One major manifestation of this dedication could be seen in the initiative, led in part by Dr. Grossman, involving care of the sick poor. This population included recipients of Aid to Families with Dependent Children, the disabled and the elderly.

Among the issues being raised in the new private initiative atmosphere that was developing in the 1980s were the following questions: How can the needs of the sick poor be accommodated? What kind of training should be emphasized? Can the resources used in hospitals for both private and government-supported patients be reduced without undermining hospital care? Where are sources of private support?

One of the specific challenges facing planners in 1981 was the possibility that a prepayment plan for Medicaid patients could reduce costs of care without reducing the quality of care provided. New England Medical Center was involved in a pilot project to test out the feasibility of such a plan.

It might be noted here that prepayment for welfare was a tenet of the original Dispensary program starting in 1796, and that the patients were provided care to the fullest extent that medical knowledge and medicines of that time allowed.

The early 1980s was a period of seeking answers to similar problems in changed circumstances. Dr. Grossman believed that finding answers required specific research; and that this research was just as important as the research being carried on to seek causes and remedies for various diseases.

Thus the New England Medical Center in the 1980s was moving forward in the tradition of its long and successful past: building on its unique strengths to develop viable responses to new challenges. In the 1980s, those challenges were of limited resources, inefficient organization, and demands for high quality care to the same populations of patients as always. By remaining financially viable and treating experimentation in these new economic and industrial areas as research and development along the medical analogy, New England Medical Center was continuing its tradition of excellent and innovative leadership in medical care, research and teaching.

Asked to comment on Dr. Grossman's outline for the future in terms of the traditions, practices and people of the past, Dr. Proger said he was gratified that Dr. Grossman planned to build on the strengths demonstrated in the past. These include, he noted "a continued effort to get and keep outstanding people with special talents for special functions, a dedication to development of programs in which such talents can flourish, and the maintenance of fiscal strength to assure their support."

With respect to the Proger building, which also bears the name Health Services building, Dr. Proger said, "I am pleased that this building bears the Health Services name because we do have a responsibility, indeed a primary responsibility, to serve people. It is in the provision of service that literally everyone in the institution makes his or her vital contribution.

"I hope that the hospital will always strive to provide the highest quality of health care in an environment of scholarly and creative effort, and with a deep concern for the well-being of every person who seeks its help."

1. Biewend Building
2. Parking Garage
3. Floating Hospital Building
4. Tufts University School
   of Dental Medicine
5. Proger Building
6. Ziskind Research
   Building
7. Pratt Building
8. Farnsworth Building
9. Holmes Building
10. Common Services
11. Boston Dispensary
12. Jackson Building

13. Center Building
14. Rehabilitation Institute
15. Nursing Classroom Building
16. Hemenway Building
17. 17 Nassau Offices
18. Employee Student Health & Offices
19. Tufts Veterinary School & Offices
20. Orthopedics
21. Posner Hall Dormitory
22. Tufts University School of Medicine
23. Nutrition Research Center

STUART ST

TREMONT ST

Washington
Entrance

Jackson
Building
Entrance

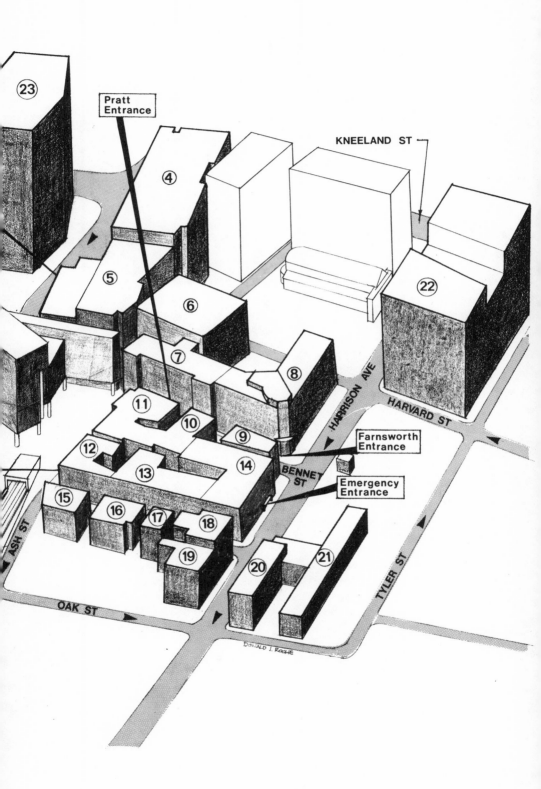

# Founders of the Boston Dispensary:
## Original Subscribers, 1796

Samuel Adams
Seth Adams
Jeremiah Allen
Jonathan Amory
John Amory
Mrs. Elizabeth Amory
John Amory, Jr.
Jonathan Amory, Jr.
Francis Amory
Thomas C. Amory
Jonathan Amory, III
John Andrews
John T. Apthorp
Nathaniel Balch
Tristram Bernard
Thomas Bartlett
Samuel Blagge
Kirk Boott
Elizabeth Bowdoin
Thomas Brewer
Peter C. Brooks
William Brown
Benjamin Bussey
Joseph Callender, Jr.
Gardner L. Chandler
Mary Coffin
John Codman
Joseph Coolidge
James Cutler
George Deblois
Thomas Dennie
Ebenezer Dorr
Samuel Dunn
Joshua Eaton
Maj. Gen. Simon Elliot

Joseph Field
Moses Gill
Nathanial Goodwin
Samuel Gore
John Gore
Stephen Gorham
John Gray
Richard Green
Benjamin Greene
Joseph Greene
David Greene
John Huskins
Elizabeth Huskins
Moses M. Hays
Stephen Higginson
Stephen Higginson, Jr.
Oliver Holden
Abigail Howard
Jonathan Hunnewell
Henry Jackson
John Coffin Jones
Thomas J. Jones
Susanna Kneeland
William Lambert
John Lowell
John Lowell, Jr.
Thomas McDonough
John Marston
Rev. Jedediah Morse
William Newman
Rev. Samuel Parker
John Parker
Samuel Parkman
Gorham Parsons
William Payne

Sarah Payne
David Pierce
Levi Pierce
Samuel Penhallow
Thomas H. Perkins
Joshua Pico
William Pratt
Joseph Roby
Hannah Rowe
Estate of Thomas Russell
Samuel Salisbury
James Scott
William Shattuck
William Shaw
Anne Smith
William Smith
Elizabeth Sparhawk
Rev. Samuel Stillman
Benjamin Morgan Stillman
James Sullivan
Joseph Taylor
Elizabeth Temple
Joshua Thomas
Samuel Torrey
William Tudor
Edward Tuckerman
Charles Vaughan
James Vila
Henry Wainwright
Oliver Wendell
Rev. Samuel West
David West
Robert Wier, Jr.
William Woods

# Governors, Trustees and Medical Staff of the New England Medical Center, 1982

James J. Gallagher, M.D.
*Anesthetist*

Morton Rosenberg, D.M.D
*Anesthetist*

Janet Wunderlich, M.D.
*Anesthetist*

Heinrich Wurm, M.D.
*Anesthetist & Chief, Adult
Anesthesia Section*

Michael R. England, M.D.
*Assistant Anesthetist*

Joanne C. Hudson, M.D.
*Assistant Anesthetist*

Robert L. Kirkman, M.D.
*Assistant Anesthetist*

Scott F. Shapiro, M.D.
*Assistant Anesthetist*

Arthur W. Stratton, M.D.
*Assistant Anesthetist*

Sabita Weirick, M.D.
*Assistant-in-Anesthesia*

### Cardio-Thoracic Surgery

Richard J. Cleveland, M.D.
*Cardio-Thoracic Surgeon-in-
Chief & Director, Surgical
Services*

Harold F. Rheinlander, M.D.
*Senior Surgeon*

Benedict D. T. Daly, M.D.
*Surgeon*

Philip A. Faraci, M.D.
*Surgeon*

Douglas Payne, M.D.
*Surgeon*

Joseph J. Stetz, M.D.
*Assistant Surgeon*

Joseph J. Zocco, M.D.
*Assistant Surgeon*

Richard S. Blacher, M.D.
*Psychiatrist, with joint
appointment in Department of
Psychiatry*

### Community & Ambulatory Care

James F. Patterson, M.D.
*Senior Physician, with joint
appointment in Department of
Medicine*

Lon Curtis, M.D.
*Physician, with joint
appointment in Department of
Surgery*

Arthur Z. Mutter, M.D.
*Physician, with joint
appointment in Department of
Psychiatry*

Peter B. F. Randolph, M.D.
*Physician, with joint
appointment in Department of
Psychiatry*

Helen Toomey, M.D.
*Assistant Physician, with joint
appointment in Department of
Medicine*

### Dentistry

H. Chris Doku, D.M.D.
*Dentist-in-Chief & Chief, Oral
Surgery Service*

Edmund Cataldo, D.D.S.
*Chief, Oral Pathology Service*

John L. Giunta, D.M.D.
*Assistant Oral Pathologist*

Philip Maloney, D.M.D.
*Senior Oral Surgeon*

William Gilmore, D.D.S.
*Assistant Oral Surgeon*

Kenneth Stern, D.M.D.
*Assistant Oral Surgeon*

Joseph P. O'Donnell, D.M.D.
*Chief, Pedodontic Service*

George E. White, D.D.S.
*Senior Pedodontist*

John P. Ficarelli, D.M.D.
*Assistant Pedodontist*

Anthi Tsamtsouris, D.M.D.
*Assistant Pedodontist*

Max J. Perlitsch, D.M.D.,
M.S.
*Periodontist*

Joseph Evans, D.D.S.
*Chief, Restorative Dentistry
Service*

Hilde H. Tillman, D.M.D.
*Assistant Dentist*

Thomas J. Vergo, Jr., D.D.S.
*Assistant Dentist*

### Dermatology

David Feingold, M.D.
*Dermatologist-in-Chief*

Stephanie Pincus, M.D.
*Dermatologist, with joint
appointment in Department of
Medicine*

Stephen E. Gellis, M.D.
*Assistant Dermatologist, with
joint appointment in
Department of Medicine*

### Gynecology & Obstetrics

Robert D. Kennison, M.D.
*Acting Gynecologist-in-Chief*

Martin Farber, M.D.
*Senior Gynecologist*

Song Hi An-Foraker, M.D.
*Senior Gynecologist, with joint
appointment in Department of
Pathology*

Douglas J. Marchant, M.D.
*Senior Gynecologist*

R. Nuran Turksoy-Marcus,
M.D.
*Senior Gynecologist (Endo.)*

Donald Edinger, M.D.
*Gynecologist*

Charles Kawada, M.D.
*Assistant Gynecologist*

Harold Michelwitz, M.D.
*Assistant Gynecologist*

Cornelius O. Granai, M.D.
*Assistant-Gynecology &
Obstetrics*

Amos Madanes, M.D.
*Assistant-in-Gynecology &
Obstetrics*

### Medicine

Sheldon M. Wolff, M.D.
*Physician-in-Chief*

Jerome P. Kassirer, M.D.
*Associate Physician-in-Chief*

Robert I. Levy, M.D.
*Senior Physician*

Donald E. Hricik, M.D.
*Assistant-in-Medicine*

William B. Schwartz, M.D.
*Senior Physician & University
Professor*

### ALLERGY SERVICE

Ross E. Rocklin, M.D.
*Allergist-in-Chief*

Steven Findlay, M.D.
*Assistant Physician*

Keith McAdam, M.D.
*Assistant Physician*

Lanny Rosenwasser, M.D.
*Assistant Physician*

## AMBULATORY INTERNAL MEDICINE SERVICE

James R. Patterson, M.D.
*Chief*

Mark Molitch, M.D.
*Physician*

Elaine S. K. Choi, M.D.
*Assistant Physician*

Helen Toomey, M.D.
*Assistant Physician & Chief, Employee & Student Health Service*

## CARDIOLOGY SERVICE

Herbert J. Levine, M.D.
*Chief*

Modestino G. Criscitiello, M.D.
*Physician*

Shapur Naimi, M.D.
*Physician & Director, Coronary Care Unit*

Stephen G. Pauker, M.D.
*Physician*

Deeb Salem, M.D.
*Physician & Director, Adult Cath. Lab*

Jeffrey Isner, M.D.
*Assistant Physician, with joint appointment in Department of Pathology*

Marvin A. Konstam, M.D.
*Assistant Physician, with joint appointment in Department of Radiology*

Peter Libby, M.D.
*Assistant Physician*

Robert D. Rifkin, M.D.
*Assistant Physician*

## DIVISION OF CLINICAL DECISION MAKING

Stephen G. Pauker, M.D.
*Chief*

Jane Desforges, M.D.
*Senior Physician*

Jerome P. Kassirer, M.D.
*Senior Physician*

## CLINICAL PHARMACOLOGY SERVICE

David Greenblatt, M.D.
*Chief, with primary appointment in Department of Psychiatry*

Darrell R. Abernathy, M.D.,
*Assistant Physician, with primary appointment in Department of Psychiatry*

## DERMATOLOGY SERVICE

David Feingold, M.D.
*Chief, with primary appointment in Department of Dermatology*

Stephanie Pincus, M.D.
*Assistant Physician, with primary appointment in Department of Dermatology*

Stephen E. Gelllis, M.D.
*Assistant Physician, with primary appointment in Department of Dermatology*

## EMPLOYEE & STUDENT HEALTH SERVICE

Helen Toomey, M.D.
*Chief*

Emile S. Hitron, M.D.
*Assistant Physician*

John Mazzullo, M.D.
*Assistant Physician*

Geetha Narayan, M.D.
*Assistant Physician*

## ENDOCRINOLOGY SERVICE

Seymour Reichlin, M.D.
*Chief & Director, Clinical Study Unit*

Ivor Jackson, M.D.
*Physician*

Mark Molitch, M.D.
*Physician*

Ronald M. Lechan, M.D.
*Assistant Physician*

## EXPERIMENTAL MEDICINE DIVISION

Sheldon M. Wolff, M.D.
*Chief*

Charles Dinarello, M.D.
*Assistant Physician*

Jeffrey A. Gelfand, M.D.
*Assistant Physician*

Mark S. Klempner, M.D.
*Assistant Physician*

Peter Libby, M.D.
*Assistant Physician*

Keith McAdam, M.D.
*Assistant Physician*

Stephanie Pincus, M.D.
*Assistant Physician*

## GASTROENTEROLOGY SERVICE

Marshall M. Kaplan, M.D.
*Chief*

Mark Donowitz, M.D.
*Physician*

Karim A. Fawaz, M.D.
*Physician*

Richard A. Norton, M.D.
*Physician*

Andrew G. Plaut, M.D.
*Physician*

Robert Russell, M.D.
*Physician, & Chief of Clinical Investigation, Nutrition Research Center*

## GENERAL INTERNAL MEDICINE

John T. Harrington, M.D.
*Chief*

James F. Patterson, M.D.
*Senior Physician*

Joseph Rogers, M.D.
*Senior Physician*

James D. C. Gowans, M.D.
*Physician (Rheumatology)*

Jerome H. Grossman, M.D.
*Physician*

Jonathan I. Morrison, M.D.
*Physician*

Richard Chamberlin, M.D.
*Assistant Physician & Medical Director, Bingham Associates Fund*

Jennifer Daley, M.D.
*Assistant Physician*

Margaret R. Dozark, M.D.
*Assistant Physician*

Susan Hou, M.D.
*Assistant Physician, with appointment in Nephrology Division*

Oscar M. Jankelson, M.D.
*Assistant Physician*

Richard I. Kopelman, M.D.
*Assistant Physician*

Keith McAdam, M.D.
*Assistant Physician*

# Appendix

GEOGRAPHIC MEDICINE
DIVISION

Gerald Keusch, M.D.
Chief

Ross E. Rocklin, M.D.
Physician

Keith McAdam, M.D.
Assistant Physician

Robert Ryder, M.D.
Assistant Physician

David Wyler, M.D.
Assistant Physician


HEMATOLOGY-
ONCOLOGY SERVICE

Robert S. Schwartz, M.D.
Chief

Jane F. Desforges, M.D.
Senior Physician

Bernard M. Babior, M.D.
Physician

Eugene M. Berkman, M.D.
Physician & Director, Blood
Bank

Syamal Datta, M.D.
Physician

Bruce Furie, M.D.
Physician

Julius Kritzman, M.D.
Physician

Stuart B. Levy, M.D.
Physician

Richard Rudders, M.D.
Physician

Stephen Louie, M.D.
Assistant Physician

James Mier, M.D.
Assistant Physician

Kenneth Miller, M.D.
Assistant Physician

Steven W. Papish, M.D.
Assistant Physician

David Parkinson, M.D.
Assistant Physician

Rita Blanchard, M.D.
Assistant-in-Medicine


INFECTIOUS DISEASE
SERVICE

Sherwood Gorbach, M.D.
Chief

Richard H. Meade, III, M.D.
Senior Physician, with joint appointment in Department of Pediatrics

Michael Barza, M.D.
Physician

Francis Tally, M.D.
Physician

Te-Wen Chang, M.D.
Assistant Physician

Jeffrey A. Gelfand, M.D.
Assistant Physician

Mark S. Klempner, M.D.
Assistant Physician

David R. Snydman, M.D.
Assistant Physician


NEPHROLOGY SERVICE

Jordan J. Cohen, M.D.
Chief

John T. Harrington, M.D.
Physician & Medical Director,
Dialysis Unit

Nicolaos E. Madias  M.D.
Physician

Susan Hou, M.D.
Assistant Physician

Andrew Levey, M.D.
Assistant Physician,
Chief, Hemodialysis Unit

Michael Madaio, M.D.
Assistant Physician


PULMONARY SERVICE

Barry L. Fanburg, M.D.
Chief

Leonard Sicilian, M.D.
Assistant Physician


RHEUMATOLOGY & CLIN-
ICAL IMMUNOLOGY
SERVICE

Raymond E. H. Partridge, M.D.
Acting Chief

Vincent Agnello, M.D.
Physician

James D. C. Gowans, M.D.
Physician

Kenneth Pariser, M.D.
Assistant Physician


## Neurology

Theodore L. Munsat, M.D.
Neurologist-in-Chief

Walter Bradley, M.D.
Associate Neurologist-in-Chief

Edward F. Rabe, M.D.
Neurologist & Chief, Pediatric
Neurology Service

Thomas E. Twitchell, M.D.
Neurologist

Bruce L. Ehrenberg, M.D.
Assistant Neurologist

John Growdon, M.D.
Assistant Neurologist

Michael Pessin, M.D.
Assistant Neurologist

Benjamin G. Zifkin, M.D.
Assistant Neurologist

### Neurosurgery

William Shucart, M.D.
Neurosurgeon-in-Chief

R. Michael Scott, M.D.
Senior Neurosurgeon

David Kasdon, M.D.
Neurosurgeon

Stephen Dell, M.D.
Assistant Neurosurgeon

Jack Stern, M.D.
Assistant Neurosurgeon

### Ophthalmology

Bernard Schwartz, M.D.
Ophthalmologist-in-Chief

Jules L. Baum, M.D.
Senior Ophthalmologist

Moseh Lahav, M.D.
Ophthalmologist

Thomas R. Hedges III, M.D.
Assistant-in-Ophthalmology

### Orthopedics

Henry H. Banks, M.D.
Orthopedist-in-Chief

Seymour Zimbler, M.D.
Associate Orthopedist-in-Chief

Joseph D. Ferrone, M.D.
Senior Orthopedist

Michael J. Goldberg, M.D.
Senior Orthopedist

John Harris, M.D.
Senior Orthopedist

Won Oh, M.D.
Senior Orthopedist

Leonard Ruby, M.D.
Senior Orthopedist

Clifford Craig, M.D.
*Orthopedist*

William Donaldson, M.D.
*Orthopedist*

Larry Karlin, M.D.
*Assistant Orthopedist*

Mark R. Belsky, M.D.
*Assistant-in-Orthopedics*

John C. Richmond, M.D.
*Assistant-in-Orthopedics*

## Otolaryngology

Werner D. Chasin, M.D.
*Otolaryngologist-in-Chief*

Victor E. Calcaterra, M.D.
*Senior Surgeon*

Parviz Janfaza, M.D.
*Senior Surgeon*

Collingwood S. Karmody, M.D.
*Senior Surgeon*

Arnold Katz, M.D.
*Surgeon*

Daniel Vogel, M.D.
*Assistant Surgeon*

## Pathology

Martin H. Flax, M.D.
*Pathologist-in-Chief*

Hubert J. Wolfe, M.D.
*Associate Pathologist-in-Chief*

Eugene A. Foster, M.D.
*Senior Pathologist*

Amiel G. Cooper, M.D.
*Pathologist*

Yogeshwar Dayal, M.D.
*Pathologist*

Ronald A. DeLellis, M.D.
*Pathologist*

Carl Hirsch, M.D.
*Pathologist*

Vivian Pinn, M.D.
*Pathologist*

Homa Safaii, M.D.
*Pathologist*

Hisashi Tamura, M.D.
*Pathologist*

Lester Adelman, M.D.
*Pathologist-Neuropathology*

Ina Bhan, M.D.
*Assistant Pathologist*

Philip R. Daoust, M.D.
*Assistant Pathologist*

Song Hi An-Foraker, M.D.
*Assistant Pathologist, with joint appointment in Department of Gynecology & Obstetrics*

Arthur K.-C. Lee, M.D.
*Assistant Pathologist*

Miguel Stadecker, M.D.
*Assistant Pathologist*

Arthur S. Tischler, M.D.
*Assistant Pathologist*

Angelo Ucci, M.D.
*Assistant Pathologist*

Jeffrey Isner, M.D.
*Assistant Physician, with joint appointment in Department of Medicine*

## Pediatrics

Marshall B. Kreidberg, M.D.
*Acting Pediatrician-in-Chief & Chief, Cardiology Service*

Richard C. Talamo, M.D.
*Senior Pediatrician*

Mary G. Ampola, M.D.
*Assistant Pediatrician*

Richard Kearsley, M.D.
*Assistant Pediatrician & Co-Director, Infant Development Program*

*AMBULATORY PEDIATRICS SERVICE*

Anna Binkiewicz, M.D.
*Chief & Assistant Endocrinologist*

Betsey Busch, M.D.
*Assistant Pediatrician*

Stephan R. Glicken, M.D.
*Assistant Pediatrician*

Lorena M. Siqueira, M.D.
*Assistant Pediatrician*

John W. Kulig, M.D.
*Director, Adolescent Medicine*

*BIRTH DEFECTS SERVICE*

Murray Feingold, M.D.
*Chief*

Hermine M. Pashayan, M.D.
*Pediatrician*

Louis E. Bartoshesky, M.D.
*Assistant Pediatrician*

Marylou Buyse, M.D.
*Assistant Pediatrician*

Margaret Siber, M.D.
*Assistant Pediatrician*

*CARDIOLOGY SERVICE*

Marshall B. Kreidberg, M.D.
*Chief*

Harvey L. Chernoff, M.D.
*Senior Cardiologist*

Kyung Chung, M.D.
*Assistant Cardiologist*

David Fulton, M.D.
*Assistant Cardiologist, Associate Director, Pediatric Intensive Care*

Kanta Nagpaul, M.D.
*Assistant Cardiologist*

*ENDOCRINOLOGY SERVICE*

Boris Senior, M.D.
*Chief*

Abdollah Sadeghi-Nejad, M.D.
*Endocrinologist*

Anna Binkiewicz, M.D.
*Assistant Endocrinologist*

Joseph I. Wolfsdorf, M.D.
*Assistant-in-Endocrinology*

*HEMATOLOGY SERVICE*

Lucius F. Sinks, M.D.
*Chief*

Shiao Woo, M.D.
*Assistant Hematologist*

*INFECTIOUS DISEASE SERVICE*

Richard H. Meade, III, M.D.
*Chief*

Cody Meissner, M.D.
*Assistant Physician*

*NEONATOLOGY SERVICE*

Timos Valeas, M.D.
*Chief, Associate Director, Pediatric Intensive Care*

Fergus Moylan, M.D.
*Associate Chief & Chief, Pediatric Intensive Care*

*NEUROLOGY SERVICE*

Edward F. Rabe, M.D.
*Chief, with joint appointment in Department of Adult Neurology*

Jerome S. Haller, M.D.
*Neurologist*

William Singer, M.D.
*Neurologist*

Leo R. Sullivan, M.D.
*Neurologist*

PULMONARY SERVICE

Henry L. Dorkin, M.D.
*Chief*

## Psychiatry

Richard I. Shader, M.D.
*Psychiatrist-in-Chief*

Carol Nadelson, M.D.
*Associate Psychiatrist-in-Chief*

David A. Adler, M.D.
*Psychiatrist*

Richard S. Blacher, M.D.
*Psychiatrist, with joint
appointment in Department of
Cardio-Thoracic Surgery*

Dan H. Buie, M.D.
*Psychiatrist*

Marc Frader, M.D.
*Psychiatrist & Director, Adult
Ambulatory Service*

Cornelis Heijn, M.D.
*Psychiatrist*

Malkah T. Notman, M.D.
*Psychiatrist*

Peter B. Randolph, M.D.
*Psychiatrist*

George Sigel, M.D.
*Psychiatrist*

Elisabeth Small, M.D.
*Psychiatrist, with joint
appointment in Department of
Gynecology & Obstetrics*

Makesh Goklaney, M.D.
*Assistant Psychiatrist*

Annette Hanson, M.D.
*Assistant Psychiatrist*

Woodrow W. Havens, M.D.
*Assistant Psychiatrist*

Randall H. Paulson, M.D.
*Assistant Psychiatrist*

Jonathan Schindelheim, M.D.
*Assistant Psychiatrist*

Mark Thall, M.D.
*Assistant Psychiatrist*

DIVISION OF CHILD
PSYCHIATRY

Arthur Z. Mutter, M.D.
*Chief*

Joseph J. Jankowski, M.D.
*Psychiatrist*

Alan N. Marks, M.D.
*Psychiatrist*

Kenneth Robson, M.D.
*Psychiatrist*

Barbara Coffey, M.D.
*Assistant Psychiatrist*

Beverly Dudek, M.D.
*Assistant Psychiatrist*

Margaret Polly Gean, M.D.
*Assistant Psychiatrist*

Jonathan Horowitz, M.D.
*Assistant Psychiatrist*

DIVISION OF CLINICAL
PHARMACOLOGY

David J. Greenblatt, M.D.
*Chief, with joint appointment
in Department of Medicine*

Darrell R. Abernathy, M.D.
*Assistant Physician, with joint
appointment in Department of
Medicine*

## Radiology

Robert E. Paul, Jr., M.D.
*Radiologist-in-Chief*

Jeffrey P. Moore, M.D.
*Associate Radiologist-in-Chief*

ADULT DIAGNOSTIC
SERVICE

Jeffrey P. Moore, M.D.
*Chief*

James B. Dealy, Jr., M.D.
*Senior Radiologist*

Ervin Philipps, M.D.
*Radiologist*

Mark Bankoff, M.D.
*Assistant Radiologist*

Stephen Bloom, M.D.
*Assistant Radiologist*

Marc Homer, M.D.
*Assistant Radiologist*

Robert Sarno, M.D.
*Assistant Radiologist*

ANGIOGRAPHY SERVICE

Victor G. Millan, M.D.
*Chief*

Oun Kwon, M.D.
*Assistant Radiologist*

Samuel L. Maxwell, Jr., M.D.
*Assistant Radiologist*

E.N.T. COMPUTERIZED
TOMOGRAPHY

Barbara L. Carter, M.D.
*Chief*

Richard I. Herman, M.D.
*Assistant-in-Radiology*

NEURORADIOLOGY &
C.T. HEAD SCANNING

Samuel Wolpert, M.D.
*Chief*

Robert J. Prager, M.D.
*Assistant Radiologist*

Frederic J. Barnett, M.D.
*Assistant-in-Radiology*

Catherine M. Mills, M.D.
*Assistant-in-Radiology*

NUCLEAR MEDICINE &
ULTRASOUND SERVICE

Paul C. Kahn, M.D.
*Chief*

Frederick J. Doherty, M.D.
*Assistant Radiologist*

Marvin A. Konstam, M.D.
*Assistant Radiologist, with
joint appointment in
Department of Medicine*

Nancy A. Gadziala, M.D.
*Assistant-in-Radiology*

Magdi Semine, M.D.
*Assistant-in-Radiology*

PEDIATRIC RADIOLOGY
SERVICE

John C. Leonidas, M.D.
*Chief*

Donald B. Darling, M.D.
*Senior Radiologist*

Roy G. K. McCauley, M.D.
*Radiologist*

Alan Schwartz, M.D.
*Assistant Radiologist*

## Department of
## Rehabilitation Medicine

Bruce M. Gans, M.D.
*Acting Physiatrist-in-Chief*

Dennis Gordan, M.D.
*Assistant Physiatrist*

Kamal Labib, M.D.
*Assistant Physiatrist*

Agatha P. Culbert, M.D.
*Assistant-in-Physiatry*

Lynn Alan Curtis, M.D.
*Assistant-in-Physiatry*

Parminder Phull, M.D.
*Assistant-in-Physiatry*

## Surgery

Richard J. Cleveland, M.D.
*Director of Surgical Services &*
*Chairman, Department of*
*Surgery (General & Cardio-*
*Thoracic)*

### GENERAL SURGERY

Allan D. Callow, M.D.
*Chief*

Lon E. Curtis, M.D.
*Senior Surgeon*

Ralph A. Deterling, Jr., M.D.
*Senior Surgeon*

Harry H. Miller, M.D.
*Senior Surgeon*

Sang In Cho, M.D.
*Surgeon & Chief, Renal*
*Transplantation Program*

John M. Kellum, M.D.
*Assistant Surgeon*

Thomas F. O'Donnell, M.D.
*Assistant Surgeon*

Thomas J. Smith, M.D.
*Assistant Surgeon*

### PEDIATRIC SURGERY

Lucian L. Leape, M.D.
*Chief*

### PEDIATRIC TRAUMA SURGERY

Burton H. Harris, M.D.
*Chief*

### PLASTIC SURGERY

Michael B. Lewis, M.D.
*Chief*

Matthias Donelan, M.D.
*Assistant Surgeon*

## Therapeutic Radiology

Hywel Madoc-Jones, M.D.
*Radiotherapist-in-Chief*

Donald F. H. Wallach, M.D.
*Senior Radiotherapist &*
*Director, Division of*
*Radiobiology*

Olubumni Abayomi, M.D.
*Assistant-in-Radiotherapy*

Hyesook Chang, M.D.
*Assistant-in-Radiotherapy*

Gene Kopelson, M.D.
*Assistant-in-Radiotherapy*

Lily Lawn-Tsao, M.D.
*Assistant-in-Radiotherapy*

James Santoro, M.D.
*Assistant-in-Radiotherapy*

Henry Wagner, Jr., M.D.
*Assistant-in-Radiotherapy*

Bernard Willett, M.D.
*Assistant-in-Radiotherapy*

## Urology

Edwin M. Meares, Jr., M.D.
*Urologist-in-Chief*

George T. Klauber, M.D.
*Senior Surgeon (Urologist) &*
*Chief, Pediatric Urology*

John A. Heaney, M.D.
*Surgeon (Urologist)*

George A. Barbalias, M.D.
*Assistant Surgeon (Urologist)*

### SPECIAL & SCIENTIFIC STAFF

## Child Psychiatry

William Costello, Ph.D.
Beverly Gomes-Schwartz, Ph.D.
Irving Hurwitz, Ph.D.
William F. Monahan, D.S., M.Ed
J.D.
Sidney Mondell, Ph.D.
Catherine Roff, Ph.D.
Judith Rubenstein, Ph.D.
Lyn Stycznyski, Ph.D.
Ellen Wilson, Ph.D.

## Chiropody

Richard Vallon, D.Sc.

## Community & Ambulatory Care

Jane Jones, Ph.D.

## Electron Microscopy

Walter Krawczyk, D.D.S.

## Gynecology & Obstetrics

Allyn H. Rule, Ph.D.

## Medicine

J.A. Andre-Schwartz, M.D.
Carl Deneke, Ph.D.
Susan Deneke, Ph.D.
Barbara C. Furie, Ph.D.
Barry Goldin, Ph.D.
Joseph J. Lanzillo, Ph.D.
James Mayhew, Ph.D.
Martha H. Mulks, Ph.D.
Miercio Pereira, E.A., Ph.D.,
M.D.
Grace Thorne, Ph.D.
Kenneth S. Weinberg, Ph.D.
Margo Woods, Ph.D.

## Neurology

John Knott, Ph.D.
Chaundri G. Rasool, Ph.D.
Richard Scheife, D. Pharm.
Barbara R. Talamo, Ph.D.
Suzanne Roffler Tarlov, Ph.D.

## Neuropsychology

Homer B.C. Reed, Ph.D.
James Reed, Ph.D.
Lynne Reed, Ph.D.

## Nutrition

Johanna Dwyer, D.Sc.

## Ophthalmology

Howard Harrison, O.D.
Ralph Levine, O.D.
George McCarty, Ph.D.
Anne Moskowitz-Cook, Ph.D.
Paul Nagin, Ph.D.
Samuel Sokol, Ph.D.
Takenori Takamoto, PhD.
Vernon L. Towle, Ph.D.

## Pathology

William J. Martin, Ph.D.

## Pediatrics

Joseph Bleiberg, Ph.D.
Ronald W. Berninger, Ph.D.
Edward Heck, Ph.D.
Francesca LaVecchio, Ph.D.
Lorene Ware, Ph.D.
Philip Zelazo, Ph.D.

## Podiatry

Donald D. Donovan, D.Sc.

### Psychiatry

Harold N. Boris, M.A.
John Gerrein, Ph.D.
William Hudgins, Ph.D.
Robert Jampel, Ph.D.
Jonathan H. Slavin, Ph.D.
Herbert L. Wasserman, Ph.D.
Martin L. Zelin, Ph.D.

### Rehabilitation

James L. Cockrell, Ph.D.
Gerben DeJong, Ph.D.
Kenneth I. Kolpan, J.D.
Sarah McCarty, Ph.D.
Mitchell Rosenthal, Ph.D.

Cheryl Trepagnier, Ph.D.
Mary J. Willard, Ph.D.

### Rehabilitation Engineering

William J. Crochetiere, Ph.D.
Richard A. Foulds, M.A.
James O'Leary, M.S.

### Speech & Hearing

Hubert L. Gerstman, D.Ed.

### Surgery

Raymond J. Connolly, Jr., Ph.D.

### Therapeutic Radiology

John F. Brenner, Ph.D.
Christodoulos Constantinou, Ph.D.
Peck-Sun Lin, Ph.D.
Ross B. Mikkelsen, Ph.D.
Boris Schiller, Ph.D.
Rupert Schmidt-Ullrich, M.D.
Edward S. Sternick, Ph.D.
Surendra P. Verma, Ph.D.
Andrew Wu, Ph.D.
David J. Zahniser, Ph.D.
Robert S. Zamenhof, Ph.D.
Robert D. Zwicker, Ph.D.

---

In addition to the full-time staff, during 1982 there were 574 doctors on the hospital's associate and consulting staffs, and there were 418 interns, residents, clinical and research fellows. On the average, 300 medical students receive clinical training at The New England Medical Center each year.

---

# Institutional Affiliations of
# New England Medical Center

Through collaborative clinical and educational programs, consulting services, patient transfer agreements and service contracts, New England Medical Center has affiliations with the following institutions:

Baystate Medical Center
Beverly Hospital
Bon Secours Hospital
Boston City Hospital
Boston State Hospital
Brockton Hospital
Cambridge Hospital
Cardinal Cushing Hospital
Carney Hospital
Choate/Symmes Hospital
Eastern Maine Medical Center
Emerson Hospital
Faulkner Hospital
Goddard Memorial Hospital
Kennedy Memorial Hospital
Laboure Mental Health Center
Lakeville Hospital
Lawrence Memorial Hospital
Lemuel Shattuck Hospital
Lynn Hospital

Marlborough Hospital
Massachusetts General Hospital
Matthew Thornton Health Center
New England Baptist Hospital
Newton-Wellesley Hospital
North End Community Health Center
North Shore Children's Hospital
Quincy City Hospital
St. Anne's Hospital
St. Elizabeth's Hospital of Boston
St. Margaret's Hospital for Women
South Cove Community Health Center
South Shore Hospital
Tufts Associated Health Plan
University Hospital
Veterans Administration Medical Center
Winchester Hospital
Women's and Infants Hospital
of Rhode Island

# Index

Abbot, Gardiner, 56
Adams, John Q., 129
Adams, Dr. Raymond, 111
Affiliated Publications, 85, 87
Aid to Families with Dependent Children, 188
Alden, John, 26
Alfred T. Sloan Foundation, 133
Alzheimer's disease, 179
American Academy of Arts and Sciences, 103
American Cancer Society, 137, 163
American College of Cardiology, 104
American College of Surgeons, 63
American Heart Association, 43
American Medical Association, 40, 78, 104, 112
*American Medical Association Bulletin*, 68
American Society for Clinical Investigation, 70, 104
*Amerika*, 144
Amherst College, 26, 36
Anderson, J. R., 28
Andover Theological Seminary, 26
Angina pectoris, 50
*Aphrodite* (yacht), 55
Architects Collaborative, The, 136
Area Health Education Centers (AHECs), 94, 143, 144–145, 147, 148
Association of American Physicians, 104
Astwood, Dr. Edwin B., 113
Atherosclerosis, 50
Augusta (Maine) General Hospital, 90
Averback, Mrs. David, 119

Bader, Richard E., 120–121
Banks, Dr. Henry H., 177

Barnard, Chester I., 101
Barr, Joseph R., 87, 95, 97, 138
Barr and Barr, 87, 138
Barron, Dr. Elmer W., 163
Barry, Robert, 120
Bartlett, Thomas, 16
Bates College, 65
Baty, Dr. James Marvin, 163
Bay Cove Mental Health Center, 178
Bellevue Hospital (New York), 2; Medical School, 39
Berg, Dr. Hans, 82
Berkeley Temple, 24; Christian Endeavor Society of, 26
Berkowitz, Abram, 108
Berkshire Medical Institution, 38
Beth Israel Hospital, 40, 80, 103, 153
Biewend, Cameron, 119, 120, 121, 131, 137, 138
Biewend, Lillian, 121
Biewend Building, 120, 121, 164
Bigelow, Dr. Jacob, 20
Bingham, Charles William, 54, 57
Bingham, Harry Payne, 56
Bingham, Mary Payne, 54, 55, 57
Bingham, William, 2nd, 50–51, 85, 96, 99, 108; and birth of Bingham Program, 62–67 *passim*; characterized, 54, 56–58, 59–60; charitable funds of, 99, 120, 123; estate of, 56; and Farnsworth Building, 99; lineage of, 54–55; medical philanthropy of, 53, 54, 55, 65, 112, 118; and Pratt Clinic, 76–78; and success of Bingham Program, 68–70
Bingham Associates Fund of Massachusetts, 97, 99, 101, 103, 105

Bingham Associates Program for the Advancement of Rural Medicine, 12–13, 50, 51, 56, 57; assessment of, after fifty years, 141–151; birth of, 61–67; contributions of Sidney Davidson to, 85; historical precedents established by, in Maine, 88–94; and Pratt Clinic, 75–76; success of, 68–73; trustees of, 53, 123
Blair, Dr. Murray R., Jr., 175
Block, Roger T., 164
Blodgett, Mrs. Frederick N., 131
Blossom, Elizabeth B., 56
Blossom Street Health Center of the City of Boston, 40
Blue Cross, Blue Shield, 75, 174
Blumgart, Dr. Herrman L., 70
Bolton, Frances Payne, 54, 56–57, 58, 66–67
Born, Emilie, 91, 147, 148, 149
Boston Chamber of Commerce, 15, 76, 188
Boston City Hospital (BCH), 2–3, 15, 40, 65, 71, 98; clinical and research laboratories at, 43; Mallory Institute of Pathology at, 10, 65, 93; Dr. Pratt's work at, 10–11; Thorndike Laboratory at, 6, 11, 68, 69–70
Boston Dental College, 41
Boston Dispensary, 2–3, 24, 26, 33, 36, 74; affiliation of, with Tufts Medical School, 9, 23; and Bingham Program, 62–63, 68–69; demise of, 98; early accomplishments of, 19–20; and early Boston Floating Hospital, 28; Dr. Ettinger's contributions to, 81–82; Dr. Farnsworth's work at, 62; financial difficulties of, 96, 97–98; Frances Stern Nutrition Center of, 20–23, 150; German physicians at, 81–85; history of, 15–23 passim; Home Medical Service clinics of, 5–6, 9; and Pratt Clinic, 76–78; presidents and directors of, 44–45; private contributions to, 75; Dr. Proger's work at, 3–6, 23, 43; Rehabilitation Institute of, 98, 116, 127–128, 162
Boston Floating Hospital, 6, 36, 74, 116, 117; Birth Defects Center at, 164; Family Participation Unit at, 163; history of, 24–35 passim; importance of philanthropy to, 33–35; Jackson Memorial Building of, 33, 34; new building for, 87, 160–168 passim, 169; origin of name of, 24; private contributions to, 75; ship, fire on, 24, 31–33

Boston Globe, 18, 31, 85–87, 100, 123; on Boston Floating Hospital ship fire, 31; on Frances Stern Nutrition Center, 23; interview with Dr. Leape in, 167–168; on Dr. Pratt, 14; and relations between medicine and press, 115
Boston Herald, 26
Boston Medical Library, 92
Boston Pops Orchestra, 6, 123
Boston Redevelopment Authority, 136, 165, 188
Boston Symphony Orchestra, 44, 123
Boston University, 3, 130; School of Medicine, 38
Bowditch, Dr. Henry I., 31
Bowdoin College, 62, 65, 66, 67; Medical School, 38, 89, 92
Brainerd, Henry, 34–35
Brainerd, William Hungerford, 34
Breck, Dr. Samuel, 28
Briggs, G. Loring, 29
Brjgsch, Dr. Heinrich, 84
Brown, Dr. Samuel, 106
Buck, Dr. Robert, 85
Burns, Frances, 100, 115

Cabot, Charles C., 45, 96, 97, 131; and Pratt Clinic, 77–78, 87; his Subcommittee on Legal Affairs, 129
Cabot, Dr. Richard, 11–12
Cabot, Dr. Samuel, 20
Callow, Dr. Allan D., 114, 130, 177, 179
Cameron Biewend Fund, 121
Canadian Task Force Study (1973), 151
Cancer treatment, 178
Cannon, Ida, 12
Capen, Elmer, 39–40
Cardiology, 43
Carley, Warren, 179
Carmichael, Dr. Leonard, 80, 97, 104–105, 140
Carnegie Commission on Higher Education, 144
Carnegie Foundation, 40
Carney Hospital (Dorchester), 40, 173
Carter, Ledyard and Milburn, 85
Casals, Pablo, 122
Casassa, Aida, 106
Case Western Reserve University, 61; Frances Payne Bolton School of Nursing at, 67
Castle, Dr. William, 70, 93
Cavazos, Dr. Lauro, 113, 146, 175–176
Central Maine General Hospital, 89, 90
Chamberlin, Dr. Richard T., 146–147, 148, 149
Cheever, Dr. David W., 20

Chiang, Madame, 121–122
Chiang Kai-Shek, 121–122
Child, Dr. Charles G., 176
Children's Hospital, 43
Chinese community, 179–180
Chipman, Dr. William R., 38–39
Clarke, Dr. B. G., 114
Clement, Thomas, 19
Cleveland, Dr. Richard J., 125, 177
Cleveland Clinic, 79
*Clifford* (first Floating Hospital), 26–29
Clinical decision making, program in, 178–179
Coffin, Dr. John G., 20
Colby College, 65
College of Physicians and Surgeons, 37
Collins, John, 162, 187–188
Columbia Presbyterian Hospital, 77
Columbia Presbyterian Medical Center, 53
Columbia University, College of Physicians and Surgeons at, 66
Community Fund, 115
Cornell Medical College, 55–56
Coronary thrombosis, 46
Councilman, Dr. William T., 10
Cousens, John Albert, 40–41, 87
Crandall, Dorothy, 23
Crile, Dr. George, 51
Crile Clinic (Cleveland), 51
Crosby, Dr. William H., Jr., 135
Curley, James Michael, 100–101
Curran, Dr. Jean A., 10–11, 56, 57–58, 97
Cushing, Dr. Harvey, 5, 68

Dameshek, Dr. William, 106, 113
Dartmouth Medical School, 38, 39, 89
Davidson, Robert T. H., 86, 123
Davidson, Sidney W., 70, 95, 97, 123, 131; and Bingham's charitable funds, 99, 120; contribution of, to Pratt Clinic, 85; New England interests of, 85–87; and Proger Building, 137, 138, 140
Dearborn, Benjamin, 18–19
Dejerine, Dr. Joseph Jules, 14
Dental Health Sciences Building, 41–42, 136, 139
Dentistry, 41–42
Desforges, Dr. Jane, 179
Deterling, Dr. Ralph A., 125, 177
Diarrhea, treatment of, 29
Dubinsky, Eli, 90–91
Dudley, Dr. Henry W., 38–39
Dukakis, Michael, 146
Dunks, Abbie, 19, 45, 133

Eastern Maine General Hospital, 89, 90, 146
Eastern Maine Medical Center, 145
Ehrlich, Edward, 179
Eisenhower, Dwight D., 157
Electrocardio(grams)(graphs), 44, 46, 61, 91
Emerson Hospital (Concord), 173
Emory Medical School, 2
Emory University, 2
Etsten, Dr. Benjamin, 114
Ettinger, Dr. Alice, 81–82, 101
Evangeline Booth maternity hospital, 40
Everhart, David, 122

Farnsworth, George, 51, 62
Farnsworth, Mrs. George, *see* Gehring, Mrs. John George
Farnsworth, Dr. George Bourne, 51, 53, 70, 95, 104–105; and Bingham Program, 61–67 *passim*, 89–90; death of, 99; and Pratt Clinic, 76–78
Farnsworth Building, 51, 53, 67, 116, 125, 136; opening of, 99–101, 114, 176. *See also* Pratt Clinic
Faulkner Hospital (Jamaica Plain), 173
Federal Housing Administration, 165
Feingold, Dr. Murray, 163–164, 167
Fiedler, Arthur, 6, 123
Fiedler, Mrs. Arthur, 123
Field, Hermann H., 136, 187
Finland, Dr. Maxwell, 70, 93
First National Bank of Boston, 99
Fishman, Dr. William H., 114
Fleet, Dr. John, 17
Flexner, Abraham, 41; report of, on medical schools, 40, 130
Fluoroscopy, 82
Foley, Mrs. Henry E., 131
Ford, Joseph, 108
Ford Foundation, 108
Frances Stern Nutrition Center, 20–23, 150
Franklin, Benjamin, 16, 154
Franklin County (Maine) Memorial Hospital, 90
Freeman, Lewis, 24–26
Freud, Sigmund, 158
Friedlander, Edward M., 115–116
Friendly Visitors, 12
Fuller, Dr. A. J., 64–65

Gardner, Mrs. Jack, 122
Garfield, James, 131
Garland, Joseph E., *Experiment in Medicine*, 63

Gehring, Dr. John George, 14, 50, 58, 59,
    92; and birth of Bingham Program, 61,
    62, 63, 64; death of, 52, 53, 65;
    psychiatric therapy of, 51–52, 54
Gehring, Mrs. John George, 51, 52–53,
    62, 63, 70, 92
Geiger, Dr. Jack, 115
Gellis, Dr. Sydney S., 135, 136; his role at
    Boston Floating Hospital, 162–167
    passim
General Medical Associates (GMA), 172
George Robert White Fund, 71
German physicians, at Pratt and
    Dispensary, 81–85
Gerrish, Dr. Frederic H., 92
Gerrish Memorial Library, 92
Gibson, Dr. Count, 115
Gilbert, Carl J., 97
Ginsberg, Frances, 91–92
Good Samaritan, 17, 19, 169
Gottlieb, Dr. Julius, 93
Gottlieb, Dr. Leonard S., 65, 93
Gould Academy, 52, 58, 65, 85, 153
Government National Mortgage
    Association, 165
Great Depression, 44
Great Northern Paper Company, 91
Grossman, Dr. Jerome H., 14, 172, 173,
    179; and Chinese community, 179–180;
    on future of New England Medical
    Center, 183–189; and HMOs, 174; his
    reports to trustees, 182–183, 185;
    variety of his training and expertise,
    170–171, 182
Group therapy, 13–14
Grover, William A., 31
Growdon, Dr. John, 179
Guest Residency Program, 148

Hale, Edward Everett, 26; In His Name,
    28; The Man without a Country, 28;
    Ten Times One Is Ten, 28
Hall, Dr. Walter L., 38–39
Hallowell, Dr. Burton C., 134
Hanley, Dr. Daniel, 65–66, 67, 145–146
Harrington, Dr. John, 172, 178
Harvard Business School, 170
Harvard Club, 14
Harvard Community Health Plan, 171,
    173–174
Harvard Medical School, 12, 17, 39, 62,
    66, 111; and Bingham Program, 90;
    and Boston Floating Hospital, 28, 31;
    Countway Library of, 92; endowment
    of (1981), 37; first black professor at,
    20; opening of, 16; opposition of, to
    opening of Tufts Medical School, 36–37

Hauptmann, Dr. Alfred, 83–84
Haussermann, Oscar W., Jr., 131
Hayman, Joseph, 128
Health Maintenance Organizations
    (HMOs), 112, 117, 173–174
Heart attack, 46, 157
Heart disease, Dr. Proger's research on,
    102–103
Hill-Burton Hospital Construction Act,
    94, 143, 144
Hinton, Dr. William A., 20
Hitler, Adolf, 46, 65, 81, 83, 84
HMOs, see Health Maintenance
    Organizations
Holmes, Dr. Oliver Wendell, 18, 20
Holmes Building, 19
Holy Cross College, 36
Homans, Dr. John, 20
Home Medical Service, 5–6, 9
Homeopathic College of Physicians and
    Surgeons, 37–38
Hope, Dr. John M., 114
Howland, Weston, 127
Human Nutrition Research Center, U.S.,
    150, 174–175, 186–187
Hyams Fund of Boston, 108
Hynes, John B., 100, 187

Igersheimer, Dr. Joseph, 84
Independent Practice Association—Health
    Maintenance Organization, 174
Ingelfinger, Dr. Franz, 140

Jackson, Henry Clay, 33–34, 161
Jackson, Paul Wilde, 33–34, 161
Jackson Memorial Building, 33, 34
Jacobs, Dr. Arthur R., 174
Johansen, Dr. Erling, 176
Johns Hopkins Medical School, 3, 39, 65
Johns Hopkins University Hospital, 3, 50,
    156
Johnson, Harold U., 131
Johnson, Mr. and Mrs. Howard, 121
Johnson, Dr. John W., 38–39
Johnston, John, 19
Jonas, Dr. Albert M., 175
Jordan, Eben, 86, 87
Jordan Marsh Company, 35
Joslin, Dr. Elliott P., 11
Joslin Clinic, 11
Journal of the American Medical
    Association, 11
Junior League of Boston, 127

Kaplan, Dr. Marshall M., 124–125
Kaplan, Nancy Proger, 103, 124
Kassirer, Dr. Jerome, 179

Katz, Geneva, 133, 136, 161, 162, 163
Keefer, Dr. Chester, 70, 93
Kemp, Sylvia, 14
Kennebec Valley Regional Medical Care
  Development Agency, 145
Keusch, Dr. Gerald, 172
King, Alice, 78
Kissinger, Henry, 121
Kiwanis Foundation of New England,
  116, 167–168, 186, 187
Koussevitzky, Serge, 44, 123
Krehl, Dr. Ludolf, 10, 45, 46
Kreidberg, Dr. Marshall B., 167

Lahey, Dr. Frank, 79
Lahey Clinic, 43, 74–75, 79, 80
Lakeside Hospital (Cleveland), 56
LaVine, Edward, 124
LaVine, Susan Proger, 70, 103, 124
Lawrence Memorial Hospital (Medford),
  173
Leadbetter, Dr. Weyland, 111, 176
Leape, Dr. Lucian L., 167–168
Lend-a-Hand Clubs, 28–29
Leonard, Dr. John C., 95–96
Levine, Dr. Samuel, 46
Levy, Dr. Robert I., 176, 179
Logue, Edward, 188
Longley, James B., 146
Lowell, Ralph, 31–33, 34, 99, 118, 131;
  his association with Boston Globe, 87;
  and Proger Building, 138

McCarty, Dr. Eugene M., 64
McCombs, Dr. Robert P., 114
McCormack, John W., 137–138
McKusick, Dr. Victor, 65
McKusick, Vincent, 65
McLaughlin, Loretta, 167
McMahon, Dr. H. Edward "Ted," 69, 87,
  114
McTernan, Edmund J., 133
Madoff, Dr. Morton A., 79–80, 114, 147,
  174
Magendantz, Dr. Heinz, 82–83
Maine, University of, 65, 145, 147
Maine Medical Association, 92, 147
Maine Medical Center, 89, 145
Maine Medical Society, 67
Mallory, Dr. Frank B., 10
Mallory Institute of Pathology, 10, 65, 93
Malnutrition, 17
Mansfield, Frederick W., 71
Marchant, Dr. Douglas J., 178
March of Dimes Birth Defects Center
  (Foundation), 116, 164
Mary Hitchcock Hospital, 38

Massachusetts, University of, 36, 130;
  Medical School, 146, 147
Massachusetts Dental Society, 41
Massachusetts General Hospital (MGH),
  12, 13, 43, 62, 80, 111; ambulatory
  care health center at, 170; and Bingham
  Program, 91; opening of, 16; publicity
  for, by Dr. Paul Dudley White, 123;
  tuberculosis clinic at, 11
Massachusetts Health and Educational
  Facilities Authority, 165
Massachusetts Heart Association, 104
Massachusetts Hospital Association, 99
Massachusetts Institute of Technology
  (MIT), 34, 170
Massachusetts Medical Society, 78, 85,
  102, 104, 112; Postgraduate Medical
  Institute of, 146, 147
Massachusetts Public Health Council,
  164–165
Mayer, Dr. Jean, 150, 174–175, 179
Mayo Clinic, 79, 156
Medicaid, 98, 188
Medical Care Development, Inc., 145,
  148–149
Medicare, 98
Memory disorder clinic, 179
Meserve, Robert W., 129, 131
Metropolitan Center, Inc., 120
MGH News, 11
Miller, Dr. Harry, 177
Miner, Rev. Alonzo A., 37
Minot, Dr. Francis, 20
Minot, Dr. George Richards, 68
Mitchell, Dr. George, 114
Modern Hospital, 64
Monday Evening Club, 26
Morse, Alan R., 131
Muskie, Edmund S., 65
Myerson, Dr. Paul G., 177

National Health Service Corps, 149
National Institutes of Health, 171, 176,
  183
National Library of Medicine, 178
Neurological Institute of New York, 53,
  62
New England Baptist Hospital, 13, 75
New England Cardiovascular Society, 104
New England Center Hospital, 102, 118;
  Pratt Clinic renamed, 99, 116; Dr.
  Proger's recruitment of staff for, 110–
  114; Dr. Proger's role at, 103, 110;
  public relations at, 115–116; Ziskind's
  contributions to, 108. See also Pratt
  Clinic

New England College of Osteopathic
    Medicine (NECOM), 149
New England Deaconess Hospital, 75
New England Hospital Assembly, 99
New England Hospital for Women and
    Children, 40
*New England Journal of Medicine*, 43–44,
    48, 88, 90, 103, 140
New England Medical Center:
    contributions of Sidney Davidson to,
    85; current status of, 169–181;
    Department of Medicine of, 125, 126;
    Department of Surgery of, 125;
    formation of, 24, 33, 36; future of,
    182–189; hospitals making up, 97, 99,
    116–117, 127–128; importance of
    philanthropy to, 18, 33–34, 50, 53;
    merger of units at, 131–134, 135; name
    of, changed to Tufts-New England
    Medical Center, 128; Oliver Wendell
    Holmes building at, 19. *See also*
    Bingham Associates Program; Boston
    Dispensary; Boston Floating Hospital;
    New England Center Hospital; New
    England Medical Center Hospital(s);
    Pratt Clinic; Tufts University School of
    Dental Medicine, School of Medicine,
    *and* School of Veterinary Medicine
New England Medical Center Hospital(s),
    45, 50, 54, 63, 65, 131; hospitals
    making up, 116. *See also* Boston
    Dispensary; Boston Floating Hospital;
    New England Center Hospital
New England Pediatric Trauma Institute,
    116, 167–168, 186
New England Red Cross, 44
Newton-Wellesley Hospital (Newton
    Lower Falls), 173
New York Hospital, 3
New York Public Library, 56
Nilson, George, 147, 149
Nixon, Richard, 121
Nordblom, Robert C., 119
North Carolina, University of, 143
Northeastern University, 41
Nothman, Dr. Martin, 84
Nott, Dr. Albert, 38–39

Office of Cancer Control (OCC), 178
Office of Economic Opportunity, 17
Osler, Dr. William, 5, 10

Paine, Dr. Alonzo K., 87
Pan American Health Organization, 171
Park, Ellery C., 64
Parker, Augustin H., Jr., 129, 131
Parker, Charles, 120–121

Parker, Franklin, 179
Parran, Dr. Thomas, 93–94, 143, 144
Pauker, Dr. Steven, 179
Paul, Dr. Robert H., Jr., 135
Paullin, Dr. James E., 3–4, 5, 48, 70
Payne, Henry (Harry), 55
Payne, Nathan, 55
Payne, Oliver Hazard, 54, 55–56, 58
Payne-Aldrich tariff legislation, 55
Peabody, Francis W., 10–11
Perkins, Paul F., Jr., 131–133, 181
Peter Bent Brigham Hospital, 13, 43, 46,
    68, 80, 113; academic affiliations with
    Harvard of, 79
Phaneuf, Dr. Louis, 87
Phillips Academy, 14, 26, 55
Polio epidemic (1954), 162
Pollution, environmental, 158
Pope, Edward W., 29, 33
Posner, Mr. and Mrs. Harry, 119
Posner Hall, 87, 119
Powers, John, 119
Pratt, Dr. Joseph Hersey, 6, 41, 45, 48,
    53; and William Bingham 2nd, 50–51;
    and Bingham Program, 62–64, 68–71;
    *Boston Globe* on, 14; characterized, 9,
    12, 13; distinguished career of, 3–5, 12,
    13, 23; education of, 9–10; and Dr.
    Ettinger, 82; Dr. Farnsworth's
    preceptorship under, 62; and Dr.
    Gehring, 50, 51; and Mrs. Gehring, 52;
    group therapy of, 13–14; later years
    and death of, 14; and Dr. Osler, 10;
    and Pratt Clinic, 76–78, 81; his studies
    in Germany, 10; tuberculosis patients
    of, 11–12; work of, at Boston City
    Hospital, 10–11
Pratt, Martin van Buren, 9–10
Pratt, Rebecca Adams (Dyer), 10
Pratt Clinic (Joseph H. Pratt Diagnostic
    Hospital), 14, 63, 67, 136, 173; and
    Bingham Program, 75–76, 88;
    contributions of Sidney Davidson to,
    85; events leading to establishment of,
    76–80; German physicians at, 81–85;
    name of, changed to New England
    Center Hospital, 99, 116; opening of,
    74–75, 81; people involved in
    construction of, 87; plans for adding
    surgical wing to, 95–97, 98–99. *See
    also* Farnsworth Building; New England
    Center Hospital
Proger, Evelyn Levinson, 6–8, 48, 78, 82,
    121; children of, 103; marriage of, to
    Dr. Proger, 7, 44
Proger, Nancy, *see* Kaplan, Nancy Proger
Proger, Dr. Samuel Herschel, 11, 19, 43,
    53, 145, 185; and Bingham Program,

62, 64, 69–73, 88–93; on character of
William Bingham 2nd, 59–60; and
James Michael Curley, 100–101;
decision of, to remain in Boston, 48;
early years of, in Boston, 1–9;
education of, 2; on education vs.
patient care, 130; on equilibrium, 4,
46–48; and estate of Oliver Hazard
Payne, 56; his friendship with Arthur
Fiedler, 6, 123; on future of New
England Medical Center, 189; and Mrs.
Gehring, 52; and Sydney Gellis, 163;
and German physicians at Pratt and
Dispensary, 82–85; on heart disease,
102–103; marriage of, to Evelyn
Levinson, 7, 44; his membership in
medical and scientific organizations,
104; and new building for Boston
Floating Hospital, 164–165; and New
England Medical Center merger, 131;
observations of, on medical profession,
152–159; and opening of Farnsworth
Building, 100; patients of, 118–126;
personal life of, 7–8, 103–104; posts
held by, 103, 139–140, 170; and Pratt
Clinic, 74–80 passim, 95–96; and
Proger Building, 136–137, 138, 139,
140, 189; on John Quarles, 131; his
recruitment of staff for New England
Center Hospital, 110–114; on
relationship between laboratory and
bedside, 4, 48–49; research papers
published by, 43–44; role of, at New
England Center Hospital, 103, 110; his
studies in Germany, 45–46, 48; his
work at Boston Dispensary, 3–6, 23,
43; and Ziskind Research Building,
106–108
Proger, Susan, see LaVine, Susan Proger
Proger Health Services Building, 87, 121,
136–140, 163, 169, 189
Provident Institution for Savings, 120
Psychiatry, 177–178
Psychotherapy, 13–14, 50, 158
Public Health Service, United States, 93,
108

Quarles, John R., 97, 100, 123, 128, 181;
on lack of cooperation among New
England Medical Center hospitals, 128,
129; and New England Medical Center
merger, 131, 134; and Proger Building,
138

Raben, Dr. Maurice S., 114
Regional Medical Program (RMP), 94,
144, 145, 147

Rehabilitation Institute, 98, 116, 127–
128, 162
Revere, Paul, 41
Rheinlander, Dr. Harold F., 65, 114, 177
Richardson, Elliot, 138
Rizzo, Michael, 31
Robertson, Dr. George J., 145, 146
Robert Wood Johnson Foundation, 172–
173
Robinson, Dr. Charles V., 114
Rockefeller, John D., 55
Rockefeller Foundation, 83, 101, 171–172
Rogers, Dr. David R., 173
Roosevelt, Franklin D., 3, 44
Rosenthal, Dr. Joseph, 5–6
Rotch, Arthur G., 44, 45, 71, 97
Royal College of Physicians, 114
Rumford, Maine, Community Hospital,
63, 64, 68, 69, 71, 75

Sackler, Dr. Arthur M., 175
Sackler, Dr. Mortimer D., 175
Sackler, Dr. Raymond S., 175
Sackler School of Graduate Biomedical
Sciences, 175
St. Elizabeth's Hospital (Brighton), 173
St. Margaret's Hospital for Women
(Dorchester), 173
Saltonstall, Eleanor Brooks, 181
Saltonstall, Leverett, 181
Saltonstall, Richard, 181
Saltonstall, William, 171, 179, 181
Salvation Army, 40
Saphir, Grace McIntyre, 78
Saphir, Dr. Nelson, 78
Sargent, Mrs. George L., 181
Schloss, Dr. Jacob, 84, 106
Schmidt, Dr. Gerhard, 84–85, 114
Schwartz, Dr. Robert S., 113
Schwartz, Dr. William B., 114, 139, 171
Selverstóne, Dr. Bertram, 114
Shader, Dr. Richard I., 177
Shattuck, Dr. James G., 20
Simmons, Phyllis, 92
Smallpox, vaccination against, 19
South Cove (Chinese) Community Health
Center, 180
South End Diet Kitchen, 20
Spiker, Ellwyn D., 133
Stearns, A. Warren, 105
Stearns, Dr. Norman, 147–148
Stern, Frances, 20, 150
Stevenson, Adlai, 8
Stimson, Lee, 168
Sullivan, Dr. John F., 83, 114
Surgery, 95–97, 98–99, 176–177
Swenson, Dr. Orvar, 161

Talamo, Dr. Richard C., 167
Taylor, Charles H., 86
Taylor, Davis, 87
Taylor, John, 87
Ten Times One Society, 28–29
Thannhauser, Dr. Siegfried, 83, 106
Thayer, Dr. Charles P., 38–39
Thayer, Dr. W. S., 50
Thibodeau, Dr. Arthur, 114, 177
Thorndike Laboratory, 6, 11, 68, 69–70
T-NEMC Corporation, 133–134, 179
Tobey, Rev. Rufus Babcock, 24, 26–28
Trauma Institute, see New England
    Pediatric Trauma Institute
Truman, Harry, 100
Tuberculosis, 11–12, 13
Tufts Alumni Association, 158
Tufts Associated Health Plan, 173–174,
    186
Tufts Associated Hospitals, 173, 177
Tufts Delta Health Center (Mound Bayou,
    Mississippi), 115
Tufts-New England Medical Center, 12,
    37, 76, 80, 116; Birth Defects
    Information Service at, 164; Dental
    Health Sciences Building of, 41–42,
    136, 139; Human Nutrition Research
    Center at, 150, 174–175, 186–187;
    name of New England Medical Center
    changed to, 128; organization of, 133;
    powers and influence of, 133–134. See
    also New England Medical Center
Tufts University, 24, 33, 36, 37, 38, 63;
    admission of women to, 39
Tufts University School of Dental
    Medicine, 6, 74, 87; current status of,
    169, 176; history of, 41; move of, to
    Harrison Avenue, 104–106; tuition at
    (1980s), 39
Tufts University School of Medicine, 6,
    12, 17, 69, 74, 79; admission of women
    to, 39–40; appointment of Julius
    Gottlieb to, 93; Boston Dispensary's
    affiliation with, 9, 23; current status of,
    169, 173, 174; Department of Medicine
    at, 103; Department of Radiology at,
    82; endowment of (1981), 37;
    enhancing of image of, 115; Harvard's
    opposition to opening of, 36–37;
    history of, 37–41; move of, to Harrison
    Avenue, 104–106; professorship of
    Gerhard Schmidt at, 85; tuition at
    (1980s), 39
Tufts University School of Veterinary
    Medicine, 175
Tupper, Earl, 123
"200 Club," 119

United Fund, 162
United States Trust Company of New
    York, 99
University Hospital, 65, 130

Vermont, University of, Medical School,
    39, 128
Veterans Administration, 116
Viguers, Richard T., 99, 128, 133, 135,
    137
Volunteers, assistance of, 181

Walter, Dr. Arthur L., 53, 99
Wang Laboratories, 180
Warren, Dr. John Collins, 20
Washington, George, 15, 154, 169
Weinstein, Dr. Louis, 111, 113
Weiss, Dr. Soma, 70
Welch, Dr. C. Stuart, 96, 100, 113–114,
    176
Welch, Dr. William H., 10
Wellesley College, 153
Weltman, David, 109
Weltman, Mrs. Sol W., 108, 109, 119,
    131, 137
Wessell, Dr. Nils Y., 129, 130, 131, 133,
    134
Wheatley, Dr. Frank C., 38–39
White, Kevin, 131
White, Dr. Paul Dudley, 10–11, 43, 122,
    123–124, 157
Whitney, Flora, 56
Whitney, Harry Payne, 56
Whitney, Payne, 56
Whitney, William C., 56
Who's Who in America, 155
Williams College, 36, 38
Wing, Frank, 44–45, 98, 161
Wise, Dr. Robert E., 79
Wolf, Dr. George A., Jr., 128–129, 133
Wolff, Dr. Sheldon M., 126, 171–173
Women, policies regarding admission of,
    to medical schools, 39–40
Wood, John M., Jr., 129, 131
Works Progress Administration (WPA),
    44, 45
World Health Organization, 171
Wyler, Dr. David, 172

Yale Law School Association, 86
Yale University, 55, 56, 86

Ziskind, Jacob, 118–119, 137, 138;
    medical philanthropy of, 106–109
Ziskind Research Building, 106, 108–109